T. H. S. (Thomas Hay Sweet) Escott

Politics and Letters

T. H. S. (Thomas Hay Sweet) Escott
Politics and Letters
ISBN/EAN: 9783337079512
Printed in Europe, USA, Canada, Australia, Japan
Cover: Foto ©ninafisch / pixelio.de

More available books at **www.hansebooks.com**

POLITICS AND LETTERS.

BY

T. H. S. ESCOTT.

LONDON: CHAPMAN AND HALL,
LIMITED.
1886.

CHARLES DICKENS AND EVANS,
CRYSTAL PALACE PRESS.

CONTENTS.

I.

A PERSONAL RETROSPECT 1

II.

MR. GLADSTONE. 41

III.

MEN OF LETTERS ON THEMSELVES . . . 64

IV.

LORD HOUGHTON . . 90

V.

TWO CITIES AND TWO SEASONS—ROME AND
LONDON, A.D. 408 AND 1875. 109
(*Reprinted from* MACMILLAN'S MAGAZINE.)

VI.

JOHN BRIGHT 141

(Reprinted from The Century.*)*

VII.

A CHILD'S AUTOBIOGRAPHY 173

VIII.

MR. HAYWARD 189

IX.

SMALL TALK AND STATESMEN . . . 213

X.

BERNAL OSBORNE 252

POLITICS AND LETTERS.

I.

A PERSONAL RETROSPECT.

AFTER two decades of unremitting exertion, the worker in the arduous passes of London journalism is perhaps entitled to feel that he has reached a table-land on which he may pause to take breath, and whence he may, for a few minutes, survey the retrospect. If no commanding eminence has been gained, the up-hill track of an opposed career has been steadily trodden, experience has been acquired, and at every step the ground has been made fairly sure. Journalism affords to those who have been moderately successful in it the satisfaction of knowing that the results secured have been honestly won, that they are the reward of industry and merit alone, and that the sphere of labour in which they have been reaped is one where nothing but his own capacity and deserts can be of any assistance to the labourer. No such thing as a spurious reputation exists in journalism. Books may occasionally be puffed into notoriety by friendly critics, and in that case the laurels of literary triumph wither as quickly as they are gathered. But no friends, however powerful or loyal; no backers, however energetic or unscrupulous; no letters of commendation, however unqualified; no conversational advertisements, however loud and systematic, can establish the writer for the periodical press in a position that is worth five minutes' purchase. An impostor in journalism is a contradiction in terms. His whole existence is an ordeal of search—a series of competitive examinations, or, to vary the metaphor, of addresses delivered to a jury of his countrymen, who, though they may not always be quick to discriminate between niceties of thought and *nuances* of style, have the eye of a hawk for blunders or fallacies, and are stoutly intolerant of anything approaching to nonsense.

For these reasons, twenty years of London journalism means twenty years of tried and genuine work. To him who has lived through them, and who looks to live through more, it must necessarily be an eventful period. For other reasons of a less selfish and personal character, the interval of time which, in the press of London, separates 1865 from 1885 must be regarded as eventful also in no common degree. The contrast between the two epochs, if even superficially examined, will prove sufficiently striking.

When, twenty years since, I adopted—very rashly

as I was informed by many older and wiser heads, on the strength, I suppose, of the failure which had attended one or two chance ventures—journalism as a profession, only two of the London newspapers now in existence were published at a penny—*The Daily Telegraph* and *The Standard*. The former of these was already an assured triumph; the latter was growing in favour and prosperity from day to day, though its proprietors and conductors were not able to divest themselves of all misgivings. *The Morning Post* and *The Daily News* cost each of them threepence; so did *The Morning Herald*, published from *The Standard* office, and, with the exception of the leading articles and the quality of the paper, identically the same journal as *The Standard;* so, of course, as it continues to be, did *The Times*. *The Morning Star*, the reputed organ of Mr. John Bright and the advanced Radicals who followed him, dragged on a precarious existence at the same price as *The Daily Telegraph*. It was discontinued some dozen years ago, while just seventeen years ago *The Herald*, which proved a dead loss, was merged in *The Standard*, already a fine property. In the higher class weekly press, there were *The Saturday Review*, *The Spectator*, *The Examiner*, and *The Economist*. Of these, *The Examiner*, one of whose latest proprietors was Lord Rosebery, has alone passed away. Of what are known as "Society papers," not one had sprung into being. *The Saturday Review*, then under the guidance of Mr. Douglas Cook, formerly editor of *The Morning Chronicle*, published every week two or three articles of the same kind that now regularly appear in *The World*, and that the rejuvenated *Saturday* would now reprobate as intolerably flippant or personal. The chief writers for *The Saturday Review* at its commencement were Sir William Harcourt, Sir Henry Maine, the learned author of "Ancient Law" and of the series of articles that have recently been reprinted from *The Quarterly Review* entitled "Popular Government," and the Rev. W. Scott, a clergyman in the City and editor of *The Christian Remembrancer*. In the course of the ten years which in 1865 had elapsed since the *Saturday's* first appearance, the dimensions of the journal had grown greatly, and a host of writers, most of them very occasional ones, had gathered round it. It was then, as it may, for all I know, be now, the practice of the proprietors of *The Saturday Review*, Mr. Beresford Hope and Mr. Douglas Cook, to entertain their contributors—the word, as I have always understood, including any one who had written for the periodical during the past year—at the "Trafalgar" or the "Ship Tavern," at Greenwich. The only one of these banquets I ever attended—I certainly did not write more than two or three articles for *The Saturday Review*—was in 1866, when more than one hundred gentlemen of all sorts and conditions, college dons, country parsons, barristers, professors, soldiers and doctors sat down under the presidency of the sociable, yet choleric, Douglas Cook—surely the oddest, most irascible as well as shrewdest and canniest of Aberdonians who ever filled an editorial chair. He had chambers in the Albany, where on every Tuesday he saw his more favoured and regular contributors. He had also a little house, which he subsequently much enlarged, at Tintagel in Cornwall. He was a great gourmet, and was supplied with the most succulent treasures of the deep by the staff of fishermen whom he maintained in the far west. He had a real love for his Cornish home, and his hospitalities were exercised in it on a princely scale. In a slope of Tintagel Churchyard, facing the Atlantic, his body lies buried. The contents of his cellar, which was remarkably well stocked, he left to his scholarly friend, the clergyman of Tintagel, the Rev. W. Vinsman, and his house itself to Lady Hayter, the daughter of the late Adrian Hope, and now known as one of the chief hostesses in London of the Liberal party.

Journalism in 1865, and for some years afterward, differed *in toto* from the journalism of to-day. Telegraphic enterprise was almost in its infancy. The machines which now throw off tens of thousands of copies an hour, and which enable the London papers to go to press at four or five o'clock in the morning, with the certainty that they will appear on the breakfast tables, or at the latest the luncheon tables of the provinces, were unknown. As a consequence, the despatches of special correspondents in the European capitals, instead of being hurriedly wired at the eleventh hour, were communicated in the shape of written letters, and if they did not record, as they record now, the impressions of the instant, were more trustworthy, since they were composed with greater deliberation, and, perhaps, even more instructive, than can be the case under a *régime* of universal electricity. In the same way, the leading articles, written under different circumstances, were written also upon different principles. To-day, during the parliamentary session, the editorials of the London journals are often little more than *résumés* of Parliamentary discussions, of official papers, or of despatches flashed by the electric wire from "our own" or "our special correspondent" in some remote corner of the earth. The great thing is to present articles "newsy" and fresh to the public; to supply the readers, it may be, with arguments, but to supply them with facts as well, and make it clear that they have been written at the very latest moment, and with all the advantages of the freshest intelligence.

The first journalist of distinction with whom, after Douglas Cook—and Cook I knew better as a friend than an editor—I had anything to do, was Thornton Hunt, a son of Leigh Hunt, and the assistant editor at *The Daily Telegraph* office, a bright, courteous gentleman somewhat past middle age, and reminding me very forcibly of the portraits of Edgar Allan Poe. Tom Hood, now long since dead and gone, had given me an introduction to Mr. Edward Lawson, the editor as well as part proprietor of *The Daily Telegraph*, and Mr. Lawson had referred me to Mr. Hunt. At this time, Thornton Hunt, on whose domestic complications with George Henry Lewes I need not dwell, was living in Euston Square. It was there that I met at dinner a young Scotchman, as he was in those days, now dead also, whom *The Daily Telegraph* had attracted to London from the office of *The Scotsman* in Edinburgh, edited by Mr. Alexander Russel, a name that is never likely to be forgotten on the other side of the Tweed, so long as Scotch journalism and Scotch salmon-fishing, of which he was an ardent devotee, endure. London journalism has boasted very few, if any, more brilliant ornaments or more capable writers than James Macdonald. He had received a thorough training in his profession not only at Edinburgh, but at Newcastle-on-Tyne, before he came about 1865 to London. Like most Scotchmen, he had a marvellous head for philosophy and theology, but, unlike most Scotchmen, and as a happy consequence of an innate literary faculty nourished and formed by careful study of the great masters of French publicism, especially Paul and Jean Courier, he had a singular aptitude for and appreciation of literary style. He was employed in the office of *The Daily Telegraph* first, I believe, rather as an assistant editor and as a coadjutor of Mr. Thornton Hunt. Afterward, when for several years I was in the habit of meeting him and my old friend, Mr. Justin McCarthy, then a leader writer for *The Daily News*, at the back of the reporters' gallery in the House of Commons, he had given up all editorial work and was simply a writer of leading articles for the paper. It must have been, I think, in the year 1876 that he severed his connection with *The Daily Telegraph* and went over to *The Times*. He was, indeed, supposed to have written articles for *The Times* while he was still connected with *The Telegraph*. Ten years ago a recrudescence of the war between France and Germany was generally apprehended. The English public was taken by storm one morning by a leader in *The Times* appealing to Prince Bismarck to avert the struggle. This was attributed, and I have since been told, correctly, to James Macdonald. He died some three or four years later. He was never a strong man. There were times when he looked appallingly ill. Nor can there be any doubt that he was one of the many whom the terrific struggle of daily journalism, pitiless and incessant, brought to an early grave.

At the time of which I now speak, *The Daily Telegraph*, with the possible exception of *The Times*, of the writers for which the outside world, even of journalism, knew little or nothing, possessed the most remarkably gifted staff of writers. The destinies of *The Times* were directed then, as they continued to be during many years subsequently, by Delane, and secrecy was one of the traditions of the office. Certain men, such as Mr. Leonard Courtney, now a Member of Parliament ; Mr. G. C. Brodrick, now Warden of Merton College, Oxford ; Mr. Wace, now Principal of King's College, London, from whose pen came, it is understood, all the more important leaders which appeared in *The Times* during the civil war in America ; Mr. L. J. Jennings, subsequently editor of *The New York Times*, whose extraordinary ability and energy have since enabled him to make a name for himself in English literature; Mr. Charles Austin and several more, were all known in a vague kind of way as connected with *The Times*, but they made it a point of never discussing their connection of their particular work even in the society of intimates. It was different in the case of *The Daily Telegraph*, and, doubtless, the other daily London papers. *The Times* went later to press than any of its contemporaries, and the men who wrote for it were mostly free till 9.30 o'clock at night, when they were expected to be in Printing House Square, or, if they were not free, they associated but little with other journalists. Even the writers on Parliamentary subjects, whose business it naturally was to attend debates, shunned the reporters' gallery and were accommodated with a seat in that quarter of the House reserved for private secretaries,

officials, and sometimes strangers, in the gallery under
the clock. With Mr. Delane I had only a social
acquaintance, and that a slight one. Introduced to
him in '68 by Bishop Wilberforce, I was invited to
lunch with him in the company of that amiable,
witty, and entertaining prelate, at what he used to
call his dingy little house in Serjeants' Inn, Fleet
Street. The general elections were then in progress,
and the Archbishop of Canterbury was seriously ill.
I shall never forget the twinkle in his eye, and the
quiet chuckle in his voice with which, when the
Bishop (who had been unusually outspoken in his
remarks and severe in his political criticisms) left the
room to keep an appointment, Delane said : " I think
our right reverend friend has his eyes keenly fixed
just now on Lambeth"—Lambeth is the London
house of the Primate, and a vacancy in the primacy
naturally seemed just then possible. I sat chatting
with the great man for an hour after this. I had
a vague sort of expectation that he might ask me to
join the staff of *The Times*. But when I told him
that I was pretty well occupied as a writer of leading
articles for *The Standard*, he congratulated me on
my success, and never held out to me any prospect
of promotion to Printing House Square. In those
days I was very full of Oxford interests. Probably
I talked too much about them, and being then only
twenty-four years of age, I believe I looked even
younger than I was. It always occurred to me that
any notion which Delane may have had—assuming

that he had any at all—of inviting me for a trial on *The Times* was dispelled by the juvenility of my appearance, and, perhaps, the academic artlessness of my prattle. In late years I met him frequently. The last time I ever saw him was in his house at Ascot, not many weeks before his death. His brain was then softening rapidly, and he looked melancholy in the extreme. He had ceased for about two years previously to be editor of *The Times*, and if his friend, Abraham Hayward, was to be trusted, he never got over the curtness with which his retirement was forced upon him by Mr. Walter. The letter containing the intimation that his services were no longer required in Printing House Square was shown by Delane to Hayward immediately after he received it. I never saw it myself, but I can trust Hayward's memory, and my own, and it was almost verbally to this effect: "My dear Delane,—The time has come when it is no longer to your advantage or to that of *The Times* that you should remain its editor. Your successor will be Mr. Thomas Chenery, whose talent and capacity for the post we all recognise, and your pension will be £2,000 a year." I have been informed that *The Times* was worth to Delane during, at any rate, the latter portion of his editorship, between £4,000 and £5,000 a year. This may seem a large income even for a publicist in the incomparably commanding position of the great Jove of the Thunderer. But it must be remembered that while

Delane (who was of a far higher calibre than that of an ordinary Cabinet Minister, and the greatest expert in the interpretation, and sometimes, by four-and-twenty hours, the anticipation of public opinion, a man whom it would not have been flattery to compare to his friend Palmerston) devoted his existence to the journal, he consolidated and created its reputation as the first newspaper in the world, and sacrificed his life for it, dying, ere yet he had touched the threshold of old age, of a disease incurred by his unremitting attention to his work.

When I first penetrated into the interior of *The Standard* office, its proprietor, Mr. Johnston, was in the prime of a vigorous middle age, and its editor was a Mr., or as he was sometimes called, Captain Hamber, the son of an old friend of Mr. Johnston. The City editor and manager was Mr. David Morier Evans, and it was the habit of these two gentlemen to see their contributors successively between certain, or perhaps uncertain, hours in the afternoon. Mr. Hamber, who is now the editor of *The Morning Advertiser*, and whom I regard as one of the best and kindest friends I have ever encountered in journalism, was and is one of the hardiest, pluckiest, toughest, and quickest men who ever trod the pavement of Fleet Street or Shoe Lane. Whether he was intended by nature for a journalist, whether instead of being a captain of the pen he should not have been a captain of horse, is possibly doubtful, or, as it may be said, not doubtful at all. As journalist, however, he possessed remarkable swiftness of insight, and, when he wrote himself, great power of vigorous and sometimes epigrammatic expression. Educated at Oxford, he had mixed much with politicians, with some of whom he was well acquainted. Lord Salisbury, certainly in the year 1866, and I believe a little later, when he was Lord Robert Cecil, with no thought that he would ever inherit the marquisate of his house, wrote leading articles for the paper. Among the editorial staff were Mr. Alfred Austin, whose connection with the paper has lasted without interruption to this day, who wields a pen unsurpassed for felicity and velocity in the ranks of London journalism, and whose genius has displayed itself in much exquisite and effective poetry as well as in reams on reams of admirable political writing; Mr. Percy Grey, son of W. Rathbone Grey; Mr. H. E. Watts; Mr. Horace St. John, and a certain Mr. George Painter, who first attracted the notice of the Shoe Lane authorities by some anonymous paragraphs in which the high faluting of *The Daily Telegraph*, called by the parodist the *Gaily Beligraph*, were parodied, and who, when he became attached to the paper, was told off to deliver himself on the dullest of topics, which he did in the most ponderous of styles; Mr. Burton Blythe, renowned for his knowledge of German politics, and Mr. Sydney L. Blanchard, son of Laman Blanchard. Blanchard, whose great enemy was his almost idiotic vanity, subsisting as it did upon a diet of dismally feeble jokes, is dead. So, I fancy, is St. John; and Painter, though I trust he is now restored to health, broke down completely some years ago. *The Standard* went through many mutations before it settled into its present splendidly triumphant stride. Mr. Hamber's services were abruptly dispensed with about 1872, Mr. Johnston appointing his own son, who, from the accident of his father's proprietorship in Shoe Lane, was imagined, I suppose, to have contracted some *soupçon* of journalistic knowledge, as editor, his technical address being Mr. Blythe, who subsequently assumed the full or a qualified editorial responsibility. The arrangement did not work, and when he could no longer disguise from himself the fact that it was a failure, astute Mr. Johnston took the boldest, the most perspicacious, and the cleverest step he ever took in his life. He offered the editorship of his newspaper to a gentleman who was then its manager (charged, that is, with making all the arrangements for the report of speeches and incidents of all descriptions), and who had previously served the paper as a reporter in the gallery of the House of Commons. His name was Mudford, and Mr. Mudford has since raised *The Standard* to the rank of the first newspaper in England, and one of the best newspaper properties, while he has placed himself at the head of the newspaper editors of the United Kingdom. Practically Mr. Mudford's position is at the present nearest that of the occupant of a journalistic freehold. Mr. Johnston by his will appointed him editor and manager for life at a handsome salary, while the Court of Chancery subsequently allowed him a share of the profits. For some half-dozen years I served under Mr. Mudford. Indebted to him as I am, and as I am also to every editor and nearly every colleague with whom I have been brought into contact, for much personal kindness and consideration, I speak entirely without bias when I describe in the language I have, his own peculiar and eminent powers and qualifications. *The Standard* has during its ever increasingly prosperous career confronted occasional opposition. *The Day*, which lasted for a few weeks or months, was started by the Conservative Adullamites, as they were called, who opposed Lord Beaconsfield's Reform Bill of 1867, and in 1873 or thereabouts there was founded *The Hour*, by Mr. Hamber and Mr. Morier Evans, who had, like his friends, seceded from *The Standard*. I was asked myself to join, on very handsome terms, the new Conservative print, and, feeling that my position at *The Standard* office during the provisional period, which I saw clearly was setting in, could not but be precarious and disagreeable, I accepted the offer. *The Hour* continued with chequered fortunes for some three or four years, when it fell a victim to pecuniary embarrassments. These, however, never affected me, and I owe it to my good friends, Hamber and Evans, to say that from the first week to the last my salary was paid to me with the regularity of clockwork. When *The Hour* expired, I took advantage of the leisure which a short cessation from the grinding labours of daily journalism seemed to offer me to complete a project that had long been in my mind. This was a work which should be as nearly as possible exhaustive and accurate on the contemporary condition of my native country. "England: its People, Polity, and Pursuits"—the alliterative sub-title of which I believe has occasioned some of my irreverent friends matter for parody—was first published a little more than seven years ago. It was the result of much work and observation, and of frequent peregrinations over all parts of the country. I was not satisfied with obtaining from books or in any way second hand, information on the subjects of my inquiry when first-hand knowledge was possible. The book, I hope, has interested and instructed others. To me the writing of it was a kind of education. It gave me a touch of the opinion of whole classes of my countrymen of whom I had previously been in ignorance. It also made me many acquaintances, and, I hope, friends, especially among the industrial orders of the population. Altogether, had the commercial success of the work been much less than has actually proved the case, I should still have had good reason not to regret that for six months or a little longer I held entirely aloof from daily newspaper work.

It has, I suppose, fallen to the lot of few men being so little acquainted with London at the beginning of their metropolitan career as I was in 1865 to have seen so much of it since, to have formed from practical experience so full an idea of most, or of very many, of its aspects, and to have stayed in it so continuously and with such little change. From 1868 to 1878 I was only absent from London—not, of course, counting an occasional "Sunday out"—twice for ten days and once for three weeks. I attribute entirely any success which, in journalism or in current literature, I have achieved mainly to the tenacity with which throughout this strenuous decade I stuck to my work, the amount of work I was able to do passably well, and the uniformly good health with which I was blessed. I had, moreover, other occupations than those which were not purely literary. For some years I was Professor of Logic at King's College, London, and during the greater portion of one year acted as the deputy of my friend, Mr. Lonsdale, then invalided, Vice-Professor of Greek and Latin. It was not till 1878—not, that is to say, before thirteen years of sustained industry had come to a close—that I felt at all sure of my position, or that I was conscious of the conviction that I had been justified at a period considerably anterior to this in flinging aside all academic or educational props and trusting entirely to my pen.

When, in 1865, I settled in a London lodging,

my only personal acquaintance among literary men was the late Tom Hood. To Mr. Masson, to Mr. Macmillan, and to an eminent educationalist, a Dr. W. B. Hodgson, living at that time in a pretty house in St. John's Wood, I had received letters of introduction from my friend and private tutor at Oxford, Professor John Nichol.

Tom Hood I had known, as schoolboys say, "at home." He had been my senior at Oxford by rather less than a decade, and had left behind him a brilliant reputation. To me he was the first friend in literature whom I possessed, and though toward the close of his life I saw little of him, and I fancied, I know not for what reason, his cordiality had worn off, I shall always cherish his memory with gratitude and affection. Hood's house in South Street, Brompton, was, at the time of which I write, a pleasant little centre of literary and dramatic Bohemianism. He was editor of *Fun*, and he had gathered round himself a remarkably bright band of personal friends and contributors, the two terms being in almost every instance identical.

Chief among these were Arthur Sketchley, whose real name was George Rose, then giving his delineations of Mrs. Brown, who, I understand, never quite took the fancy of the Americans, at the Egyptian Hall; Tom Robertson, the dramatist, author of "Society," "Ours," "Caste," "School," "Play," and many other performed and unperformed comedies;

W. J. Prowse, H. S. Leigh, Paul Gray, Tom Morten, William Brunton, W. S. Gilbert, and Clement Scott. Most of these have long since followed poor Tom Hood and his wife into the land of shadows. Sketchley, educated at Oxford, and a contemporary of Delane and Dasent, was originally a clergyman of the English Church. When he went over to Rome he was supposed to have allied himself with the Jesuits, and, be this as it may, he was a zealous proselytiser. Inordinately stout in body, he had a remarkably fine and handsome face, and was accounted, I believe, an excellent impersonator of Falstaff on the amateur stage. His two chief friends at that era, and the most indefatigable of Tom Hood's guests at his Friday evenings—evenings of unconstrained fun and unaffected sociality, free from all pretence, the only repast served at which was a joint of cold beef, flanked by hot roast potatoes—were Clement Scott and Paul Gray, both of them, like Sketchley, Catholics, and the former well known to-day as a journalist, dramatic critic, playwright, essayist, and poet of unprecedented fecundity and grace.

Tom Robertson, dead—as, too, are Brunton, Morten, Sketchley, Prowse, Leigh, the three Broughs, Robert, John, and William, only the two latter of whom were personally known to me from meeting them at the Savage Club, Robert Brough having passed away before my time—was just about to make his first hit on any stage with "Society."

I was present, and so, I suppose, were all his personal friends, at its inaugural performance. The curtain had not been up five minutes when it was plain that the piquant and most artistic acting of Marie Wilton, Mr. Hare, and the rest of the company had ensured its triumph. There were some solecisms in the piece, such, for instance, as the meeting between the young patrician maiden and her lover after dark in the garden of a London square. There was also a great deal of genial and laughter-moving satire. If the children of fashion were lashed in some parts, so was Bohemianism also; and the scene in the Sly-by-Nights Club, in which one gentleman of the society, asking another for a loan of five shillings, received the answer: "I have not got it myself, my dear boy, but I will get it for you "— the same request and the same reply being passed on to every one in the room—was recognised by those who knew the original as true to the life. A greater air of actuality was further imparted to the incident by a resemblance which two or three of the stage club men bore to actual and living prototypes, notably to Mr. Buckingham, the dramatic critic of *The Morning Star* and son of Silk Buckingham, and to Mr. Horace Green, each of them an habitué of a literary and theatrical club facing the Thames at the bottom of Salisbury Street, Strand, the Arundel. Tom Robertson really shone in conversation. He was full of sardonic humour, of biting satire, of ironic badinage, and of paradox which not unfrequently bordered on profanity. Although he was then, as the result proved, in a fair way to make his mark, he had passed through a terrible probationary ordeal of failure. He indemnified himself for all that he had suffered by making fun of the most mordant sort upon all persons, upon all institutions, human and divine His manner was bright and breezy, although a little boisterous, and he delighted in running a tilt at the conventionalities of the respectable as flimsy hypocrisies. In doing this he did but reflect, if in an accentuated shape, the temper of those about him.

To-day the Prince of Wales, accompanied by an equerry, dines with and is an honorary member or president of the Savage Club. Twenty years ago, when that society used to hold its Saturday dinners in a long low room in Radley's Hotel, Henrietta Street, Covent Garden, looking out on Maiden Lane, the Savages would have been not more incredulous or cynically contemptuous if they had been told that the Heir Apparent would shortly be of their company, than if the Archbishop of Canterbury had taken it into his head to stroll in, supported by Mr. Paul Bedford and Mr. J. L. Toole. Mr. Prowse (Jeff Prowse, as he was known among his friends) wrote the most charming articles on all matters nonpolitical for *The Daily Telegraph*. He was a humorist of a very fine order, and his conception of Nicholas, who was quite as real a personage to all readers of *Fun*, was equal in its way to the Jeames De la Plush or the Mr. Snob of Thackeray. Had he lived, he might, and doubtless would, have touched the very highest level of excellence in the lighter department of English literature. To an uncommon gift of pathos and taste, he added a fastidious appreciation of style. His imagination was nimble and his metaphors apt. But the life of London told upon his health. His lungs gave way, and he was compelled to betake himself to Nice, where eventually they laid him to rest, at the age of thirty-three, under the orange and palm trees of the Riviera. He himself had shrewdly prognosticated his coming end in some touching and exquisite lines, which he had written four years earlier, entitled, "My Lost Old Age:"

> I'm only nine-and-twenty yet,
>   Though young experience makes me sage,
> So how on earth can I forget
>   The memory of my lost old age?
>
> Of manhood's prime let others boast,
>   It comes too quick or goes too soon;
> At times the life I envy most
>   Is that of slippered pantaloon.

H. L. Leigh, who wrote not a few ballads equal in merit to any of Frederick Locker, survived his friend Prowse some ten years, and with him there may be said to have departed the last of the highly-gifted Bohemians of London.

Leigh's muse was really exquisite. His existence slipped away between his chambers in Furnival's Inn, the Savage Club, and a few chosen taverns and restaurants. There is, I imagine, very little of the

Bohemianism of which Leigh was the representative in London to-day. Had Tom Robertson been alive he would have been not only famous but wealthy, and might be living in the same splendour as Mr. W. S. Gilbert enjoys to-day in South Kensington. Gilbert, when I first knew him, was writing his "Bab Ballads," and was essaying to take his first flight as a dramatist. He was a man of reserved and rather rugged manner, of biting and saturnine wit, saying the oddest things, and making the most bizarre of comparisons, in a rasping tone of voice. His first piece, I believe, was played upon a London stage as a burlesque, entitled "Dr. Dulcamara." It was produced at the St. James's Theatre, and it followed "Hunted Down," in which Henry Irving was making his *début* in the metropolis, playing admirably the part of the villain, with Miss Herbert as his wife. It must have been in the year 1866 that I was introduced to Irving, who, I recollect, was seated, as I entered the room, together with Gilbert, on a couch in the Arundel Club—then one of the favourite haunts of journalists, essayists, playwrights, and playactors. It is a fascinating theme, that of the literary Bohemianism of London twenty years ago. Artemus Ward, who had no sooner taken up his dwelling in the metropolis than he was made a member of the Savage Club, saw it, enjoyed it, and was highly popular in it. Sala had passed through it, and he was not at the time I speak of a prominent member of it. He was too busy, and above all things too constantly absent from London as the Special Correspondent of *The Daily Telegraph* in foreign parts. He used to turn up unexpectedly sometimes at the Savage Club, more frequently in the café portion of the old supper room at Evans's, now transformed into the New Club. His conversation was always full of brilliancy and knowledge, and what must have struck every one most in listening to him was the extraordinary flush of animal spirits which he possessed. This he had in common with Dickens and the great majority of those who belonged to the school of Dickens. Of the author of "David Copperfield" I can say little more than *vidi tantum*. I was introduced to him by my friend of now nearly twenty years' standing, Edmund Yates, about the time that Dickens had met Lord Beaconsfield, then Mr. Disraeli, at Lord Stanhope's at dinner. Dickens was much attracted by the Conservative statesman. "Had," he remarked regretfully—not in my presence, the story is Mr. Yates'—"Disraeli devoted himself to literature, he might have done something. What on earth can have made him throw himself away on politics?" Andrew Halliday was another prominent figure of the group of which I now speak, a canny Aberdonian who was occupied with the writing of essays for Dickens's *All the Year Round*, and with the adaptation of Sir Walter Scott's plays for the stage, which he found exceedingly profitable. He had commenced his career in commerce, and had acquired in it habits of business which stood him in excellent stead in after life.

Occasionally these convivial gatherings were visited by James Hannay and his henchmen. Hannay was an extraordinary talker, with a good deal of literary, antiquarian, and classical knowledge, very loose and inaccurate in his statements, sometimes exceedingly epigrammatic, and always, when his humour was exuberantly social, audacious in his criticisms on the company to the point of impudence and even insolence. It was the great object in Hannay's life to revive in London the patrician and the feudal ideas which he had derived from Sir Walter Scott and the bibulous traditions of the "Noctes Ambrosianæ." In the intellect of very few men can it be said that the associations of conviviality played so large a part. One of his first books was entitled "Biscuits and Grog," and the best copy of light verses which he ever wrote was called "Nothing Like Hock." I have omitted two names, without some mention of which the most hurried glance at the literary life of London a couple of decades, or even a decade ago, would be grievously incomplete. These were John Oxenford and J. W. Davidson, the dramatic and musical critics of *The Times* respectively. Both men were exceedingly well informed on all subjects, acute reasoners, powerful conversational controversialists. When the labours of play-going or opera-going were past they would meet over a friendly supper and not stinted potations at the "Albion

Tavern." Fate, freewill, foreknowledge, the origin of evil, the existence of a Deity — these were the topics which they were never weary of debating. I remember as if it were yesterday the air of triumph with which Davidson rose after one of these polemical encounters, and remarked to his friend, "And now, Oxenford, having brought your cosmic God to his last ethical fence, I shall go to bed."

It has also been my lot to mix with what are called literary circles of a very different character, and upon quite another social level. I first made my bow to George Eliot at one of the Sunday receptions she was in the habit of giving at her house in North Bank, now inhabited by Mr. Wilson Barrett, the actor. She was then Mrs. Lewes, and the late G. H. Lewes was alive. The function was more like a religious ceremonial than a social reunion, and Mr. Lewes played to perfection the part of Hierophant. The gifted lady, whose autobiography we have all recently devoured, sat in the centre of a little crowd of worshippers, of whom some were permitted to hold personal converse with her. But the majority gazed at her reverently and mutely from afar, as if they were looking upon the beatific vision. If any one spoke in too loud a tone, or spoke at all, when George Eliot happened to be speaking herself, he was at once met with a "hush" of reprehension by Mr. Lewes, and made to feel that he had perpetrated a sort of iniquity. George Eliot had unquestionably immeasurable charm of mind, manner, and conversation for those who knew her well. But as in these desultory reminiscences I record nothing of which I had not personal cognisance myself, I must say that I never advanced beyond the outer circle of worshippers, and that I always felt myself one of the Levites at the gate. The poet, Browning, assisted frequently at the intellectual mysteries of North Bank, and it was in that august atmosphere that I first set my eyes upon one of the finest heads I have ever seen, and the handsome presence, incorporating, perhaps, the most penetrating, powerful, and sympathetic intellect, of our day. Browning remained on terms of the most intimate friendship with Mrs. Lewes, to the last—after, that is, she became Mrs. Cross. There were several other houses where, at this time, the literati of the period of both sexes were in the habit of congregating. At Mr. Grant Duff's country house, whether in Buckinghamshire or subsequently at Twickenham, at Lord Houghton's breakfasts and dinners, at Thomas and William Longman's, to name only a very few out of a multitude. Grant Duff's Saturday to Monday parties were always exceedingly agreeable. Among those whom one most frequently met there were FitzJames Stephen, with his leonine presence and his home-like manner; George Selwyn, full of literature and politics, enthusiastic, humorous, and capital company; Sir Thomas Erskine May, socially and politically omniscient, and a good talker also; Sir John Lubbock, who was, as indeed he is, himself the most hospitable of men both in London and at his country house near Hayes, in Kent, High Elms, where for years Darwin was his neighbour and Herbert Spencer and Alfred Russell Wallace his most frequent visitors.

Charles Reade once did me the honour of dining with me (now nearly fifteen years ago) at a club in St. James's Street. He talked incessantly, without quitting the dinner table, till nearly two o'clock in the morning, and very interesting as well as aggressively original much of his talk was. I do not suppose I could have met him upon half a dozen other occasions, and one of these, the only one, indeed, I can now remember, was at a garden party given by Mrs. Maxwell—Miss Braddon. Like Wilkie Collins, he went into general society exceedingly little. I have the honour of calling Mr. Collins my friend, but I have only been seated twice at the same dinner table with him, once upon the occasion already mentioned, when I first met Dickens at Edmund Yates's; next at a little dinner at which I and a few others entertained Edmund Yates some five or six years ago. The late Lord Lytton, being well acquainted with many members of my family, took some trouble to be polite to me, and one of my most interesting recollections is a Sunday I passed with him many years ago at Knebworth.

I cannot help thinking that when I was with him he must have been engaged in writing one of the most perfect of the essays contained in the volume entitled "Caxtoniana"—"The Increased Attention to Outward Nature in the Decline of Life." In the first place, his manner was that of one rehearsing "Adiocomes," which he had either prefaced or was preparing. In the second place, many of the sentiments which this charming composition contains were identical with his remarks to me. His manner impressed me as that of the most abstracted and artificial person, at once the most self-conscious and the most dreamy I have ever seen. As was the man, so were his house and his surroundings, a perfect epitome of picturesque sincerity. Of George Lawrence, the author of "Guy Livingston," and the founder of a school of English novelists, I caught occasional glimpses in the course of his troubled and tempestuous career. Lever I met, and I can remember his conversation, but I did not know him. Whyte-Melville had been good enough to notice me when I was a boy at Oxford, giving me then a piece of advice which I have never forgotten. "Ride straight to hounds, say nothing, and all men will speak well of you," and I believe he took a kind interest in my modest career. With Captain Mayne Reid, who was becoming old and even dilapidated when I first settled in London, I have passed many an afternoon and smoked many cigars in a little tavern in Air Street, Regent Street, which, I believe, ceased to exist many years ago. Tavern life was a recognised thing in London, and especially Stone's bar and parlour in Posterham Street, Haymarket, were the haunts of men connected with literature, art, or law.

The great centre of the literary and intellectual life of London in its social aspects then, as now, was, as it is, the Athenæum Club. Of this institution I have never been, am not, and probably never shall be a member; but I have been favoured with the friendship of some of its greatest ornaments, and at this moment there lies before me a letter in which Abraham Hayward, who was a kind of despot of the establishment, dominating it with his will and his presence, is good enough to express his regret that I had not the *entrée* to the place, "because," he adds, " I have organised a dinner-party for to-night there which you would enjoy." Hayward, on whom I have written at some length elsewhere, was not, as he has been represented, a wit or humorist at all. He was far too earnest to be anything of the kind, and one of his greatest objections to his friend, Bernal Osborne, was that his lively sallies of humour rendered serious conversation impossible. Even of Lord Houghton he once said to me: "It is a pity so fine an intellect is so spoiled by whim and paradox." Hayward liked political argument of the most practical kind. Fond of discussing politics, he never talked about them in the speculative tone of a philosopher, but always with something of the responsibility of the statesman, and as one who would be prepared, if he were in power, to translate into action the opinions he expressed. One of Hayward's great arts was that of telling a story with entire lucidity, yet in the fewest possible words. No man had a greater horror of boredom or so successfully avoided inflicting it on his fellow creatures.

Bernal Osborne, on the other hand, was a wit, a humorist, an anecdotist and a farceur. All he required was a butt, some one who was present for preference, some one who was absent, or some incident in which those of the company might be interested, of necessity. The first time I ever met Osborne was some three-and-twenty years ago in a country house. The post had brought him a letter from a young lady to whom he was closely related, and this letter proved to be, in the main, a eulogy upon the young gentleman on whom she had set her affections. This Bernal Osborne took as the text for a running commentary of infinite mirth and merriment, which lasted throughout the whole of breakfast, and kept the table in a roar. The man who knew and appreciated and liked Bernal Osborne better than any one else, is my much-respected old friend, A. W. Kinglake, the historian of the Crimean War, who, by his "Eothen," an epoch-making book, if ever there was one, has done more than any man living to exercise a permanent influence on English literature. It was with the help of Mr. Kinglake—though at his express desire I abstained from mentioning his name—that I wrote in *The Fortnightly Review* an article on Bernal Osborne, which, I believe, on the whole, gave a fair idea of the man. Kinglake and Froude are probably the two greatest writers of the English language now alive. Certainly, if one adds to these names those of Cardinal Newman, John Morley, and Matthew Arnold they are conspicuous among the greatest. Nothing better, or even half so good of its kind, was ever done as "Eothen." It unconsciously gave Mr. Oliphant a model for imitation in his "Piccadilly," and its lightness of touch and power of graphic illumination in the smallest number of words possible, have powerfully affected all writers of the lighter kind of English since. Mr. Kinglake, I am happy to say, though he must be now within five or six years of fourscore, is hale and well, and, as he ever was, the very ideal of an English gentleman of the most perfect possible breeding. Nothing could be more chivalrous or touching than the attention with which he nursed Abraham Hayward during his last illness. There is one story which Mr. Kinglake is fond of telling, and which he will, I believe, forgive me if I repeat here. In the year '46, Hayward, though a Peelite, remained a member of the Carlton Club. The present Lord Ranelagh, seeing him there one day at luncheon, offered, in a tone intended to be audible, some observations as to the impropriety of Hayward's continuing in an institution from the political principles of which he had apostatized. Hayward immediately sent him a challenge through Kinglake, and Kinglake informed Lord Ranelagh that he should be dining that evening at the Travellers' Club, and would gladly see any friend of his lordship's between 9 and 11. About 10 o'clock Sir William Bagge, a Norfolk squire, was announced, and Kinglake received him in a separate room. Sir William may have been dining wisely, but he had been dining well, and his honest face was flushed with the juice of the grape. His manner was jovial, and he began with expressions of hope that the matter might be arranged amicably. He then proceeded to say in the rich voice of vinous good fellowship: "You know, Mr. Kinglake, I am one of those who contend that Ranelagh is a gentleman." At this sentiment Mr. Kinglake bowed stiffly, and remarked in his iciest tones: "That I assume. In fact, the business in hand rather implies it." In a moment the colour fled from the rubicund cheeks of the jolly country baronet, and he became white as a sheet. "I had," says Mr. Kinglake, "frozen him sober, and this is the only little piece of acting in my life I ever attempted."

I have alluded to the literary influence of such a book as "Eothen," and I think, as I have said, this influence is reflected more or less in the lighter periodical writing of our time. This was conspicuously the case in what was, I suppose, the parent, or at least the herald, of the so-called Society journals of these latter days. *The Owl* was started some five-and-twenty years ago, mainly by Mr. Lawrence Oliphant and Sir Algernon Borthwick, now the editor-in-chief as well as proprietor of *The Morning Post*, and the doyen of London journalism. Many other writers, not the least among them Mr. T. Gibson Bowles, there were. The journal appeared fitfully during the parliamentary session, and, in addition to

much early and exclusive information about politics
and diplomacy, published some capitally written
little essays, admirable verses, and first-rate *jeux
d'esprit*. The enterprise was profitable, though it
was not started for purposes of profit, and it
was arranged that anything which stood to the
credit of the contributors to *The Owl*, after all business expenses had been paid, should be devoted to the
ends of pleasure. As a consequence, many amusing
Owl dinners and symposia were held. The paper
continued till absence, other occupations, and the
disintegrating influences of life generally practically
broke up the staff. The next paper of the same sort
which appeared was the *Tomahawk*, under the editorship of Mr. Arthur A'Beckett. It was something
between *Punch* and *The Owl*, but dealt with certain
events of the day in a caustic and severe way peculiar
to itself. Its great feature was an exceedingly sen-
sational cartoon drawn by Mat Morgan. The writers
for this little print, in addition to Mr. A'Beckett,
were Mr. Gilbert A'Beckett, Mark Marshall, Mr.
T. G. Bowles, Mr. Alfred Thomson, and one or two
more. Gradually *The Tomahawk* went the way of all
such ephemeral prints, and then Mr. Bowles floated
Vanity Fair. Strange as it may seem, *Vanity Fair*
had been in existence five or six years before another
journal, organised upon anything like the same lines,
was started. *The World*, the first number of which
appeared in July, 1873, may be described as, in a
measure, of Transatlantic origin. That is to say, as

my friend Mr. Yates has himself explained in his "Recollections," it was the circumstance, beginning with his American trip, that he had acquired leisure for reflection, which caused him to map out the whole scheme of the "journal for men and women." Long before this Mr. Yates had written a weekly article, summing up the social events of the past seven days, full of shrewdness and remarkable for its antithetical felicity of expression, in *The Morning Star*, entitled " The Gleaner." *The World* was really in its inception, as it has been in its continuation, a blend between the brightest features of *The Saturday Review* in its old days and the series of brilliant, social, and more or less personal jottings which appeared from the pen of Mr. Edmund Yates, I know not for how long, in *The Morning Star*. When he projected the paper he was good enough to invite my collaboration, chiefly or exclusively as a political writer. It was gratifying to me to discover that he had been so favourably impressed with a few compositions of mine which had appeared under his editorship in *Temple Bar*. I gratefully accepted his proposal, and I hope I have never given him reason to regret that it was made. So far as I am aware, *The World* is solely indebted for the large success it has achieved to the brightness, the originality, and the organising and administrative skill of its editor and proprietor.

Since this journal first shot above the literary horizon of London it has provoked many imitations.

It inaugurated, if the word be not too pretentious, an era. Of many of these imitations I am ignorant even of the name. The most prosperous of *The World's* rivals is Mr. Labouchere's *Truth*. Only a man of Mr. Labouchere's brilliance, versatility, and power could have done what his opportunities have enabled him to accomplish. One of the results brought about by *The World* and *Truth* is the depression of the influence and the popularity of *The Saturday Review*. *The Spectator* has probably not felt the competition at all, but that is because *The Spectator*, unlike *The Saturday Review*, has been able to command and retain a special public of its own, as over and above, of course, a considerable section of the general public.

It is not an easy thing for a person in my position to say much of the distinguished public men who have honoured him with their acquaintance. I well recollect some years ago being a guest at a house where Lord Beaconsfield and Lord Granville were of the company. The latter, who was then leader of the Opposition in the House of Lords, asked the former, who was Prime Minister, what he thought of Delane. "I think," replied Lord Beaconsfield, affecting to hesitate for a moment, "I would sooner answer that question when Delane is dead." A mere publicist has no title to pronounce an estimate of public men into whose company he may chance to have been thrown, whether they are alive or dead, for the simple reason that it is, in the nature of things, impossible he should ever have acquired much real insight into their character, while, if he is bold enough to think that he possesses such insight, he will be very rash or very foolish if he does not keep it to himself. Circumstances have caused me to be more or less, though always superficially, acquainted with some of the chief personages who have manufactured the history of this generation.

Almost, I believe quite, my earliest recollection is that of seeing the great Duke of Wellington, Sir Robert Peel, and Lord Lyndhurst walking on the bowling-green of my uncle's house in West Somersetshire on a Sunday afternoon. I was not more than five years old at the time, but I can remember that the Duke suggested a game of bowls. Sir Robert Peel said: "But it is Sunday; think of the servants." Lord Lyndhurst laughed, and my uncle told the servant to bring the bowls. The game, notwithstanding that it was the Sabbath, was played. A little after this I was taken by the same relative to the House of Commons, and heard Sir Robert Peel make either his last speech or his last speech but one. When my uncle drove me back to his house in John Street, Mayfair, I can recollect his asking the servant, who opened the door, whether any one was waiting for him. The reply was: "Only the Prince," and the prince to whom I was presently presented was Louis Napoleon, shortly to be Napoleon III., Emperor of the French. It must have been in the year '62, when the Second

Empire was at the height of its glory, that, being then an undergraduate at Oxford, I paid my first visit to Paris. With the boundless assurance of extreme youth, I sent a note to his Imperial Majesty at the Tuileries, intimating that I was in the capital of his empire. When I returned that afternoon to my hotel, I found that one of the Imperial carriages was waiting to convey me and my luggage to the palace.

Having during the last twenty years been comparatively little abroad, I have known or seen very few European statesmen of eminence. With Gambetta, thanks to the introduction of Sir Charles Dilke, I was acquainted for three or four years, and was in the habit of seeing him once or twice a year. He was so good as to authorise me to publish in the first number of *The Fortnightly Review* for which I was responsible (November, 1882), an account of his views on French and European affairs. The article was not actually written by him, but was dictated by him to one of his secretaries. It was untouched by any further hand, and, such as it is, possesses, I believe, even at this day a historical value. Of Lord Beaconsfield I had next to no personal knowledge; but he was so kind as to ask me once to see him at Hughenden, and he showed me, with much thoughtful attention, round its exceedingly picturesque gardens. He was particularly proud of some beautiful specimens of the birds sacred to Juno, and, on my venturing to remark to him that these were calculated to interfere with his flowers, he said: "It may be so; but I prefer the peacock to a flower." This saying of his is an interesting commentary on the culture of the primrose which has been recently established in Lord Beaconsfield's honour.

Though I could add much to these disjointed reminiscences of interesting and illustrious persons, I will for the present bring them to a conclusion. The retrospect I have taken covers not perhaps a long, but certainly an eventful period. Within its limits there has been witnessed an entire revolution in the status and opportunities of journalism. On the one hand, journalism has, as a profession in England, become more organised than at any previous period. On the other hand, the enormous number of those who write— and write, if not excellently, yet passably well—in newspapers has so increased that journalism is to-day, to an extent it never was before, the occupation or the pastime of the educated classes generally. There is probably no calling in the world which is at once so tempting to a man of mediocre abilities, and yet in which mediocrity will so surely fail to make any mark. There is none either in which the general average of mind is so high. Yet anything above this standard is unusual, and it thus follows that journalism is and will continue to be more of a career to those possessing exceptional capacities than any other. Thus much is certain. The really good political writer of knowledge and power, if he devotes himself heart and soul to newspapers, if he does not form too high an estimate of the rewards that await him, may have no reason to regret his selection of journalism as a pursuit. If, however, he does not possess these attributes, he will do well to reflect seriously before he essays to make a living by contributing to the periodical press of Great Britain. What is true of Great Britain and London is true, for all I know to the contrary, of every other capital and country in the world.

II.

MR. GLADSTONE.*

THE place which will ultimately be assigned to Mr. Gladstone in the ranks of English statesmen can only be fixed by one who is prophet as well as critic. At the present moment he is seen by opponents, and even by friends, through so disturbing a medium of prejudice and partiality; he is presented to the public by those who pass judgment upon him, in so grotesque and inconsistent a variety of aspects and disguises; he is to such an extent the victim of contradictory and antagonistic superlatives; above all, the exact quality of his influence upon the course of events, and the members of his party, is so difficult to define; the results, in some cases even the tendencies, of his statesmanship are so incalculable—that only the very rash, foolish and ignorant would presume to anticipate the verdict of posterity on the Liberal leader.

It is a task, at once less perilous and more profitable, to measure and classify the attributes by which he has acquired the position he now holds; to summarise a few of the idiosyncrasies of a man who is

* Reprinted from *The Fortnightly Review* for November, 1884.

admitted by his bitterest detractors and enemies to be a commanding force in the political life of England; to define some respects in which he differs from the most distinguished of his contemporaries, and some peculiarities which, in his seventy-sixth year, have accompanied the successive stages of his political development.

Fifty-two years ago, Mr. Gladstone entered Parliament as Tory member for Newark. Since then he has travelled the whole distance which separates the early Toryism of Sir Robert Peel from the Liberalism of Cobden and Bright, and far more than the distance which separated Sir Robert Peel's Protectionism from his conversion to Free Trade. The contrast between Sir Robert Peel and Mr. Gladstone, and between Mr. Gladstone and Mr. Bright, is striking. The changes of opinion undergone by Sir Robert Peel are surpassed in the changes illustrated in the career of Mr. Gladstone. But in the case of Mr. Gladstone they have been accomplished far more gradually and laboriously than in the case of Sir Robert Peel. During the debates on the Irish Church Act, the severest reproach which Mr. Disraeli could bring against the author of the measure was that he had formerly been a champion of the Protestant Establishment in Ireland, and that he had spoken in its favour when an undergraduate at Oxford. Neither Mr. Disraeli nor any one else could taunt Mr. Gladstone with having, like Peel, been returned to power to give effect to one policy and then espousing and executing another.

To say this is not to bring any charge against the memory of one of the greatest Ministers of the century, and, according to Lord George Bentinck's biographer, "the greatest Member of Parliament who ever lived." Peel's hand was forced by famine. The arguments with which imminent pestilence, bred of starvation, and the murmurs of approaching revolution supplied him, were unanswerable. He would have been no true patriot or statesman if he had held out against them. But though the desertion of his principles was prescribed by a destiny whose decrees he could not withstand, the fact of their unexpectedly sudden desertion remains.

If Mr. Gladstone's position has been established on the ruins of his old beliefs; if he destroyed that Irish Church of which he was once the enthusiastic advocate; if, in other fields of legislation, he has led his followers to the attack of strongholds which he once defended—it has been after due notice and upon clear and unambiguous pretences. In "A Chapter of Autobiography" he has demonstrated the processes by which he arrived at the conclusion that the Established Church in Ireland, which he had formerly held reconcilable with civil and national justice, could not be perpetuated without gross injustice. His original case, he says, was that "the Church of Ireland must be maintained for the benefit of the whole people of Ireland, and must be maintained as the truth, or it cannot be maintained at all." The latter condition was violated by the Maynooth grant; the former was disposed of by existing facts. "I never held," writes Mr. Gladstone in this chapter, "that a National Church should be permanently maintained except for the nation. I mean either for the whole of it, or at least for the greater part, with some kind of real concurrence or general acquiescence from the remainder."*

This language explains how it was that in the spring of 1868, in the debate on Mr. Maguire's motion, Mr. Gladstone first declared that "for the settlement of the Irish Church, that Church as a State Church must cease to exist." Mr. Disraeli's comment was that "the right honourable gentleman had come upon them all of a sudden like a thief in the night." But this suddenness—and it was naturally exaggerated by the Tory leader—was an entirely different thing from the adoption of a policy the exact opposite of which his party and the country had entrusted to a Minister; and when Mr. Gladstone came into office six months later, it was with a special commission to disestablish the Irish Church.

The contrast between Mr. Gladstone and Mr. Bright is even more strongly marked than that between Mr. Gladstone and Sir Robert Peel. As he now draws towards the end of his career, Mr. Bright cannot be charged with having abandoned, violated, or withdrawn a single principle that he ever proclaimed. Not a flaw of inconsistency or blemish of self-contradiction is to be seen in his whole career.

* "Gleanings of Past Years," vol. vii., pp. 112, 113, et seq.

Others have come round to him; he has lived to behold the convictions, which he firmly embraced and which were condemned as extravagant and absurd, incorporated into the accepted doctrines of the Liberal party and of all parties, and into the unquestioned traditions of English policy. But though Mr. Gladstone's record and retrospect are of the most opposite character, his mutations have never had anything in them of vacillation; they have partaken from the first of the nature of a slow growth, and have indicated the successive periods of an intellectual development.

Slowly, but with the certainty of daybreak, his horizon has expanded. He has himself told us that when he entered public life, he had but an imperfect sense of the ineffable blessings of liberty. This deficiency was not unnatural to one who had been brought up in the straitest school of authority and tradition, and who in early manhood was, in Macaulay's familiar words, "the rising hope of the stern and unbending Tories." As men rise on stepping-stones of their dead selves to higher things, so Mr. Gladstone has throughout his whole public life been engaged in bursting, and disentangling himself from, the cerements of his dead faiths. Whether he would have been greater or less than he is but for this progressive movement of his mind may be questioned; it is certain that he is indebted to it for much of the power which he exercises over those who are associated with him, however remotely or indirectly, in public life.

It is because Mr. Gladstone has been so consistently inconsistent, because the continuity of his views and beliefs has known such decisive, if slowly consummated, solutions, that he has carried with him so large a group of politicians, and so overwhelming a majority of the English people. The process of self-education has enabled him effectually to educate others. Those who have themselves learned slowly, at school or college, were declared by Dr. Arnold to make the best schoolmasters, because they could most easily place themselves in the position of unreceptive schoolboys. The wealth of words which Mr. Gladstone expends upon any proposal he introduces to the House of Commons; the variety of the points of view from which he looks at it; his minute weighing of every sort of counter consideration; the nice and, as they may seem, the tedious and sophistical distinctions which he draws between shades of thought and forms of words—each of these reflects or suggests some experience of his own mental discipline. There are few objections to any policy or scheme of legislation which he has not appreciated, and which consequently he does not set himself to remove.

For this reason he is in his treatment of public topics the least dogmatic of statesmen. Mr. Bright, who has neither receded from nor advanced beyond the tenets with which he first entered public life, cannot avoid a certain autocracy and absolutism in a statement of opinion. He has been troubled with no doubts, and even his fertile imagination can make little allowance for doubters. But it is to the doubters, the most illustrious of whom he himself has been, that Mr. Gladstone chiefly addresses himself. Hence the extraordinary complexity and comprehensiveness of his argumentation; hence what may be called the metaphysical quality in his eloquence, the subtle series of appeals to the consciousness of his hearers which runs like an undertone through his most splendid orations, and which is perhaps the secret of their occasional verbosity and even obscurity.

Whatever history may say of Mr. Gladstone, it will not say that he was a perfect leader of the House of Commons. He fails to be this for the very reasons which make him a great popular leader in the country. He understands more of man in the abstract than of man in the concrete; more of the passions which sway humanity in the bulk, than of the motives to which individuals are amenable, and the treatment to be applied to them. He is at his best when he is the exponent not so much of the policy of a party as of the ideas which animate that policy, and which touch the heart of nations. It was not till he had made his famous "flesh-and-blood" speech that Mr. Gladstone was really recognised as a great popular leader, and struck a responsive chord that still vibrates in the breasts of the English people. He had hitherto been best known as a financier, as the greatest Chancellor of the Exchequer England ever had, and as somewhat academic, narrow, and exclusive in his sympathies and tastes. But this phrase, to which additional effect was given by the glow of the language and the atmosphere of ideas associated with it, produced an instantaneous and almost electrical result.

The place into which he may be then said to have leaped, he has continued to hold. Notwithstanding his temporary retirement and the eclipse which, with the metropolitan public, his popularity suffered in the melodramatic days of Jingoism, events have conclusively shown that Mr. Gladstone surpasses all his contemporaries in his power of interpreting, and placing himself at the head of, public feeling, when it is deeply moved. The Bulgarian atrocities supplied him with one of those opportunities exactly congenial to his character and gifts. His Midlothian campaigns, whether in their oratorical labours or in the results that followed them, form a monument which supplies a fair measure of the greatness of the man. He took his stand upon general principles, upon those elementary ideas of justice, of humanity, which all can understand, and which he had, in his reply to Lord Palmerston thirty years earlier during the Don Pacifico debate, clearly foreshadowed. This reply is so remarkable, so appositely prophetic of the attitude which in foreign policy Mr. Gladstone has since repeatedly assumed, and so comparatively little known, that no apology need be offered for quoting an extract from it here:

The noble lord (Lord Palmerston) vaunted, amid the cheers of his supporters, that under his administration an Englishman should be, throughout the world, what the citizen of Rome had been. But, I ask, what then was a Roman citizen? He was a member of a privileged caste; he belonged to a conquering race, to a nation that held all nations bound down by the hand of Imperial power. For him there was to be an exceptional system of law; for him principles were to be asserted and rights were to be enjoyed, that were denied to the rest of the world. Is such, then, the view of the noble lord as to the relation that is to subsist between England and other countries? Does he make the claim for us that we are to be uplifted on a platform high above the standing-ground of other nations? It is indeed too clear that too much of this notion is lurking in his mind; that he adopts, in part, that vain conception that we, forsooth, have a mission to be the censors of abuses and imperfections among the other countries of the world; that we are to be the universal schoolmasters, and that all who hesitate to recognise our office should have the war of diplomacy, at least, forthwith declared against them. And certainly, if the business of a Foreign Secretary is merely to carry on a diplomatic war, all must admit the perfection of the noble lord in the discharge of his functions. But it is not the duty of a Foreign Minister to be like a knight-errant, ever pricking forth, armed at all points, to challenge all comers, and lay as many adversaries as possible sprawling, or the noble lord would be a master of his art; but to maintain that sound code of international principles which is a monument of human wisdom, and a precious inheritance bequeathed by our fathers for the preservation of the future brotherhood of nations.

This language explains why in foreign policy Mr. Gladstone has at times reached the heart of the multitude, precisely in proportion as he has dissatisfied the cooler critics of the House of Commons, and tried the patience of foreign statesmen and chancellors. It is literally true of Mr. Gladstone to say that, Trojan or Tyrian, Englishman, Egyptian, or Ethiopian, Bulgarian peasant or Lancashire artisan, he holds any one of them in no difference. To him the inhabitant of any country, in whatsoever quarter of the globe, and whatsoever his complexion, is first of all a man; to him he appears denuded of all the accidents of his nationality, isolated from the influence exercised on him by custom and antecedents, merely a member of the great family of the human race. As Bacon assumed that the *ingenia* of all men were equal, so Mr. Gladstone seems to assume that all who are born into this world have, innate in them, the same capacity as Englishmen of the nineteenth century, to become the orderly and prosperous subjects of a constitutional and popular Government. There is steadily fixed in his imagination the *idea* of a man, to which all existing types of humanity under heaven are conformable —an idea gathered from his experience of his fellow-men within the four seas.

This generous appreciation of the happy possibilities latent in a universal humanity, this tendency to reduce mankind to a common yet beatified denominator, commends itself to the fancy of the multitude just as it exasperates those statesmen and diplomatists to whom human beings are merely pawns on the chess-board—the creatures of circumstance, dependent for their capacities solely on geographical and physical conditions. Whatever misconception of Mr. Gladstone may exist in the mind of Prince Bismarck, or of any other Continental statesman, arises entirely from the circumstance that the point of view from which he regards human nature is diametrically opposite to that from which Prince Bismarck regards it. Hence, too, the difference which divided him from Mr. Disraeli, who, in the tactical skill with which he dealt with men as the members of a party, was as much superior to Mr. Gladstone as Mr. Gladstone is superior to Mr. Disraeli in his insight into the control of those perennial forces which dominate mankind in the aggregate.

It is an often cited instance of Lord Althorp's influence with the House of Commons that once, in answer to a speech of Croker, he rose and merely observed that he had made some calculations which he considered as entirely conclusive in refutation of the right honourable gentleman's arguments. But, unfortunately, he had mislaid them, so that he could only say that, if the House would be guided by his advice they would reject the amendment; which they accordingly did. Nothing of exactly the same kind is recorded of Mr. Gladstone, but in many cases he has exercised, if not in the House of Commons, yet in the country, an analogous authority. This prerogative has been displayed not only among professed Liberals, but among those very Conservatives who are most of all impervious to new ideas—country gentlemen, merchants, and country clergymen.

It may be doubted whether the Irish Church would have been abolished, or the Irish Land Act of 1881 passed so easily, except for the personal ascendency of the Prime Minister. There is so large and active a Conservative element in his nature that, when he has advocated an organic change, some

Conservatives, even though the leaders of the great mass of the party may have denounced him with all the bitterness and rancour which the English vocabulary can express, have secretly felt that Mr. Gladstone must be the victim of a great and overmastering necessity. He has carried the day rather by his moral influence than by his political cunning, and this influence has in its turn been based upon his conviction. And here it may be noticed that the doubts cast upon Mr. Gladstone's sincerity, the abuse with which, for qualities the exact opposite of sincerity, he has been assailed, have only tended to confirm the impression that above all things he is in earnest. When men are denounced for hypocrisy, with the animus which has characterised these denunciations in the case of the Prime Minister, one may be pretty sure that the real gravamen of the charge is an inconvenient devotion to an unwelcome faith.

Mr. Gladstone's sincerity reveals itself in various ways, some of them perhaps equivalent to congenital defects in his judgment and character. Among the many peculiarities of his mind few are more remarkable than its extraordinary casuistical learning, coupled as it is with intense interest in ecclesiastical questions. The two traits together find their expression in refinements of ratiocination which are often most puzzling to his warmest admirers, and in occasional displays of a want of anything like a due sense of proportion. Thus he is frequently as much agitated about and concerned in matters of the veriest detail as about affairs involving the highest principles. During the session of 1884, for instance, Mr. Gladstone showed an eagerness for the Bishopric of Bristol Bill not inferior to, and sometimes more aggressively visible than, his eagerness for the Franchise Bill. "Our miraculous Premier," *The Times* remarked in an article unusually discriminating and able, "has just given us another opportunity of admiring his many-sidedness and versatility. To-day begins an extraordinary and probably momentous session of Parliament, for which both sides have been preparing by two full months of the most strenuous agitation. . . . This is the occasion which he selects for issuing a letter, more than a column in length, to a Welsh Bishop on the subject of the Disestablishment of the Church. It would seem, indeed, that except for the little interlude of a run into Scotland, with the twenty or thirty speeches which that entailed, the Prime Minister's holiday has been given to topics much less mundane than the extension of the suffrage to county householders. There was a preface to write to the new edition of Hamilton's Catechism; there was the question of the Hittite Empire, and its possible alliance with Troy, to be taken in hand."

Closely allied with the quality just noticed is his persistent attention to debates which to others seem duller than Saturnian lead. He has been known, and doubtless will be known again, to sit for hours in the House of Commons with only a score of members present, listening, not merely with indefatigable patience, but with positive enthusiasm, to a succession of bores holding forth on a subject of no general interest. Could there be a more touching testimony to the infinite toleration of the Prime Minister? The charges often levelled at him by his opponents are absolutely inconsistent with this attribute. It may be observed incidentally, too, that they are mutually destructive. If Mr. Gladstone is tossed about by every gust of Radical passion, eager only to anticipate the will of his revolutionary associates, how can he be described as a despot and dictator?

Nor is the common impression that he is arrogant and imperious in his official capacity less at variance with the facts. In the Cabinet he is modest and conciliatory to a fault. Again and again, when a word from him would settle a question, he allows it to be discussed at length, and accepts without objection the decision of the majority. What is the explanation of a conventional accusation, absolutely unfounded upon any experience? The answer is not difficult. Power gravitates to the side of knowledge and ability. Water does not find its own level more sure than ascendency comes to the hands of the man who has the qualifications for it. Mr. Gladstone is the most commanding figure in the House of Commons. He is the best debater in it; he has had an unrivalled acquaintance with office and with affairs. He is, in a word, the first man in the popular Chamber of the Legislature, and his so-called dictatorial arrogance is merely an admission of the fact.

One of the reasons of Mr. Gladstone's influence with the English middle class may not yet have received the attention due to it. He is himself one of the most brilliant ornaments that the middle class, from which he himself is sprung, has ever possessed. He is the true representative of many of the most characteristic sentiments of this social order. Like Sir Robert Peel, he has a thorough sympathy with the aspirations of the commercial aristocracy, and in a far greater degree than Sir Robert Peel he has flung over the middle class a glamour higher than that derived from mere material prosperity. Mr. Gladstone is, in some respects, to look at him for a moment not as a statesman but as an English gentleman, the highest product of Eton and Oxford. As such he would have won social distinction if he had never plucked a single political laurel. The middle class, therefore, is proud of him on grounds independently of his achievements in statesmanship. At bottom it admires him even when it may not quite understand him. The very obscurity, which comes from subtlety, is accepted by the persons now spoken of as flattering to themselves, since it is the attribute of one who is in a measure their progeny.

Mr. Gladstone's oratory is, as for that matter all oratory is, the reflection of the intellectual being of the orator. It is laboured and lengthy because the mind and brain, which furnish the tongue with language, are so keenly appreciative of the difficulties which may suggest themselves to hearers. If Mr. Gladstone seldom touches a theme without adorning it, he never touches a theme which he does not, for the immediate purpose in hand, exhaust. His oratory is didactic, homiletic, beseeching, commentatorial, and microscopically minute, because he does not forget how tardy the process of conviction is, and how many obstacles must be disposed of before the desired result is obtained. It is not long since one of his colleagues gave an account of the difference between his own oratorical method and that of the Prime Minister. "When," he said, "I speak, I strike across from headland to headland. But Mr. Gladstone coasts along, and whenever he comes to a navigable river he cannot resist the temptation to explore it to its source."

All the dissertations on rhetoric since the world began, from Aristotle to Cicero, Tacitus and Quintilian, down to Whately, Alison, and Arnold, may be searched before so happy and terse an illustration is encountered. For the reason embodied in this figurative definition of two oratorical schools, some of Mr. Bright's single speeches are better than anything of Mr. Gladstone's. Yet it may be doubted whether there is anything finer in nineteenth-century oratory than Mr. Gladstone's impromptu speech on Mr. Disraeli's budget of 1853, or than his peroration before the division on the second reading of Lord Russell's Reform Bill was taken in 1866. In the same way his tribute to the memory of Lord Beaconsfield in 1881 was not only a masterpiece of taste and judgment, but of that peculiar class of oratorical composition to which it belonged. It also furnished a remarkable illustration of Mr. Gladstone's felicity in quotations, an ornament of debate now practically obsolete. On the whole Mr. Hayward's estimate of Mr. Gladstone as a speaker leaves nothing unsaid : " It is Eclipse first, and all the rest nowhere. He may lack Mr. Bright's impressive diction—impressive by its simplicity—or Mr. Disraeli's humour and sarcasm. But he has made ten eminently successful speeches to Mr. Bright's or Mr. Disraeli's one. His foot is ever in the stirrup ; his lance is ever in the rest. He throws down the gauntlet to all comers. Right or wrong he is always real, natural, earnest, unaffected and unforced. He is a great debater, a great parliamentary speaker."

He is also an eminently persuasive speaker, and that explains why he is less condensed than Mr. Bright. There is no writer the tones of whose voice it is easier to hear with the ear of imagination in the inflections and convolutions of his literary style than Mr. Gladstone. There are few speakers whose speeches it is less satisfactory to read. Yet nothing is more certain than that if Mr. Gladstone's oratory were better literature it would have been less fruitful of results. The style is the man. The persistency and even the prolixity of the orator are the counterparts and supplements of those qualities—the earnestness, the zeal, the wide-stretching sympathies—which have made the statesman great. And if, as has been admitted, there are single speeches of Mr. Bright's or Mr. Disraeli's of a higher literary and intellectual merit than any single speech of Mr. Gladstone's, Mr. Gladstone has still delivered a host of speeches, every sentence of which is stamped with intellectual power, that could have come from no other statesman of the day except himself.

To this order the first of his series of Midlothian addresses in which he explained the whole history of the Franchise Bill, belongs. Nor perhaps was he ever surpassed in the faculty of carrying the whole House with him in a dialectical whirlwind when in the session of 1884 he demolished Sir Stafford Northcote. Never, again, did he astonish and delight the House with a finer display of physical and intellectual vigour than when, after having been worried for a couple of hours in the Commons, he spoke for nearly three hours subsequently on the Eastern question. On the whole the very finest speech delivered by him during the lifetime of the late Parliament was that delivered on the Bradlaugh case. One quality is unquestionably wanting in Mr. Gladstone as an orator. He has little or no sense of humour. He seldom makes a joke; he seldom tries to do so; and if he tries, he very seldom succeeds.

If this were the place in which to say anything about Mr. Gladstone as a private member of society, it would, perhaps, be enough to remark that the fullest materials for information on this point may be found in the memoirs of distinguished men not long since departed and some of them still with us, which have recently been published. Lord Malmesbury has recorded that when he first met the present Prime Minister, then a rising young man, in 1842, he found him exceedingly agreeable. Much more copious materials for his personal portraiture will be discovered in the life of the late Bishop Wilberforce, written by his son. On the whole, however, those who will probably be spoken of as Mr. Gladstone's equals know little or nothing more of him than they know from their habitual contact with him in public. Few statesmen of the first order possess many very intimate associates among their political peers or allies. Most of those who were once Mr. Gladstone's peculiar friends have been carried away by death. The few who still survive are either ranged in a hostile camp or belong to a sphere of action and thought so different that personal communication with them has become impossible.

The persons who are now in his private confidence appear to be chosen for reasons of the validity of which Mr. Gladstone alone can judge. Before the Prime Minister of England all doors fly open, and even beyond the social limits of Liberalism or Whiggism Mr. Gladstone is welcomed, and is agreeably, though, as should probably be said, superficially, known. The subjects in which he takes an interest are multifarious. He reads immensely, and within five years of fourscore his intellectual activity and resourcefulness are such that time is never wanting to him when any subject he is deeply interested in comes to the front. Has he not just written an introduction to a devotional volume? On December 11th and 12th, 1868, he was the guest of Lord Salisbury at Hatfield, Bishop Wilberforce being one of the company. The episcopal diary for the former of these days thus mentions Mr. Gladstone: "Gladstone as ever; great, earnest, and honest; as unlike the tricky Disraeli as possible." But next day the Bishop writes: "Morning walk with Gladstone, Cardwell, and Salisbury. Gladstone was struck with Salisbury; 'never saw more perfect host.' . . . When people talk of Gladstone going mad they do not take into account the wonderful elasticity of his mind and the variety of his interests. This morning he was just as much interested in the size of the oaks and their probable age as if no care of state ever pressed upon him." That is a pleasant picture, and one intelligibly full of charm to the good prelate who drew it, and who subsequently speaks of Mr. Gladstone's power of detachment from the controversial matters of passing moment as his "chief safeguard." It may not, however, be his chief attraction to some of the more prominent members of the party which he leads. These would willingly hear him talk more about the great political struggles in which he has been and is engaged, and may attribute what seems to them his lack of attractiveness in private life to his superficial desultoriness and to his preference to discuss topics that are not of deep or living moment to him.

Few persons will be disposed to deny that the exact position which Mr. Gladstone fills in English politics, and the precise influence he wields, belong to himself alone, and that when he disappears he will leave no successor in either of these capacities. Mr. Gladstone served his parliamentary apprenticeship under the old *régime*. Canning had not passed away five years when he entered the House of Commons, and many of the men with whom he first went into the lobby were the associates and contemporaries of Pitt and Fox. No man who has caught the dying rays of the grand manner at St. Stephen's, who is so deeply imbued with the already half-forgotten traditions of the place, classical, literary, as well as political and official, has lived so long into, and has played so prominent a part in, the new order of things.

Any man who had lacked Mr. Gladstone's force of character, who had not combined even his moral influence with his early associations, would have failed to learn the era of democracy based on household suffrage, with so many ideas of an essentially Tory kind. He was, as he himself has said, brought up at the feet of Canning; and his first chief in the active business of political life was Sir Robert Peel. Whatever may be thought of Mr. Gladstone's personal merits or demerits, it will at any rate be confessed that this particular combination is not likely to present itself again. The statesman who has inhaled the traditions of Toryism with his earliest breath, who was saturated as a young man with academicism and classicism, who in religious matters was the friend of Newman and Keble, and who is indebted for much or most of the hold he has had upon the clergy—which is, after all, the most Conservative interest in the country—to his allegiance to those sentiments which found expression in his speeches on the Divorce Act, and again on the Public Worship Regulation Act, is a phenomenon on whose reappearance no one will count.

Already there has sprung up a school of political thinkers who, while they follow Mr. Gladstone's politics, have not the slightest sympathy with the sources, or the quality, of the moderating control which he exercises upon the progress of affairs. There is an immense deal in common between Mr. Gladstone and not only the old Whigs but the old Tories, and if he ever seems to go to the verge of the new Radicalism, it is with something more than a last longing, lingering look behind—with an earnest desire to which, as far as may be, he gives effect, to guard against the possible errors of precipitancy and excess. Mr. Gladstone's authority and experience have upon different occasions, and at no time more conspicuously than the present, induced his followers to limit and curtail their demands. He has stood at the parting of two ways, and by standing there has prevented a separation of the two forces of which Liberalism is composed.

The history of the Liberal party has illustrated thus far, and will illustrate yet farther, the progressive movement of Mr. Gladstone's own mind. Those who affect to deplore the encouragement he has given to advanced ideas will, when he has gone, have abundant reason to regret the check he has imposed to their translation into fact. It may be that his departure will be followed by a schism in the Liberal ranks. In that case what has happened before will happen again, and the party of movement will carry after it the party of inaction and delay. Liberalism and Radicalism are only varying modes of the same political agency. The difference between them is one, not of principle, but of chronology. The part played by Lord Palmerston has in some sort been played by Mr. Gladstone, but, as far as it is possible to frame any estimate of the political forces now at work, Toryism will for the reasons already assigned discover that the disappearance of Mr. Gladstone will be the prelude to an era of organic political change far more stirring and drastic than that which commenced with Lord Palmerston's death.

III.

MEN OF LETTERS ON THEMSELVES.*

THE two entertaining and instructive volumes in which Mr. Edmund Yates has recorded the experiences and reminiscences of a varied, animated and successful career, had as their predecessors some interesting recollections by a popular novelist, and have been followed by the narrative of "Episodes in the Second Life" of a distinguished journalist, told by himself. Certain characteristics are possessed by each of these autobiographies in common. Mr. Yates combines, or has combined, in his own person the function of Mr. James Payn and Mr. Antonio Gallenga. Like the former he is a novelist; like the latter he is, or has been, a writer of newspaper articles, and among the most locomotive and picturesque of newspaper special correspondents. With Mr. Yates, as with the two other literary autobiographers, existence has been a strenuous and prosperous affair,—full of labour and

* "Edmund Yates: His Recollections and Experiences." 2 vols. (Bentley). "Episodes of My Second Life," by A. Gallenga. 2 vols. (Chapman and Hall). "Some Literary Recollections," by James Payn. 1 vol. (Smith, Elder, and Co.).

effort, but of effort ending in fruition, and of labour sweetened by fame. Mr. Yates tells us how first, at the bidding of the Post Office authorities, he performed rapid journeys between London and foreign capitals, and how, when the Government was taking over the telegraphs, he visited nearly every portion of the United Kingdom; how next, at the bidding of the editor of *The New York Herald*, he had no sooner returned to England from America, than he was summoned to Paris, and then instructed to proceed without a moment's delay to Vienna or Madrid, to St. Petersburg or Berlin.

The correspondence of Mr. Gallenga was for the most part in a more serious vein than that of Mr. Yates. He was present at scenes of greater historic significance, and he chronicled the decision of more momentous issues. But both men were in their separate departments of journalism equally in the first rank; equally prompt, accurate, persevering, graphic. This discipline, perhaps the most trying of any that the press affords, was never submitted to by Mr. Payn, between whom, however, and Mr. Yates there exist, in spite of marked dissimilarities, some resemblances or coincidences. Both may be said to have been brought up in the school, and at the feet, of Dickens; both enjoyed in varying degrees his friendship; both formed his acquaintance about the same time, Mr. Yates in 1854, Mr. Payn two years later; both made their real literary *début* in *Household Words*. The first appearance of each in print was poetical—Mr. Yates

F

when a mere boy, sending to Mr. Harrison Ainsworth some stanzas which were inspired by Thackeray's "At the Church Gate;" and Mr. Payn at the same tender age contributing a composition entitled "The Poet's Death" to Leigh Hunt's journal.

Both have, or have had, many common friends, and many of the same famous or familiar characters appear and reappear in the pages of the books of each. The education, like the natural tastes and aptitudes, of Mr. Payn and Mr. Yates was widely different. The former, who went from Eton to Woolwich, and from Woolwich to Cambridge, was without any turn whatever for languages. "Languages," he writes, "have been always as unattainable to me as the science of music. I spent many years over French and German, but could never read, far less converse in, either tongue with facility." Mr. Yates received the rudiments of a sound classical and general training at Highgate School, was transferred to Düsseldorf and Bonn, whence in nine months' time he returned to England with a perfect command of the German vocabulary and accent. It is to his knowledge of French and German that Mr. Yates attributes much of his success in life, and notably the opportunities of studying men, manners, and cities, which his Continental missions for the Post Office supplied.

One admirable quality pervades, in a conspicuous degree, each of these works. "I do not think," writes Mr. Yates in his preface, "I have said any harsh thing of any person alive or dead. I am certain that

I have not said such a thing consciously." As a matter of fact, Mr. Yates has not said it at all. "Whatever judgment," writes Mr. Gallenga, "I may have passed upon myself, whether the picture of my character resulting from the narrative of my thoughts and deeds be too partial or too severe, I must at least be held guiltless of having indulged in any personality offensive to the dead or living."

As for Mr. Payn, he makes no professions, because he spares himself the trouble of a preface, but he is consistently amiable and genial. It is only natural that there should be more traces of a melancholy humour, bordering on bitterness, in Mr. Gallenga than in Mr. Yates or Mr. Payn. In the first place, he was a patriot and an exile. He took life seriously; he felt acutely the vicissitudes and humiliations to which, in his earliest attempts to earn a living in America and in England as a teacher of languages and a writer of magazine articles, he was compelled to submit. In the second place, though the success which Mr. Gallenga achieved as an English journalist and the command he acquired of forcible and correct English are for a foreigner unique, he never forgot that he was a stranger living among strangers. "In spite," he writes, "of the unfailing kindness and deference which I received abroad, I was full of silly complaints borrowed from Dante about the salt that savours other people's bread, and the hardship of climbing and descending other people's stairs." But he had other hardships than these, and for some years he was a man with a grievance. He could not get back his manuscripts when he wanted, or see editors when he called. "Paying editors were not many, and were accessible to none but their intimate friends." Of Delane and Morris, under whom he did much splendid work for *The Times*, he speaks in terms of unstinted admiration; but, with the exception of Mr. Sala, there is no one about whom he expresses himself with more than conventional cordiality.

Elected in 1853, after his name had been down nine years, a member of the Athenæum Club, "he did not much value the mere honour of belonging to a learned society. As," he continues, "members have to wait at least a score of years before they are balloted for, by far the greatest number consisted of twaddling and cackling fogies, whose bald pates, toothless gums, and rickety limbs sent a chill through my veins, and acted as an unpleasant reminder that I also had left the mid career of life behind me. I met but few old friends, and made fewer new ones." Again, "The Athenæum Club was to me a workshop where I saw few I knew, and hardly spoke to those few. Literary men like Bulwer and Disraeli; statesmen like Lord Clarendon, Lord Granville, Lord Salisbury, Mr. Gladstone, Mr. Forster, and Lord Hartington; diplomatists like Lord Lyons, Lord Cowley, Lord Ampthill, Lord Lytton, Lord Howden, have all come within the orbit of my acquaintance; but with all the good-will on my part and all the courtesy and amiability on theirs, the intercourse almost invariably ended where it began."

The truth is, as he explains, Mr. Gallenga was very busy, very shy, and very near-sighted. Mr. Payn, indeed, is uniformly cheery, sometimes positively chirpy. Yet a bubbling drop of something very like acrimony occasionally wells up to the smooth and smiling surface. "My experience," he says, "of men and women of letters, which has been continuous, and extends over thirty years, is that for kindness of heart they have no equals. I have known but one absolutely offensive man of letters, and even he was said to be pleasant when sober, though as I only met him some half-dozen times, and his habits were peculiar, I never had a fair chance of finding him in that condition." "I am well aware," he writes in another place, "that there are a good many people who dislike me very cordially. If they do so for a good reason I exceedingly regret it. But there are some folks whose animosity is the highest of compliments. There is, in my opinion, no more fatal weakness in human nature than the desire to be thought well of by everybody"—a doctrine to which perhaps no one can take exception.

Neither Mr. Payn nor Mr. Gallenga is as uniformly charitable and kindly, as absolutely free from all afterthought of rancour, all hinting of faults and hesitating of dislikes, as Mr. Yates, who, indeed, shows himself in these volumes to be the incarnation of buoyancy, good-nature, and good-fellowship. Mr. Payn and Mr. Yates seem both of them to be brimming over with an exuberance of joyousness which may well excite the admiration of those whose moral mercury seldom rises above a figure contemptibly low. It is not so long since, if I remember correctly, that Mr. Payn published a volume of stories called "High Spirits." Mr. Payn's title has been from his earliest youth Mr. Yates's property, and as Mr. Payn, although he was not addicted to any form of physical exercise, had as a boy a fatal propensity towards practical jokes; so Mr. Yates's inborn vivacity was so indomitable that his departmental chief in the Post Office bade him, as a preliminary discipline to the day's routine, walk from St. John's Wood to St. Martin's-le-Grand instead of being driven on the omnibus. For genuine amiability, as has been said, the palm must be given to Mr. Yates. His volumes are not only in their way a masterpiece, excellently written, whether as regards taste or literary style, with their component parts admirably arranged, the product at once of an exceedingly clever man, wielding a practised and artistic pen; they are also the product of a kindly, courteous, and considerate nature, strong and impetuous, but sympathetic even to tenderness.

Unless Mr. Yates was endowed in an unusually liberal measure with these qualities, it is certain that he would not have refrained from some animadversions which might have been pardonably severe on Thackeray. Mention is made of Thackeray by Mr. Payn and Mr. Gallenga as well. Mr. Payn tells what some persons may suppose to be a characteristic

anecdote of the great novelist. "Even B—I will
call him *B*, for indeed he was busy enough, though
he made no honey—speaking to Thackeray of Leitch
Ritchie, admitted that he was 'a very gentlemanly
man.' 'But how does B *know?*' said Thackeray."
Mr. Gallenga, as an instance of Thackeray's playful-
ness, cites the following:

> One day, at a large men's party, when we were sixteen present,
> as I was seated nearly at the lower end of the table and I was
> talking to my neighbour on the right, our host, from the opposite
> end, where the conversation was flagging, suddenly and apropos
> to nothing, called out loudly to me across the table, and asked:
> "Pray, Mr. Gallenga" (he never omitted the mister), "pray, who
> is your dentist?" There was instant silence, and most of the
> guests looked up at me. But I was ready with my answer and
> spoke out instantly: "John Heath, No. 11, Albemarle Street, the
> best in London." Upon which the guests looked at each other for
> a few moments wondering, and soon the confused buzz of voices
> went on as before. What whim was it that prompted Michael
> Angelo Titmarsh with that apparently idle question? Did it arise
> from an ill-natured desire to call attention to the havoc that time
> might have made with my jaws and at the truly marvellous skill
> with which art now repairs the grievous losses of nature? Did he
> expect me to blush or faint like any middle-aged madam, the
> mystery of whose golden chignon or rosy cheek is by some un-
> toward accident brought into light in the presence of her most
> devoted admirers? Or was that merely his pleasantry, his wish
> to give a fillip to a languid conversation by supplying a new sub-
> ject which might raise a laugh no matter at whose expense? If
> the latter was his purpose, it flew wide of the mark, for though
> some of our friends may have been struck by the strangeness of
> his sudden sally, no one seemed to perceive its drift. No one
> noticed its "fun" or humour. The joke, if joke it was, fell flat.

As there were reasons which might have excused
Mr. Yates if he had adopted a very different tone in

regard to Thackeray, so there is much in the unavoidable circumstances of a literary career which might have prompted him, as well as Mr. Payn and Mr. Gallenga, to reflections far more acrimonious than are to be found in any of the volumes I am now considering. The life of a writer was defined by Pope as "a warfare upon earth." Few warriors could have illustrated the principles of amnesty with more generosity than Mr. Yates. Speaking of literature, Mr. Payn says there is "no calling so bright and pleasant, so full of genial friendship, so radiant with the glories of success; but there is also no pursuit so doubtful, so full of risks, so subject to despondency and disappointments, so open to despair. Oh, my young friend, with a turn for literature, think twice and thrice before committing yourself to it, or you may bitterly regret to find yourself where that turn may take you."

Yet though these are Mr. Payn's sentiments, everything is rose-coloured in his autobiography, and as it is with Mr. Payn so is it in a greater degree with Mr. Yates. Now it is no sufficient explanation of this circumstance in the case of a man like Mr. Yates to say that he has been brilliantly successful. Success in most men is no remedy for resentment, and does not remove the causes of embitterment. If there ever existed a calling which could justify embitterment and resentment, it is that of the professional writer. Thackeray in one of the most acid chapters in his "Book of Snobs," after having shown that literature was full of them, exclaimed in bitter irony, "There are no snobs in literature." Mr. Yates has had a good deal more to do with journalism than Mr. Payn; he has therefore been brought more into contact with all kinds and conditions of gentlemen who write. He has had as many opportunities as an Old Bailey barrister, or Mr. George Lewis himself, of seeing the seamy side of human nature.

It is not too much to say that the social commerce and the professional intercourse inseparable from a literary life is to moderately sensitive natures a protracted torture. The competition which must be encountered and defeated before the position is won, is incessant, bitter, and frequently humiliating. When a sort of table-land of success and influence has been reached, and the competitor has at his disposal some degree of literary patronage, he is upon the threshold of fresh troubles. The responsible conductor of any literary enterprise has to deal with every sort of knavery and incapacity—as to which let the intelligent reader consult Mr. Payn's remarks in the last hundred pages of his volume. He is perpetually assailed by the importunity of incompetence and the impudence of inaptitude. He will find himself beset alternately by the entreaties and impertinences of the opinionated dullard whose conceit is a bar to his improvement, and who in his relations with the men whose kindly offices he solicits begins with flattery, then breaks into a snarl, and ends by suing with a whine. The monitions of experience are thrown away upon these persons. They are the parasites of our literary system, and it is infinitely to the credit of Mr. Yates's native kindliness that he should have been able to practise a self-control beyond that of Mr. Payn, and not have had an unkind word to say upon the subject. There is, I firmly believe, no instance on record of a man of letters who, having trodden so persistently the uphill path of an opposed career as Mr. Yates, and having gone through such a series of exertions and encounters, ever took so urbane and kind a retrospect of the past.

In his chapter entitled "The Influence of 'Pendennis,'" Mr. Yates gives us what is, from an autobiographical point of view, one of the most interesting portions of his work :

> To get admitted into the ranks of literary men, among whom I might possibly, by industry and perseverance, rise to some position, began to be my constant thought; and I was encouraged in the hope that I might succeed, perhaps more than anything else, by reading the career of "Pendennis," which, in its well-remembered yellow cover, had then been appearing month by month for the last two years, and in its complete form was just obtainable at the libraries. There is no prose story in our English language, not even the "Christmas Carol," not even "The Newcomes," not even the "Scenes of Clerical Life" or "Silas Marner"—and now I have named what are to me the most precious—which interests and affects me like "Pendennis." It had this effect from the very first. I knew most of it so thoroughly. The scenes in the provincial theatre—the Fotheringay, her father, the prompter, the company—were such perfect creations (to this day I have never seen any hint as to where Thackeray got his study of these people, who were quite out of his usual line); the position of Pendennis and his mother was so analogous to that of me and mine—her

devotion, his extravagance; the fact that I was personally acquainted with Andrew Arcedeckne, the original of Foker, in whom he was reproduced in the most ludicrously lifelike manner: all this awakened in me a special interest in the book; and when, in the course of Pen's fortunes, he enters upon the literary career, writes his verses for the *Spring Annual*, dines with Bungay, visits Shandon, is engaged on the *Pall Mall Gazette*, and chums with Warrington, who makes that ever-to-be-quoted speech about the power of the press: "Look at that, Pen! There she is, the great engine; she never sleeps," etc.—when I came to this portion of the book my fate was sealed. To be a member of that wonderful Corporation of the Goosequill, to be recognised as such, to be one of those jolly fellows who earned money and fame, as I thought, so easily and so pleasantly, was the one desire of my life; and, if zeal and application could do it, I determined that my desire should be gratified.

One can understand that men should, even from the sober eminence of middle age, look back to the novels of Marryat or Lever as the sources from which they first derived their passion for a naval or military career. But this is very different from a man of Mr. Yates's maturity and experience deliberately asserting that "Pendennis" impelled him into literature. It may be so, and there seems throughout Mr. Yates's nature a strong vein of sentiment which would partially account for the fact. But the prosaic critic may be pardoned for suspecting that he has unconsciously exaggerated the influence of the book. Mr. Yates had from the very first, partly, it may be, as a result of his thorough training in French and German, partly as a gift of nature, a real capacity for literature. He has always possessed a faculty of neat and concise expression, flavoured by wit, fun, and irony, that is exceedingly rare amongst English writers, and that renders him, in certain kinds of composition, unsurpassed by any and unapproached by most of his contemporaries. Ability of this sort would have found its right field of display, and if Mr. Yates will forgive "the young gentleman, then fresh from Oxford, who called upon him in 1866, at the Post Office, with a letter of introduction from Tom Hood," and of whose articles in *Temple Bar* he was good enough to approve, for saying it, neither "Pendennis" nor its author had perhaps as much to do as he supposes with the initial step he took on the road to literary fame. At the same time Mr. Yates ought to know—and the fact that he is now deliberately of opinion that such is the case, even if he misconceives the circumstances, furnishes a suggestive clue to, and is a significant commentary on, the appreciative, impulsive, and sympathetic aspects of his character.

It is curious that if "Pendennis" first made Mr. Yates a writer, the author of "Pendennis" should have been directly instrumental in investing the year 1858 with "the vast importance" with which, in his seventh chapter, Mr. Yates says "it was fraught to him." The reference is to the events that led to Mr. Yates's withdrawal from the Garrick Club. Both for its interest and its taste the Garrick chapter is excellent. "The most striking portion of the club in those days was the smoking-room on the ground floor, built out over the 'leads'—a good-sized apartment, comfortably furnished, well ventilated, and adorned by large pictures specially painted for it by Stanfield, David Roberts, and Louis Haghe." Among the *habitués* of the establishment were Charles Kemble, "Assassin" Smith, Clarkson Stanfield, Sir William de Bathe, Samuel Lover, Robert Bell, Charles Reade, Peter Cunningham, Frank Fladgate, better known as "Papa," and J. D., "most mellow of elderly topers, with all the characteristics of 'Bardolph of Brasenose'—a veteran who drank and swore in the good old-fashioned way, and who came to a sad end, poor fellow, dying alone in his Temple chambers, on a Christmas Eve, of loss of blood from an accident, while the men in the rooms below heard him staggering about and groaning, but took no notice, as they fancied their neighbour was only in his usual condition." Thackeray was the presiding genius of the place. As Mr. Gallenga has said in his concluding chapter, "Thackeray was a member but not much of a frequenter of the Athenæum Club, his preference being all for the Garrick, a club better suited to the free and easy, somewhat Bohemian, tastes and habits of his early days."

When Mr. Yates was first admitted to the Garrick he was not eighteen years of age. When he left it he was twenty-seven, and Thackeray, who was the cause of his leaving it, was forty-seven. The little article contributed by Mr. Yates to a paper long since dead, at which Thackeray took grave umbrage, scarcely deserves the censures passed upon it by its author. It is simply a piece of smart, hurried, impertinent, and curiously young writing. Now, as Thackeray was then twenty years Mr. Yates's senior, what one might have expected from him was, if he had been incurably wounded, silent contempt; or, if he had been merely annoyed, a sharpish caution to Mr. Yates. The article in question did not violate the sanctity of club life. It disclosed no private or semi-private conversations; it said absolutely nothing more about Thackeray than was at the time on the lips of every one, and was, therefore, public property. Thackeray, however, very absurdly, as all coolheaded persons will think, addressed to Mr. Yates a formal letter, which, as its recipient says, was severe to the point of cruelty—being, indeed, an inexplicably bitter outburst of personal feeling, and "a censure, in comparison with the offence committed, ludicrously exaggerated."

What, however, under the circumstances, Mr. Yates ought to have done is perfectly clear. Young men of twenty-seven cannot allow themselves the luxury of engaging their superiors and elders in single combat. Their business is to be conciliatory and to wait. Mr. Yates should have written to Thackeray an apologetic disclaimer, assuring the great novelist that he had misunderstood the motives with, and the conditions under, which the offending article was penned; that on re-reading it the author recognised its impropriety, and that doing this he could only cry "Peccavi!" express his extreme regret, and throw himself on his elder's consideration. One of two things must then have happened: either Thackeray would have accepted the apology and condoned the offence, or, by refusing to do so, he would have made a graceless exhibition of churlishness, and public opinion, even the opinion of the Garrick Club, would have been with Mr. Yates. The letter which Mr. Yates prepared in draft, so far from being an apology, was a challenge, a justification of all he had originally said, and a justification by reference to instances which would have been most exasperating to Thackeray. "I took the liberty," to quote his own words, "of reminding Thackeray of some past errors of his own, not the result of the hasty occupation of an hour, but deliberately extending over a long space of time, and marked by the most wanton, reckless, and aggravating personality."

I reminded him how, in his "Yellowplush Correspondence," he had described Dr. Lardner and Sir E. L. Bulwer: "One was pail, and wor spektickles, a wig, and a white neckcloth; the other was slim, with a hook nose, a pail fase, a small waist, a pare of falling shoulders, a tight coat, and a catarack of black satting tumbling out of his busm, and falling into a gilt velvit weskit." How he had held them up to ridicule by calling them "Docthor Athanasius Lardner" and "Mistaw Edwad Lytton Bulwig," by reproducing the brogue of the one and the drawl of the other, and by exhibiting them as contemptible in every way.

In regard to the Garrick Club, I called Mr. Thackeray's attention to the fact that he had not merely, in his "Book of Snobs," and under the pseudonym of Captain Shindy, given an exact sketch of a former member, Mr. Stephen Price, reproducing Mr. Price's frequent and well-known phrases; he had not merely, in the same book, drawn on a wood-block a close resemblance of

Wyndham Smith, a fellow-member, which was printed among the "Sporting Snobs," Mr. W. Smith being a sporting man; he had not merely, in "Pendennis," made a sketch of a former member, Captain Granby Calcraft, under the name of Captain Granby Tiptoff, but in the same book, under the name of Foker, he had most offensively, though amusingly, reproduced every characteristic, in language, manner, and gesture, of our fellow-member, Mr. Andrew Arcedeckne, and had gone so far as to give an exact woodcut portrait of him, to Mr. Arcedeckne's intense annoyance.

Although this letter was not sent, the spirit of Mr. Yates's actual rejoinder, approved though it was by Dickens, was scarcely more conciliatory. There is no need to pursue the details of the incident. The alternative was at last presented to Mr. Yates of apologising to Thackeray or of quitting the club. Here Mr. Yates made a second mistake. He declined to apologise, and preferred the doom of exile. That he was to a great extent in the right ought really not to have weighed with him. Matters of this sort are practically decided, not on their merits, but by the prejudices and the partialities of a majority. Mr. Yates has given the facts; only a few remarks are necessary to place them in their proper perspective. The inference is irresistible that Thackeray's feelings were worked upon from outside, and that influences hostile to Mr. Yates were from the first brought to bear upon him. Dashing and successful young men of strongly defined "personality," and superabundance of animal spirits, are never likely to be popular among their elders. It also seems reasonable to suppose there may have been a clique antagonistic to Mr. Yates in the Garrick Club, of which Mr.

Yates's friend, now deceased, who mentioned to Thackeray the authorship of the article which produced the mischief, was possibly the leader. Again, Mr. Yates's champion and adviser in the whole matter was Thackeray's rival, whom Thackeray himself, however fervently he could, as Mr. Payn shows was the case, admire his genius, personally disliked. In this matter there can be no doubt that Dickens showed himself as bad an adviser as Delane, practised man of the world though he was, did upon another occasion when Dickens invoked his services as a counsellor.

It would be exceedingly presumptuous on the part of one who never had the honour of being in Thackeray's company—except, indeed, once, some thirty years ago, when the great man, coming down to West Somerset to inspect a small country house which he then thought of buying or renting, noticed him as a child—to attempt any estimate of Thackeray's character. Anthony Trollope, who on the strength of a seven years' (though exceedingly slight) acquaintance with the author of *Vanity Fair*, dared to pen a monograph of him, was called to account with contemptuous severity by the surviving relatives of the object of his admiration.

Some of the stories told by Mr. Yates of Thackeray are as good as anything of the kind which can be expected. There are also, as we have seen, some reminiscences of him in Mr. Gallenga's work, and a few pages are devoted to him by Mr. Payn. But they really tell us nothing. Death, the great leveller, is also the great distorter, and it is the most difficult thing in the world to arrive at anything like a complete idea of the identity of so many-sided a man as Thackeray. Lord Beaconsfield in his last novel, "Endymion," drew him, as to Disraeli the younger he seemed to be, at full length in St. Barbe. But then Lord Beaconsfield may have travestied his original, just as we are assured he caricatured and calumniated John Wilson Croker. Upon those who were personally acquainted with a great man gone, death produces an effect upon the moral features of their illustrious friend analogous to that which it is said to produce upon the human physiognomy. Countenances which, while the breath remained in the body, were unlovely, harsh, angular, or coarse, are traditionally supposed to be invested with a spiritual beauty and ennoblement directly the muscles, sinew, and marrow are reduced to inanimate clay. It is the fashion nowadays for the moral being of a man to undergo a similar transformation. Again, what is called character is habitually invested with an unreal unity. Pope's celebrated couplet,

> Nothing so true as what you once let fall,
> Most women have no character at all,

is applicable to the majority of the stronger as well as to the weaker sex.

Consistency is the last thing one should look for, except amongst the most elevated, and not always with them. It is just possible that the infinite variety of the man and the inconsistency and contradictions which it involved, may be the chief reasons that render it so hard for those who never knew him personally to form a notion of what manner of man Thackeray was. What are called estimates of character are in nine hundred and ninety-nine cases out of a thousand the records of personal, of interested, and of, therefore, more or less untrustworthy impressions. They are true as far as they go and no farther. If of two mendicants, who meet a pedestrian, one at the top and the other at the bottom of the street, the former receives sixpence and the latter nothing, the estimates which they each form of the same individual will be diametrically opposite. The beggar who has pocketed the dole will heap blessings upon him; the beggar who has failed to secure a copper will pursue him with execrations. Of Thackeray no biography worthy of the name has yet been published, and even when it is published it will fail to supply us in all probability with any formula of manageable dimensions in which we can apprize the man.

> Everything about him, says Mr. Gallenga, his humour, his countenance, his voice, was changeable. In the depth of his heart I am inclined to believe he was all kindness, but all sourness and uncharitableness on the surface. Like Carlyle, he spoke precisely as he wrote. His cynicism, his misanthropy and pessimism, his hatred of mobbism and flunkeyism, were with him inexhaustible themes. But it was in a great measure mere bounce—rhodomontade and fanfaronade—and it grew louder and more blatant in proportion as his domestic fortunes improved, and his real good-nature ripened and mellowed.

Mr. Yates' volumes, apart from their purely personal interest, have—and the remark holds, to some extent, good of Mr. Gallenga's and Mr. Payn's —a genuine historical value. Mr. Gallenga's book, indeed, contains a succinct, lucid and admirably-written account of the patriotic movement in Italy which came to a triumphant close when, on that memorable 20th of September, 1870, the troops of General Cadorna passed into the Eternal City. Mr. Gallenga occupies a prominent place in that brilliant galaxy of special and war correspondents, the other bright particular stars of which are W. H. Russell, Sala, Forbes, and Cameron of *The Standard*. He has also, as a political writer, especially on foreign affairs, left behind him a reputation in Printing House Square which will never be forgotten.

Personally I do not think that any work I was allowed to do in my time was ever rewarded by a word of praise more gratifying to my self-esteem than that which Delane bestowed upon me from the beginning to the end of that seven years' severe trial. He had great confidence in my judgment and knowledge of continental affairs, and allowed me to conduct the wars and revolutions of that eventful period at my own discretion. He heard that *The Times* authority on military subjects never stood higher. He was told by club quidnuncs, who congratulated him on the war articles in the great journal, that there was only one man in England who understood such subjects so thoroughly, and that was Sir John Burgoyne, and he laughed in his sleeve as he answered that they—the quidnuncs—"were perhaps not much out in their surmises." At the same time, however, there were many anxious moments at the various stages of the Franco-German war, especially during the three great days before Metz, towards the close of the siege of Paris, or the campaign of Aurelles de Paladine and

Chanzy on the Loire, in which a sudden turn in the fortune of arms seemed probable, seemed imminent, and when, nevertheless, I pinned my faith to Moltke's genius, and staked, as it were, *The Times*' reputation on the German's complete final victory; and then my good editor came to me late in the evening pale with anxiety, begging me not to be rash, not too confident, for he had seen this, and he had heard that, and competent judges, whom he named—among others Colonel B—— had assured him that we were venturing too far, and that events would soon contradict our statements and demolish our theories, greatly to the loss of *The Times*' prestige. When Paris surrendered, and Moltke and I had triumphed over prostrate France, my dear Delane drew a long breath and wrote to me a kind letter of congratulation, stating how glad he was that he had trusted me, that I had always been right in my forecast, and had not, by one single false step during that long warlike crisis, misled the English reading public. I have still the letter before me, and I value it far more highly than any Red or Black Eagle that Bismarck could have bestowed upon me.

When, therefore, Mr. Gallenga says, "I might also feel tempted to flatter myself that my career as a journalist was not an absolute failure," he speaks with unnecessary diffidence and modesty. In talking of "the cut and dry manner which has become almost the technical and conventional style of the Press, especially since the invention of electric wires has sunk the correspondent's business to the level of that of the mere telegraph clerk," he will be held by competent judges to be in error. The influence of telegraphy upon the style of the special and war correspondent has certainly not been hostile, still less fatal, to vigour and picturesqueness; witness the marvellous despatches of Mr. Cameron and Mr. Forbes. On the other hand, it has probably robbed the resident correspondent in foreign capitals, and therefore the Press generally, of some of its own authority. Instead of the well-weighed and instructive letters on foreign affairs, which used to be highly profitable reading, and which have now almost entirely disappeared from journalism,—*The Times, The Morning Post, The St. James's Gazette,* and *The Globe* alone being permitted by inexorable exigencies of space occasionally to publish them,—we have to be content with telegraphic despatches which are admirable as viewy condensations of the latest news, but which have little permanent value, and which scarcely help the average reader to form an intelligent notion of a political situation in a remote capital.

Mr. Gallenga makes some suggestive remarks on the social revolution which has been accomplished since the period of his first stay in England. "Men," he tells us, "then travelled little; the women seldom left home, except for their three weeks' sea-bathing at Herne Bay or Broadstairs. They seldom saw the inside of a theatre, and few of them were great readers, for Mudie was not yet, nor Westerton, nor the Grosvenor, nor the London Library, and books were hard to borrow and dear to buy." When Mr. Yates first knew London, Butcher Hall Lane had not disappeared, Alton Ale houses abounded to the east of Temple Bar, Almack's was in its zenith, the Adelaide Gallery had just been taken by Laurent, the Holborn Restaurant was a swimming bath, Vauxhall, though in its decadence, "dingy, dear, and absurdly expensive," was popular, the Overland Route was on view in Waterloo Place, the Park was full of prodigious dandies, cheap chop-houses and foreign eating-houses were in vogue, Paddy Green was in his patriarchal bloom. There was none of the display, luxury, and glitter of these latter times; but there was much comfort, much geniality, and an amount of sociability, and a facility for cheap amusements now unknown. Bohemia then occupied a recognised and considerable place in the map of London. Mr. Sala was brought from Rule's oyster shop to be presented to the Duke of Sutherland, then Marquis of Stafford, who was loud in praise of "Colonel Quagg's Conversion," at the Fielding Club. Robert Brough was denouncing the sham culture of pseudo-classicists in his lyrics, and published in his "Songs of the Governing Classes" a passionate attack upon social distinctions with the refrain—

> 'Tis a curse to the land, deny it who can,
> That self-same boast, I'm a gentleman.

Mr. Edmund Byng, Mr. Yates's godfather, entertained the most select of guests with the plainest and best of dinners, and young men, "who to-day sit down to soup, fish, entrées—then called 'made dishes'—a roast, a bird, a sweet, a savoury, and a bottle of claret, would then have been content with a slice off the joint, a bit of cheese, and a pint of beer." Even Mr. Yates, when he first married, as he "could not afford to give his friends good wine, and would not give them bad," regaled them on bitter ale. Lucky friends! though one may hope that if, even in this degenerate epoch, Mr. Yates were starting afresh he would not be so far borne away by the vicious contagion of fashion as to endeavour to sap the digestion of his company by the loaded acidity which is called claret, and the abominable decoctions of sugar and petroleum known as champagne.

London, Lord Beaconsfield remarked some months before his death, which was once a very dull place, is now a very amusing place, and so from one point of view it is. But the impression left upon the reader who was not personally acquainted with the metropolis during the first decade of the Victorian era, as he lays down Mr. Yates's volumes, is, that if we have gained considerably, we have also lost not a little. There is much that is cheap and nasty now; there was much that was cheap and pleasant then. "Timmins's little dinners" had not become regular events, and the trail of Mrs. Ponsonby de Tomkins was not over us all. In yet another respect, of a far more important character, was there a distinction between the epoch when Mr. Yates commenced his active existence and the present. No such central figures in literature—Dickens, Thackeray, Macaulay—as existed then exist now. The general average of literary productiveness has immensely increased, but the stimulating influences of individual genius, placed upon a high pedestal, have disappeared. Literature, and especially periodical literature, has become more highly organised, and therefore more of a business. The result has been favourable to the social and moral welfare of the literary class, but it has involved the sacrifice of not a little freshness and of a great deal of fun.

IV.

LORD HOUGHTON.

The delusion of comparisons is as dangerous a fallacy in the estimate of character as the falsehood of extremes. If there was ever any man the surest way to misrepresent and misestimate whom would be by resorting to that classification so dear to an age of schoolmasters and auctioneers, it was the late Lord Houghton. Remarkable for many things, he was remarkable chiefly for his strong individuality. He was a great social figure for considerably more than half a century. Yet it would be impossible to place him exclusively in the category of men whose reputation was social alone. A similar remark would hold good if he were looked at from the point of view of any other of his more commanding attributes. In the same way, to assert that he was a second-rate poet—the violet a second-rate flower!—or a politician who never attained political eminence, or a man of letters who never did justice to his literary capacities, or a speaker who missed being an orator, or a student of human nature who never rose to the lofty levels of divine philosophy, would, even if it were true, be to give an altogether false idea of the brilliant and accomplished man who, less than a fortnight ago,* bade adieu to a prolonged, an eventful, and on the whole a singularly happy existence, in the manner which, above all others, he might have desired:

> Oh, that each of us might die
> When we are at the best,
> Pass away harmoniously
> To some fitting rest.

So wrote Milnes in his remonstrance upon the habit—a flat blasphemy against youth as it seemed to him—of using the words, "second childhood," as a synonym for extreme senility. There is nothing specially excellent in the lines, but they embody the aspiration for the Euthanasia that was the lot of their author. There was no dreary interval for him between enforced withdrawal from the world and the end of everything; no gloomy tarrying in the vestibule of death before the final release came. The curtain fell suddenly, and all was over. Fortunate in his life, Milnes would have assuredly esteemed himself not less fortunate in his death.

The exceptional circumstances of his earlier days must have tended to sustain and intensify the originality of a fresh and buoyant nature, which never lost the wild charm of being untamed, unsubdued. As a boy he was brought up entirely at home and by private tutors. Whatever disadvantages his inexperience of public school life may have entailed, one can hardly

* August 11th, 1885.

conceive of any conditions better calculated to stimulate the free play and spontaneous growth of his gifts. Nor were the scenes and the social environment of his boyhood less conducive to this end. Till a short time before he went to Cambridge he lived much in Italy. Who can doubt that it was the free, unfettered life beneath an Italian sky, to the influences of which he was indebted for that *abandon* which, as it is entirely the reverse of English, is without any English equivalent, and which was the dominant trait of his manner and his mind. Intellectually he was as much the child of Italy as if he had been of Italian birth, nor did the gay idiosyncrasies which he had contracted in the South desert him in after years.

At Cambridge he asserted himself and showed his quality as naturally, and with the same absence of cautious self-restraint that he afterwards showed in the turmoil of what is called London Society. To the social position he was indeed born. His father—"single-speech Milnes"—was a man well known. He was offered, and he declined, the post of Chancellor of the Exchequer by Spencer Perceval, as he was subsequently offered and refused a peerage. His son, Richard Monckton, the future Lord Houghton, married Miss Crewe, a great favourite in that social realm which associated itself with Lansdowne House; and the house (No. 16, Upper Brook Street) in which Milnes, during many years, collected all that was greatest and most intellectual, and above all most poetical, in the London world, had a "pedigree," if so we may speak, connecting it not only with the famous assemblies of Mrs. Cunliffe Offley (the aunt of Miss Crewe), but also, unless we mistake, with the "Mrs. Crewe and True Blue!" who answered the Prince of Wales's toast with her "True Blue and all of you!"

Never did there live a poet of any order who was so warm a friend of poets as Milnes. If he loved poetry much he loved the makers of poetry even more. Their merit as poets was not with him the only question. What he admired and what interested him was the poetic impulse. On the occasion of one of his daughters' marriages, he especially aimed at securing the company of all the English bards of every degree whose addresses he could discover. Nor should it be forgotten that in his capacity of the poet's friend he placed on record one illustration of his power which will always be gratefully remembered. It was under the counsel of Milnes that the Laureateship was conferred on his college friend, Tennyson. Already, as one of that little band of Cambridge undergraduates, surnamed the Apostles, most of whom became famous themselves, he had obtained a hearing for Tennyson, and had, not without difficulty, forced him upon a somewhat reluctant, and, at first, a very much puzzled world. The difficulty of the task and the unattractiveness which the Muse of the new singer had for much of the culture of the day, may be judged from a single incident. Miss Berry, one of the brightest and most intellectual women of her day, piqued herself upon her capacity for keeping pace with the intellect of the younger generations. At the instance of some of the men who, like Milnes, were then preaching up the new poet, she seriously set to work to read Tennyson. Educated in the school of Pope, and habituated to classical models, she could make nothing of him. Perplexed and chagrined, she suspected that she was the victim of an amiable imposture, and full of misgivings proceeded confidentially to interrogate a common friend of her own and Milnes' on the point.

For the most part Lord Houghton's influence was disproportionate to his position as a leading Member of Parliament, to his abilities, to his social opportunities and rank. Ascendency is to the stern, is perhaps even to the fierce, while Milnes was the most kindly, forgiving, tolerant, and indulgent of men. "Houghton," writes to me one who knew him well, "with all his high gifts, had, like most really noble men, a good deal of the woman in his nature, not only of the gentle, the merciful woman, but also of the woman excelling man by her ready initiative, by her swift sagacity transcendent of the reasoning process, and now and then by her nimble, her clever resort to a charming little bit of stage artifice. My laundress had come to me one day in a flood of tears because her little boy of eleven years old, but looking she said much younger (being small of stature), had wandered off with another little boy of about the same age to a common near London, where they found an old mare grazing. The urchins put a handkerchief in the mouth of the mare to serve as a bridle, got both of them on her back, and triumphantly rode her off, but were committed to Newgate for horse-stealing! My laundress (not wanting in means) took measures for having her child duly defended by counsel, but I thought it cruel that the fate of the poor little boy should be resting on the chances of a solemn trial, and I mentioned the matter to Milnes. He instantly gave the right counsel. 'Tell your laundress to take care that at the trial both the little boys —*both*, mind—shall appear in nice clean "pinafores."' The effect, as my laundress described it to me, was like magic. The two little boys in their nice 'pinafores' appeared in the dock and smilingly gazed round the court. 'What is the meaning of this?' said the judge, who had read the depositions and now saw the 'pinafores.' 'A case of horse-stealing, my lord.' 'Stuff and nonsense!' said the judge with indignation. 'Horse-stealing, indeed! The boys stole a *ride*.' Then the 'pinafores' so sagaciously suggested by Milnes had almost an ovation in court, and all who had had to do with the prosecution were made to suffer by the judge's indignant comment."

There were many other essentially feminine traits in his nature; prominent among them his love of domestic management. Although he was ever surrounded by the ladies of his family, and was comforted in late years especially by the society of his sister, Lady Galway, with whom as a boy he had been brought up, and who devoted herself to him with an affection and assiduity infinitely touching and beautiful, he wrote his notes of invitation with his own hand, and himself made the arrangements for the reception, the departure, and the general entertainment of his guests at Fryston.

It was owing, perhaps, to this womanly element in his nature that he sometimes elicited confessions of a sort not often vouchsafed to men. During one of the divisions on the Jew Emancipation Bill, which was taking place at a time when the success of the measure was virtually assured, Milnes, finding himself by the side of Disraeli in the Lobby, made bold to congratulate him in his character of a Jew. "Yes," observed Disraeli, "I am a Jew and a Radical, and I defy anybody to say I ever pretended the contrary." The true meaning of this little speech, which only stupidity can misconstrue, is obvious. What Disraeli desired to convey was not of course that he had never worn the Church of England and the Tory cockade, but that what he had worn was *only*, after all, a cockade, and that having enlisted with the Conservatives, he desired to help them for his own sake in fighting their battles, without really playing the hypocrite to the extent of making any intellectual man fancy that he really shared their notions.

The mention of Mr. Disraeli's name suggests another of Lord Houghton's distinguishing qualities.

In a letter written to me by the late Mr. Hayward, eight years ago, apropos of an opinion I had presumed to offer on Lord Houghton, are these words: "Houghton's is a fine intellect, spoiled by paradox." A paradox is conventionally supposed to imply something in the nature of a contradiction—to involve on the face of it some aggressive inconsistency. One should rather understand by it something that runs counter to the received opinion, and inasmuch as there is always an à priori objection to the truth of whatever does this, every paradox may be thought to bring us to the verge of romance. With Milnes, paradox was generally an instrument either for the suggestion of truth, in which case it served the same logical purpose as analogy, or for stimulating conversation and eliciting the opinions of others.

It was, thus, the precise sort of intellectual weapon natural to one who was not what the French call *un homme sérieux,* who was always pursuing truth tentatively, and who, with that aim, loved to throw out views which were not necessarily the less sound because they might be strange. When, for instance, Milnes declared some forty-four years ago that Disraeli, then strange and actually repulsive to the House of Commons, would achieve the highest place in Parliament, he was thought by those who heard him to be uttering a mere piece of uninteresting nonsense. It took the slower world years to learn that he had truly divined the future. An instance of the second kind of paradox, the paradox with a purpose, in which Milnes delighted, was the audacity with which, at a dinner table, he once improvised a vindication of deception and falsehood. The object was rendered immediately apparent because it "drew" Carlyle, who proceeded to do exactly that which Milnes had meant him to do, vehemently to take up the cudgels in favour of the Eternal Verities.

No one who has ever possessed anything like Lord Houghton's intellectual power has qualified it by so much of sportiveness. And perhaps it would not be wrong if one were to say that intellectual sportiveness and intellectual curiosity were the two dominant "notes" of his mind. In one of his poems, "The Men of Old," he contrasts the old Pagan thinkers and patriots with their latter-day successors. "I know not," he writes, "that the men of old were better than men now." Yet on the whole he gives the palm to the former, of whom he says:

> Blending their soul's sublimest needs
> With tasks of every day,
> They went about their gravest deeds
> As noble boys at play.

The words, "noble boys," carry with them a touch of illumination to those who have heard Lord Houghton talk of the intellectual friends with whom he lived at Cambridge as his "playfellows"—a pretty, and, on his lips, singularly appropriate expression. He was a worker, but he worked in his own light-hearted fashion; he was a searcher after truth, but in his own easy way. Aristippus, the Cyrenaic, often wished that he could for a short time be a woman, and there was a heroine of Greek mythology, Cænis, who, prompted by an analogous motive, actually succeeded in effecting a corresponding transformation, and was henceforth known as Cæneus. If Milnes never gave articulate utterance to the wish of Aristippus, he at least went so far in that path as to play Shakespeare's Beatrice in some theatricals at Cambridge. There was much, as will be presently pointed out, in common between the genius of Houghton and the genius of the poets of classical Hellas. He resembled, too, the more restless of the Hellenic speculators by the intensity of his intellectual inquisitiveness. His impassioned eagerness, ever of an intellectual kind, distinguished him from all other people.

"If," writes to me the friend from whose instructive letter I have already quoted, "you had had the devil himself staying with you, Houghton would have almost turned you out of your own house, in order to learn all that your guest could tell him; would have turned the conversation abruptly to the subject of 'hoofs and horns;' would have asked whether the prowess of the Angel Michael was not greatly exaggerated; and would not have gone away till he had mastered the whole subject of the Evil One, and his relations with the heavens above and the earth below. He never, like other young men, affected a love of dangers; but under the impulse of insatiable curiosity he would brave anything. I once knew him go up in a balloon. This, a descent in a diving-bell excepted, was probably the only achievement approximating to athletic which Lord Houghton ever attempted. Prodigious though as a young man, and even as a man matured or advanced in years, his energy was, it displayed itself always in an intellectual field. He was never a sportsman. He never hunted and he never shot."

There can be little doubt that what constituted to a large extent Lord Houghton's intellectual and social charm was an obstacle in the way of his political advancement. He was not naturally a good speaker. Such, however, were the pains which he took with himself that he ended by acquiring the art, and what he once said to the Prince of Wales, "The two best after-dinner speakers, sir, are your Royal Highness and myself," was literally true. On occasions of a graver character he never commanded an equal success. The intellectual inquirer was so prominent in his nature, that although he might speak quite positively without uttering a word which tended to disclose the *arrière-pensée*, he always found it impossible to induce his hearers to take him in earnest. There is reason to suppose that he was well aware of this difficulty. What he lacked by nature he endeavoured to make good by art. He even went so far as to assume in his speeches a kind of gravity or solemnity absolutely foreign to himself. Undertaking once at the Cambridge

Union to deliver an oration glorifying the genius of Milton, he attempted to rise worthily to the height of his great argument by reverently calling the author of "Paradise Lost" *Mr.* Milton. As an inevitable result, he threw the whole assembly into roars of laughter.

No one had a larger store of learning or of precepts on the subject of oratory in the House of Commons, and many are they who have profited by his counsels. Yet he could not practise what he preached. He could not make his audience take him as *un homme sérieux*. One need not, therefore, wonder that he failed to obtain the official rank which he coveted. His intellect indeed was so bright, so discursive, and his individuality so splendidly strong, that he was not a man to be put in a team under the harness of the public service. Yet he did not think so himself, and was eager to take office, singling out the most laborious office in the world—the Under-Secretaryship of Foreign Affairs; and, as his abilities were universally recognised, his knowledge vast, his speaking fully good enough for the purpose, and his acquaintance with public men abroad and at home almost universal, whilst, moreover, he enjoyed the esteem and confidence of Sir Robert Peel, the Prime Minister, and was afterwards on terms of friendship with Lord and Lady Palmerston, it might seem that there was absolutely nothing to prevent his attaining the object in view; but the one cause of the obstruction was assigned by Lady

Palmerston, in three words spoken one day when Palmerston was forming a Government. To a friend of hers who had mentioned Milnes praisingly, she said simply, "Yes, but I observe that men smile when they speak of him, as if they did not think him quite serious."

Speaking of the Palmerstons, "Milnes," again to quote my correspondent, "was with them at Broadlands in the Christmas of 1851, when no other guest was in the house. All at once—I think in the evening—there came a despatch, brought by a Queen's messenger. Palmerston read the despatch quietly without betraying any emotion, or even any particular interest, and handed it silently to Lady Palmerston. She seized its import at a glance, and putting no restraint upon herself burst out into violent wrath. The despatch was one from 'Lord John,' simply dismissing Palmerston from his office of Secretary of State for Foreign Affairs! The blow was the more startling, since 'dismissal'—unmitigated, unveiled 'dismissal' under any such conditions—had at that time become obsolete. I dare say Milnes to the utmost of his kindly nature shared the indignation of Lady Palmerston; but he loved the drama, and could not have helped being interested by seeing a blow delivered so apparently powerful and decisive, yet destined, as perhaps he foresaw, to be after all so harmless. Before many more weeks had passed, the tables were turned on 'Lord John.'"

There is a sense in which this great lover of

paradox illustrated in his life a paradox far more striking than any of those which he ever propounded in speech. Forced by the eagerness of his nature to be always in a crowd, whether in London society, in assemblies of politicians, of philanthropists, of poets, of philosophers and publicists, he was yet at heart the least gregarious of men. In his mind, at least, he never "trooped," never "flocked," never "herded" with any of the myriads of his fellow-creatures. Perhaps the man himself never spoke more sincerely, or more from the depths of his heart than in what, though I believe it has been vulgarised by being set to jingling music, is one of the finest and profoundest of his poems, "Strangers Yet." Take these two stanzas:

> Strangers yet!
> After strife for common ends,
> After title of "old friends,"
> After passions fierce and tender,
> After cheerful self-surrender
> Hearts may beat and eyes be met,
> And the souls be strangers yet.
>
> Strangers yet!
> Oh, the bitter thought to scan
> All the loneliness of man.
> Nature, by magnetic laws,
> Circle unto circle draws,
> But they only touch when met,
> Never mingle—strangers yet.

It was not any instinctive tendency to go in the beaten track of humanity but the inexhaustible kindness of his own good heart which bound him to his beloved fellow-creatures. Whether this individuality would have remained throughout so strong, whether he would have always stood firm as a rock against the examples of people about him, but for the conditions under which he had been brought up, his home education and the early Italianisation, to use a barbarous compound, of his mind, may be doubted. But of the fact itself there can be no doubt whatever.

The merit and beauty of Lord Houghton's poetic performances are in an inverse ratio to their length. He is seen at his best, his thought is most felicitous and his diction most polished, in his shorter pieces. He was, as Lord Beaconsfield described him, under the guise of Mr. Vavasour in "Tancred"—a description so admirable that it practically exhausts the man—"a poet and a real poet." But then "his life was a gyration of energetic curiosity; an insatiable whirl of social celebrity. There was not a congregation of sages and philosophers in any part of Europe which he did not attend as a brother. He was present at the camp of Kalisch in his yeomanry uniform, and assisted at the festivals of Barcelona in an Andalusian jacket." An existence of this kind could not but have the effect of withdrawing attention from his poetry. Speech in the House of Lords; meeting at Marlborough House; speech by the chairman of this society; speech by the chairman of that —no one reading of these labours every day in his *Times* would incline to turn from his newspaper to the lovely poems of Milnes' early days; and it is only now, when the grave has closed over him, that he will cease to intercept the public appreciation of his works. For years together a great critic, who never tired of declaring his exalted estimate of Houghton's genius, used to work himself into a perfect fury of passion at the spectacle of his poet appearing so constantly in public life.

Intense sympathy is, perhaps, the key-note of Houghton's poetry, as it is of his character. He did not describe so much as interpret. Instead of drawing a mere picture of Oriental personalities, or of the heroes of the old Greek mythology, he identified himself with them, and told the world what they felt. Other poets, proceeding objectively, produced more or less frigid and inanimate presentments of the heathen life of Hellas, or of the sensuous existence of the gorgeous past. Houghton brought the subjective treatment to bear on old times and made them aglow with the warmth of actual being. Contrast the treatment of classical themes, as shown in "The Tomb of Laius" or "The Flowers of Helicon," with the treatment of Shelley or Keats. Contrast his handling of the life of the harem with that of Moore, and a difference, as between that of life and death, at once discloses itself.

Houghton loved to linger on the borders of wonderland. He was for ever labouring to believe. There was no mystery of the hour in which he did not strive to initiate himself. As it was with thought-reading, so had it previously been with table-turning.

No yearning could be more insatiate than his to find that the destiny of poor mortality might not, after all, be so narrow, so meaningless, as science demonstrated it to be. He was enamoured of credulity; and although his keen, clear intellect and his sense of the ludicrous prevented the gratification of his passion, he still held that, impossible as it was to push his search after knowledge beyond the limits inexorably set, there still might be bliss, actual bliss, in belief resting on fancy. "We would," he writes in "Anima Mundi :"

> We would, indeed, be somewise as Thou art,
>   Not spring and bud, and flower, and fade, and fall,
>   Not fix our intellects on some scant part
>   Of nature, but enjoy or feel it all.
> *We would assert the privilege of a soul,*
> *In that it knows to understand the whole.*

The lines italicised seem exactly to explain the attitude of Houghton's intellect towards the problems of the universe. He was, as he may have called himself in the lines entitled "The Peace of God," "this life's inquiring traveller," endlessly busy with the unravelling of complicated truths and the solution of dark enigmas, ever analysing the complex aggregate of human sentiment, ever impressed by the hidden analogies and resemblances of things, now ready to elevate the creations of his fancy to the dignity of immortal verities, now asking whether there be such a thing at all as Truth.

In some of the most exquisite of his earlier verses

he laments the rapid, irretrievable passing away of youth. "Youth," he exclaims, "is gone away; cruel, cruel youth!" And he concludes:

> We are cold, very cold—
> All our blood is drying old,
> And a terrible heart-dearth
> Reigns for us in heaven and earth.
> Forth we stretch our chilly fingers
> In poor effort to attain
> Tepid embers, where still lingers
> Soul-preserving warmth, in vain.

But the youth whose flight the poet deplores is not merely the freshness of man's existence, it is the freshness of the world. It is more than the individual man that is growing old, it is the round earth and everything that is thereon. The ancients were the youths of humanity; we moderns, as Bacon said, are the true ancients. Houghton bewails the disappearance of the primitive Paganism of mankind as if it were a personal loss which he had himself sustained. He writes on all these subjects like one born out of his due time. In those days in which he seems to say he fain would have lived, there was no depressing consciousness of the world's failures, there were no gloomy yesterdays of aspirations baffled and sorrows accumulated on which to look back. The retrospect was bright in fancy; the prospect glorious with hope. What matter if the heathens of classic antiquity lived in an atmosphere of vain imaginings, and fed themselves only on the fictions of their fancy. It was enough for them; their fancies were to them as facts, and they therefore supplied a faith.

The feeling which Houghton betrays in his classical poems towards these men is one of almost passionate envy. With such thoughts the poetry of his best and earliest period is charged. He realised and gave articulate expression to the sentiments and aspirations of Pagan antiquity with an enthusiasm and pathos that in their way have never been surpassed and seldom approached. Again and again he speaks as from the very soul of one of his Hellenic heroes or favourites who were troubled by no doubt that their worthy resolves would be sanctioned by the approving thunders of Zeus, might even be followed by counsels from the lips of Pallas Athene herself. He could not, like the Emperor Julian, undertake to bring back into life the past which he loved so much by any positive edict, but he could testify his desire to do so, he could proclaim his sympathy with the vanished epoch through the mouth of his muse. As in Edward Bunbury's great history of "Ancient Geography" and its illustrative maps we see the small circlet of territories within the ring-fence of Oceanus, which was all that had then been irradiated by the mind and imagination of Greece, so under the spell of Houghton's genius the circlet becomes all aglow with the rapturous fervour of a life illumined and glorified, and almost created by poetry.

V.

TWO CITIES AND TWO SEASONS—
ROME AND LONDON, A.D. 408 AND 1875.

IF any one wishes to study a microcosm and epitome of the grand world in London, as it is to be seen during the present season, let him go to Hyde Park on what day he will between the hours of five and seven p.m. He will find no single feature in our fashionable civilisation unrepresented. Vienna may have its Prater, Berlin its Unter den Linden, Rome its Corso and its Pincian, Paris its Bois de Boulogne, New York its Broadway, St. Petersburg its Nevske Perspective. The spectacle of the Row in the season is unrivalled in either hemisphere. Thirty years ago the number of well-appointed equipages, which "a stranger, seated on the rails near our great captain's statue, might see pass before him to the Mall in all the pomp of aristocratic pride," within the space of two hours, was calculated by "Nimrod" at a thousand; that estimate, to be adequate, should now be quadrupled. "Old Seneca," writes the chronicler of the Chase, the Turf, and the Road, best known by his already-mentioned *nom de plume*, "tells us such a blaze of splendour was once to be seen on the Appian Way. It might be so; it is now to be seen nowhere but in London."

To discover something like a prototype for Rotten Row and the London season, it is not necessary to travel the full interval of time which separates us from the age of the great Stoic moralist. Let us ask the reader to suppose himself in the thick of a Roman season, two hundred years and more after Lucius Annæus Seneca had bequeathed to his friends and to posterity "the image of his life." We are, in fact, in Pagano-Christian Rome, about the date 408 of this era of grace. Society had its historians, its satirists, and its preachers, pretty much as society has now. It had, too, its follies, its foibles, its extravagances, much after the pattern which Babylon sets the world to-day. For our edification the records of all these survive. Ammianus Marcellinus and the Christian Fathers themselves abound in sketches which have the stamp of truth, and we must be dull indeed if we miss their application to our own epoch. It is overpoweringly hot in the Seven-hilled City. The Roman season of 408 languishes to its end. But the cypresses which line the Appian Way cast as grateful a shadow as the elms which flank Rotten Row. The gorgeously-decorated carriages are surmounted with skilfully-devised awnings, and tall footmen, stationed on the splashboard behind, hold over the heads of patrician dames gilded umbrellas with silken folds.

Still it is "quite too awful, this heat: how delicious to be in Iceland!" It was not exactly in this language that the Roman ladies of the period expressed themselves, but if Ammianus Marcellinus is to be trusted, the sentiment conveyed was identical. "Should a sunbeam," he writes, "penetrate through some unguarded and imperceptible chink they deplore their intolerable hardships, and lament in affected language that they were not born in the land of the Cimmerians, the region of eternal darkness." The crowd of carriages—*carrucæ* is the name given them by the Roman historian, and they may be said roughly to correspond to our modern barouches—grows denser every minute. At the first mile-stone from the Servian gates, and from thence to the tomb of the Scipios, hard by the hollow of the Aqua Crabra, the equipages press so closely on each other that they can only proceed at a snail's pace. Nearer to the city still, as the road becomes a street, and is intersected by various thoroughfares, the stream of vehicles disperses in different directions, and the equipages of matrons and ladies set off at a sharp trot "round the immense space of the city and suburbs. Their long robes of silk and purple float in the wind, and as they are agitated by art or accident they occasionally discover the rich tunics embroidered with the figures of various animals."

Are the fair occupants of the *carrucæ* supplied to the present generation by such purveyors as Messrs. Laurie and Marner ignorant of similar innocent little devices for displaying the elegant fit of a bodice, or the graceful fold of a mantilla?

But Rotten Row is not exclusively dedicated to the presence of ladies whose social position is well-defined and indisputable. The half-world of M. Dumas supplies a conspicuous contingent. The Marchioness of Carabas's victoria is immediately followed by Anonyma and her ponies. A very considerable sensation was once caused in Hyde Park by the pertinacity with which a certain Liliputian equipage, drawn by a pair of miniature horses, on one of which was seated a diminutive postilion, made its appearance within the fashionable enclosure day after day; and great ladies, while betraying signs of deep curiosity as to the *status* and the antecedents of the proprietress of this bijou vehicle, were heard to express their disgust at the frequent signs of recognition which she elicited from the gilded youth and the more patriarchal dandies grouped on the adjacent footpath. Strangely enough Ammianus indicates something very like a parallel to this. "If," he tells us, and he is speaking of the Roman nobles, "in their places of mixed and general resort they meet any of their favourites they do not refrain from open salutation." Unless Chrysostom grievously exaggerates the phenomena of his age, institutions closely analogous to the afternoon teas which attract a considerable proportion of the members of two Pall Mall Clubs to the neighbourhood of St. John's Wood and South Belgravia, were not unknown to the young officers of the Imperial army, taking their holiday in the Seven-hilled City after the labours of an arduous campaign among the border tribes of Scythia.

Nothing can be more dramatically complete than the entire picture presented by the historian, on whom the author of the "Decline and Fall" has so largely drawn, of high life at Rome, and of the characters and customs of an aristocracy which had long since lost its influence, because it systematically ignored its duties. And a new aristocracy, that of wealth, had asserted its existence in the social hierarchy of Rome. In nineteenth-century London, a good many highly respectable people flaunt armorial bearings, crests, and mottoes, to which they have no legal or heraldic claim, and are supplied by obliging dealers with faithful portraits of a remote and mythical ancestry. Changes of patronymic are not unknown. Neither were they unknown in the epoch of which Ammianus gives us a faithful narrative. These shoddyites — *plebecula* is the Latin expression — " contend," he remarks, " with each other in the empty vanity of titles and surnames—curiously select or invent the most lofty and sonorous appellations." Thus some wretched *terræ filius* who had made his fortune by a successful venture in Asiatic merchandise or Greek fruit, would from plain Faber, swagger before the Roman world as Reburrus or Fabunius, Pagonius or Tarrasinus—titles, observes our author, " which seem to impress the ears of the vulgar with astonishment and respect. From a vain ambition," he continues, "of perpetuating their memory, they affect to multiply their likenesses in statues of bronze and marble." Have we not here something like an anticipation of those "Portraits of a Gentleman" which now form so prominent a feature in the annual exhibition at Burlington House?

Let us select another point of coincidence between the two cities and the two seasons. The gambling hells of London no longer exist. But is the social reform which we pride ourselves on having consummated genuine? If we have no Crockford's, have we no Arlington and no Portland? If we do not play high in public, what passes in private? If there are no organisations out of doors for the promotion of *écarté* and *roulette*, is there any person at all acquainted with the *vie intime* of Mayfair and St. James's who cannot mention half-a-dozen domiciles, pretty and innocent enough as to their exterior, but to which no visitor would be welcome after the shades of night had fallen, unless he was willing to stake sums for something more than "fun" or "love," on the turn of the dice or the colour of the cards. Are there no Becky Sharpes and Rawdon Crawleys to preside over such delightful little establishments as these? "Another method," we quote the garrulously circumstantial chronicler, "of introduction into the houses and society of the great is derived from the profession of gaming, or, as it is more politely styled, of play. The confederates are united by a strict and indissoluble bond of friendship, or rather of conspiracy : a superior degree of skill in the Tesserarian art (which may be interpreted the game of dice and tables) is a sure road to wealth and reputation." Captain Deuceace and Mr. Rocketer may be glad to know that they each of them have their prototypes in Ammianus Marcellinus. Perhaps if we could recover some of the lost books of Ammianus' history, we should read of the woes of "plungers" and the sorrows of "pigeons."

The effect produced on the reader of these records resembles that which follows on a survey of the excavated remains at Herculaneum and Pompeii. We are brought face to face with a civilisation which, as we gaze at it, lives again. The Roman nobles of whom Ammianus tells us are not phantoms—they are realities. We can see their consequential swagger as they walk in the direction of the Campus Martius; our eyes are blinded by the dust-clouds raised by their whirling equipages; we are conscious of offence at the contemptuous arrogance of their manner; we do not fail to see the settled sneer that curls upon their upper lip. If we were to follow them, after the conclusion of their drive through the Appian Way, into their palaces grouped on or around the hills of the city, we should be impressed with a sense rather of glare and glitter than of elegance or comfort. Mr. Disraeli, in one of his novels, has described a certain order of banquets as marked by "coarse plenty and barbaric splendour." In the great houses of Pagano-

Christian Rome there was magnificence rather than grandeur, luxury rather than refinement. The dinners and suppers of the aristocracy were conceived on a scale of gorgeous abundance; there was a dazzling profusion of plate; the air was heavy with perfumes of sickly sweetness; but there was an absence of all humanising influences. The impression conveyed by a perusal of such a treatise as Müller's *opus magnum* on the "Genius, the Character, and the Learning of the Age of Theodosius" is one of ostentatious vulgarity.

Yet even in the chapter of Ammianus on the Roman nobility there are one or two brief passages not unsuggestive of a certain degree of parallelism. As we read of proud and wealthy senators who "when in the country welcome a casual acquaintance with such warm professions and such kind inquiries that he retires enchanted with the affability of his illustrious friend, and full of regret that he had so long delayed his journey to Rome;" as we hear the sequel—how when the provincial makes the solicited visit to his *potens amicus* in the capital, at his town house, "he is mortified by the discovery that his person, his name, and his county are already forgotten," are we not reminded of the episode in which a well-known personage replying on the flag-stones of Pall Mall to the effusive salutation of a rural acquaintance, said that as he had known him in the country before, so he should be happy to know him when he was in the country again? While rustic cousins were not more courted in Rome than in London, foreigners were in a measure the fashion. My Lord Fabunius, Viscount Pagonius, or Earl Tarrasinus welcomed with open arms the stranger who hailed from Athens or the shores of the Levant. There are members of the peerage in England who appear to believe that a sea voyage has the same effect upon the human character as on wine, and who extend to the smallest of Transatlantic authors a reception which they would shudder to give to a man of letters of their own country.

Let us suppose that the Roman season of the year 408 A.D. is over, and that the representatives of Roman fashion have retired from the capital for the purpose of recruiting after its fatigues—even as in August the broken hearts of London will wing their flight to Scarborough and the blighted beings find refuge at Cowes. Italy had both its Cowes and its Scarborough. The painted galleys which sailed upon the waters of the Lucrine lake, what were they but the forerunners of the fairy craft which flit up and down the Solent? We have heard of yachtsmen who object upon principle to lose sight of their clubhouse on the coast, and who are careful not to go so far in their expeditions as to be unable to recognise the signal which a kindly *chef* displays communicating to them the contents of the dinner *menu* of the day. The fine ladies and gentlemen who trusted themselves to the surface of the Mediterranean off Baiæ and Cayeta were, we gather from Ammianus, very fair-weather sailors indeed. " Sometimes," writes this Duc de Gramont of his age, " these heroes undertake more arduous achievements—they visit their estates in Italy, and procure themselves by the toil of servile hands the amusement of the chase."

Did Ammianus intend to make any prophetic allusion to the modern *battue?* Before we quit this part of our subject, let us give a further extract from our historian. " The acquisition of knowledge seldom engages the curiosity of the nobles, who abhor the fatigue and disdain the advantages of study. . . . But the costly instruments of the theatre, flutes and enormous lyres, are constructed for their use; and the harmony of vocal and instrumental music is incessantly repeated in the palaces of Rome. In those palaces sound is preferred to sense, and the care of the body to that of the mind. . . . The distress which follows and chastises extravagant luxury often reduces the great to the use of the most humiliating expedients, and when they desire to borrow they employ the base and supplicatory style of the slave in the comedy." We think it was Mr. Gaston Phœbus who said that the great point in the training of our governing classes is that they never "read." Have not the theatre and its accompaniments become of late a fashion to an extent only known since the model of social Paris has been set up and worshipped in London? While as for the Nemesis of insolvency which dogged the footsteps of the "extravagant" habits of the nobles in the reign of Honorius and

Constantine, has it been unknown since the accession of Queen Victoria ?

The question of the populousness of Rome at this period is one which, notwithstanding the immense amount of speculation and research that it has excited, has not been settled. Whether we fix the number of its inhabitants at 1,200,000, or at little more than half that sum, it is at least certain that in the dense crowding of its dwellings, in its close and vivid contrasts between pauperism and opulence, in the local proximity of the dens of squalor and misery to the palaces of a profligate aristocracy, Rome resembled London more nearly than any other city has ever done before or since. Then, as now, St. James and St. Giles were next-door neighbours, and had some Roman senator cared to take up such a social question, he might have found abundant material for a measure analogous to Mr. Cross's " Rookeries Bill." Into such matters as these the great world of Pagano-Christian Rome did not care to inquire ; and the languid ladies who wore all kinds of devotional and religious devices embroidered on their dainty robes—even as our own " girls of the period " burden their bosoms with crosses, and show a *penchant* for Brummagem rosaries—bestowed not a thought upon the wretched, ragged specimens of humanity whom they encountered in the course of their afternoon drive. Yet these high-born dames and demoiselles prided themselves above all things on the orthodoxy of their theological faith. The religion of Christianity had already become highly fashionable at Rome. Six years before the Gothic siege, St. Melania returned to the Italian capital after an absence of some duration for purposes of piety. On this occasion, as we learn from Paulinus Nolanus, the Appian Way was one uninterrupted blaze of splendid carriages, containing the wives and daughters of the chief nobles and senators of the city, magnificently dressed in the most elaborate toilets which the costumiers of the age could manufacture.

Rome had, in truth, come out to meet and greet the fashionable saint in much the same way that London debouches into Hyde Park when the Princess of Wales, for the first time in the season, comes forth to gladden with her presence the eyes of the motley concourse at the West End. A motley group, too, it was which welcomed, A.D. 402, the divine Melania to the city of her adoption. There, in the midst of a throng, habited in a multitude of fashions, and resplendent with all the colours of the rainbow, were a sprinkling of men and women whose garments and whose mien struck the eye as a protest against the levity and ostentation of the crowd—women in serge dresses and with covered faces; men who, as they hurried onwards to catch a glimpse of her whom Heaven was supposed to have visited with such exceptional marks of favour, muttered a prayer under their breath, described upon their breast the sign of the cross, made a gesture, as who would say,

Apage, Satanas! while their toga of coarsest cloth or untanned skin trailed behind.

It was these latter who constituted the Roman clergy, and who were the spiritual guides, pastors, and confessors of the feminine rank and fashion of the Eternal City. The resemblance presented by the interior of a fashionable church at Rome to what is to be witnessed any Sunday at any one of the Ritualistic establishments in London must have been curiously close.

> In a church that is furnished with mullion and gable,
>   With nave and with chancel, with reredos and groin,
> The penitents' dresses are sealskin and sable,
>   The odour of sanctity's Eau de Cologne.
>
> But only could Lucifer flying from Hades
>   Gaze down on this crowd with its panniers and paints,
> He would say, as he looked at the lords and the ladies,
>   "Oh, where is All Sinners, if this is All Saints?"

So has written an epigrammatist of our day, and there are passages in the writings of St. Chrysostom, St. Ambrose, and St. Augustine which read like ancient homilies on the modern text. The women, we are told by these Fathers of the Church, take their places and offer up their prayers loaded with rings and chains. The air is filled with strange scents and exquisite odours. Religion itself is made subservient to vanity and display. Even in the House of God matrons wear their hair brought up to an enormous height, especially affecting the *golden dye* [mark these words!] from which propensity they are not to be deterred by any motives of religion. In a similar vein St. Jerome, reviewing the *personnel* of the congregation which attended his own chapel, asks, in one of his sermons, "What business have rouge and paint on a Christian cheek? Who can weep for her sins as she hears the just wrath and sure judgments announced, if she knows that the tears will wash her face bare and leave furrows on her skin? With what trust can faces be lifted up towards heaven which the Maker cannot recognise as His workmanship?" St. Gregory of Nazianzen, while preaching a funeral sermon on his sister Gorgonia, takes the opportunity of satirising the feminine follies and foibles of the day, and by anticipation, of a day also for which the world was to wait some fourteen centuries. "Her only ornaments," quoth the saintly pulpiteer in reference to the object of his panegyric, "were pure manners and a pure air. She wore no jewels, no fine transparent robes, no hair crisped, no extravagant head-dress, no paint, no false colours. Gorgonia's red was given by modesty, her white by fasting." "Those pigments," exclaims Tertullian, " that ye use for your cheeks, that red dye which ye place upon your lips, that black with which ye mark your eyebrows—what are they but open disdain for God's work? In God's likeness ye were made, and of that similitude ye do your utmost to destroy all trace."

Yet, notwithstanding these very plain animadversions, delivered Sunday after Sunday from the pulpits of the Roman churches against the iniquities of fashion, the clergy were high in fashionable favour, and their sermons were listened to by overflowing congregations. The Roman ladies appear to have had the same taste in the matter of pulpit oratory as that attributed by Mrs. Oliphant in "Chronicles of Carlingford" to one of her heroines, and to have been chiefly attracted by "real, rousing-up discourses." One preacher might say that "women had always some contest with saints; and that the enmity of Jezebel to Elias, and of Herodias to John the Baptist, was typical of a strife that was being waged every day in the world." Tertullian might blindly exclaim, "You women are the cause of the sin of the world, and yet you delight thus to attract notice to yourselves;" or might, by a fanciful combination of ideas, carry his hearers in thought from the serpent to the devil, and from the devil to womankind by the following images: "Pearls, which are the ornaments of women, are taken out of the heads of serpents: this only was wanting to Christian women to be indebted to the serpent for the improvement of their beauty." Is this the way in which they seek to carry out the spirit of the prophecy, "She shall bruise his head"?

Nor was Chrysostom more reserved or complimentary. "Your fine linen," he said, "will not shield you from the flame; your purple will not keep off the fire of hell." There is nothing to show that these expostulations and invectives produced much in the way of result. It was to no purpose that these patristic Boanerges reminded their flocks that they were told by the inspired Word to work out their salvation with fear and trembling, and yet that, in the face of this Divine information, they appeared before Him week after week, with faces confident and satisfied, as if their silks, their laces, ponderous buckles and diamonds, could purchase safety for their souls. If "the body of a little woman could be made to bear a load of riches, and carry about with it an entire estate," did the wearer of that wealth remember that, as she had brought nothing into the world so she could take nothing out? When St. Jerome, as he thundered forth his eloquent and impassioned diatribes against the sins of his generation, saw depicted on the countenances of his hearers a keenly critical pleasure, and recognised in their manner a tendency to demonstrate their approval by words and signs, he indignantly deprecated any such manifestation. "Let me," he cried, "hear rather the groans of the people than their acclamations; let the only applause given me be their tears."

At this period no fewer than thirty-nine churches existed on the sites of Pagan temples. The Bishop of Rome had already become a considerable personage in the realm. His power was supreme over the urban clergy, and extended to a wide suburbicarian district as well. The clerical establishment which he ruled in the city itself was composed of forty-six presbyters, seven deacons, as many sub-deacons, forty-two acolytes, fifty-two exorcists, and a host of wardens and door-keepers. In the splendours of its ceremonial, Roman Christianity did not yield to Roman Paganism. The propriety of this magnificence in the services of the Church was not, however, undisputed. We may even trace in the difference of sentiment and practice which prevailed on the subject, the germs of that feud which has continued for centuries among professing Christians, and which divides the Church of England at the present day—between the supporters of a gorgeous symbolism in ecclesiastical ordinances and the cultivators of a studied and severe simplicity.

It is clear that then, as now, the religious world was divided into the opposing camps of Ritualism and Evangelicism. The cultus of primitive Christianity, which was distinctively Roman, had not suffered itself to be betrayed into extravagance. The increase of religious pageantry was the result of a twofold influence—first, the necessity of a successful competition with the ceremonies of Paganism; secondly, the force of the example of the Eastern Christian Church. In the age of which we write the pomp of Byzantine usage had grafted itself on the once almost puritanically simple Church of Rome. Still the innovations were (in some quarters) strongly opposed; and while it was urged, on the one hand, that religion, in winning souls to the Saviour of mankind, should without hesitation avail itself of all the allurements of sense, it was contended, on the other, that the æsthetic emotions were at best an untrustworthy basis for moral practice or for theological conviction.* Strangely enough, as if a premonitory sign of the warfare in after ages to be waged by opposite schools of thought as to the text of the spiritual songs and psalms in use in their churches, a severe conflict had already arisen on the subject of ecclesiastical hymnals and their appropriate musical accompaniment. Any person who knows the bone of contention which the publication entitled "Hymns, Ancient and Modern" is among the clergy of the present day will regard the dispute as ominously prophetic.

Old Rome—the Rome of the Cæsars, of Jupiter, of the worship of Vesta, the Rome whose glory and protection were the special care of all the members of the Olympian hierarchy—had passed away. The new order of things had been already entered upon. The religion of Christianity was popular; excommunication was a social and a fashionable penalty, and involved a species of ostracism from the most select of Roman coteries. The Church was not merely the home of piety; it was a court of modish honour. The supremacy of the pontiffs bade fair to rival that of the Emperors; and in the relations which existed between Valentinian and Damasus, we may see the

* In his "Early Christianity" (iii. 30), Dean Milman has traced the gradual transfiguration of the ritual of the Roman Church, and its social and religious results.

first beginnings of that strife between Pope and Kaiser which runs through the whole web of European history. "When I consider," says Ammianus, speaking of the contest between Damasus and Ursinus for the pontifical chair, "the splendour of the capital, I am not surprised that so valuable a prize should inflame the desires of ambitious men. The successful candidate is secure that he will be enriched by the offerings of the matrons; as soon as his dress is composed with becoming care and elegance he may proceed in his chariot through the streets of Rome; and the sumptuousness of the Imperial table will not equal the profuse and delicate entertainments provided by the taste and at the expense of the Roman pontiffs. How much more rationally would these pontiffs consult their true happiness, if, instead of alleging the greatness of the city as an excuse for their manner, they would imitate the exemplary life of those provincial bishops whose temperance and sobriety, whose mean apparel and downcast looks, recommend their pure and modest virtue to the Deity and His true worshippers!"

We need not have much difficulty in finding points of social detail in which the ecclesiastical system of Pagano-Christian Rome suggests a resemblance to that of Christian and fashionable London. The "pet parsons" and the "fast clergymen" of modern society had their faithful prototypes in the fifth century. The Rev. Morphine Velvet of Mr. Samuel Warren, and the Rev. Charles Honeyman of Mr. Thackeray, had their prototypes in the ranks of the primitive Roman hierarchy. The spirit which prompts young ladies of the present day to overwhelm the celibate curate or the rector (unattached) with gifts of slippers and curiously emblazoned book-markers, animated the matrons and the maids, whose ancestresses had bowed their pious knees in the temple of Jupiter Capitolinus. St. Jerome takes the younger clergy of his communion severely to task because they do not abstain from mingling in the giddy crowd on the Appian Way, or even from assisting at the shows of the theatre and the spectacles of the circus. "You," he exclaims with righteous wrath, in one of his addresses, "who by your vows have dedicated your lives to the Divine service, are you not ashamed to devote hours and days to attendance on these idle women, who, while they prattle about the things of the next world, have their hearts and their affections solely fixed upon the things of this ? Does no feeling of reverence and awe prevent you from laying aside the garb which is intended to proclaim to all men your sacred calling, and assuming a dress which has in it no trace of the priesthood ? Does no fear lest your souls should contract pollution from the levity and profanity of the conversation to which you must listen come over you when you take your places at those banquets of the great ?"

St. Jerome may possibly have fallen into an excess of severity in these denunciations of his weaker brethren. But he appears to describe phenomena with which we are curiously familiar. We shall be pardoned if we suggest that the number of Anglican clergymen who are to be met with in Hyde Park during the season, on the course at Ascot during the Cup day, or in the Duke of Richmond's park during the Goodwood week, in *mufti*, might cause the bones of the old Roman saint to turn with indignation in their sepulchre. It is perfectly possible to distinguish between two classes of the Christian priesthood, each of them possessing considerable social influence at Rome, and diligently cultivating the families of the Roman nobility. On the one hand, we have the monkish *heredipedists*, or legacy-hunters—the priestly successors of the *testamenti captatores* lashed by Juvenal—who, on the strength of their spiritual influence with the opulent households of the capital, laid the foundation of the temporal wealth of their Order; on the other, we have those who take advantage of their priestly position and privileges to acquire, in Gibbon's language, " the most desirable advantages of the world; the lively attachment, perhaps, of a young and beautiful woman ; the delicate plenty of an opulent household, and the respectful homage of the slaves, the freedmen, and the clients of a senatorial family."* When we remember that in the early days of the Christian Church at Rome celibacy was not uniformly compulsory on her priesthood, the position or the possible pretensions of the ecclesiastical *cavalier servente* provide us with the

* " Decline and Fall," chap. xxv.

outline of a picture that, *mutatis mutandis*, might have been drawn from the life of to-day.

In alluding to the power exercised by the Christian clergy over the fair members of their congregation, we are reminded of a change that had already taken place in the social and legal position of the entire sex, which must on the whole be allowed to bring us very near to the modern order of things. The condition of the Roman wife had become totally revolutionised. The family was no longer constructed on the principle of marital autocracy, but of co-equal partnership. The legal rights of women as regarded the tenure of property, independent of the jurisdiction of their husbands, were as complete as the late Mr. Mill would have desired. The fortunes of many of the Roman ladies were immense, and, in the manner which has been described above, not unfrequently found their way into the coffers of the Church—a destination which was by no means discontinued after the issue of Valentinian's edict illegalising testamentary dispositions made in the interest of ecclesiastics. Socially, the Roman lady was free to order her movements as she would, nor can Mayfair or Belgravia boast of more perfect specimens of feminine independence than abounded in the fashionable neighbourhood of the Palatine. Marriage was regarded, the protests of the Church notwithstanding, as a civil contract terminable at will, and one of the consequences of the practical adoption of this view was that a phenomenon which the student of English sociology will recognise as strangely on the increase in our own favoured century was very prevalent at Rome. Probably every third carriage which passed in that glittering string described by Ammianus Marcellinus down the great promenade of the city contained a *divorcée*, or a marketable widow.

St. Jerome mentions a lady of fashion at Rome who was married to her twenty-third husband, she herself being his twenty-first wife. Incompatibility of temper, difference of religious belief, mere dislike of the married state—these were admitted as sufficient causes for a final suspension of all matrimonial relations. A *divorcée* is eyed with suspicion in London or at Brighton, where they are probably more numerous than in any other town in the United Kingdom, or even in Paris. But though pulpits echoed Sunday after Sunday with denunciations of divorce as an institution ineffably offensive to the Divine will, the custom was regarded with something more than social toleration. The lady who had separated from her husband by mere process of law enjoyed a greater amount of liberty than her unmarried friend, and, in spite of the fervour of the patristic condemnation, her position suggested itself to her friends as only less desirable than that of the widow. On the widow of the period, not less than on the *divorcée*, St. Jerome is particularly severe. "They are used," he says, "to paint, to dress in silk, wear jewels, and sprinkle themselves with perfumes.

They mourn for their husbands as if they rejoiced that they are at last freed from bondage, and may look after other husbands." Before we take leave of the impassioned invective of this saintly censor, we may say that there is one class in the world of Roman fashion whom he assails with more indignant remonstrances than worldly-minded clerics, divorced wives, or frisky widows—the *passé* dowagers and the decaying dandies, who, "though the tomb is waiting to receive them, still flock to the theatres and sun themselves in the park." "You dress well," he says, speaking to some Major Pendennis of his day, "you wear rings, you adjust in proper form the few hairs that remain on your autumnal head. Has not the hour come for more serious thoughts?" St. Salvian's language is even more emphatic, and his "senes improbi mundi usibus dediti" may be translated with accuracy if not with elegance, "fashionable old sinners."

Twenty-five years ago there was no more common theme of priestly invective in the pulpits of our English churches than the stage. The Puritan animosity against the theatre as the temple of the devil and the anteroom of hell had not yet died out. For two reasons these diatribes are heard with much less frequency now: first, a more comprehensive and robust view is generally taken of dramatic art; secondly, the objections which a quarter of a century since might have been advanced, not without injustice, to the immorality of its accessories, are now anachronous. Vice itself may not have decreased; but the *venue* of vice has been shifted, and the music-hall has purged the playhouse. Even our professed teachers of religion and morality have recognised the truth, that nothing is gained by obscurantism at least here; and that if the art of the playwright or the novelist be the representation of human nature, sin and misery, crime and sorrow, come within the legitimate sphere of literary or dramatic treatment. The writings of the moralists and divines contemporary with St. Jerome are full of unmeasured strictures upon spectacles, which are sometimes roughly identified with the theatrical performances of our own time.

I venture to think it is an entire mistake to suppose that the genuine dramatic exhibitions of the nineteenth century were included by anticipation in the patristic anathemas of the fifth. The gymnastic games of the circus, and the presentation of the comedies of Plautus, Terence, and their successors, were not placed under the ban of the Primitive Church. St. Cyprian is, perhaps, of all others the writer and preacher who discusses the topic at the greatest length, and who subjects the influence of the pageants of the stage on those who throng to witness them to the most unsparing analysis. But his animadversions are only applicable to the drama in its most debased form; to the brutalising combats between gladiators and wild beasts in the amphitheatre; to the gross mimes of Liberius; and to the indecent dances of a nude *corps de ballet*. It can only be said that theatrical exhibitions were condemned unreservedly by the Fathers of the Church, when it is alleged—as with but a very partial degree of truth it can be—that the only shows which the public at Rome cared to witness were of this order. The taste of a public accustomed to have its passions stirred by the sight of mortal combats between man and man had become almost irredeemably debauched. As is ever the case, cruelty and sensuality went hand in hand, and if there were exhibitions that fairly rivalled these bloodstained prize-fights, they were exhibitions which provoked desire and symbolised lust.

Was there no species of histrionic or scenic entertainment in fifth-century Rome, occupying a mean point between these two extremes? We believe that there was. The pantomimist of the Imperial city had acquired an evil name in the days of Tacitus; the pantomime itself was not necessarily an indecorous amusement in the days of Theodosian.* With the charming account of the representation of the fable of Paris, as given by Apuleius in the Tenth Book of his "Metamorphoses," before us, it may reasonably be contended that the Roman pantomime was inferior neither from an ethical nor æsthetic point of view to

---

* The themes of these pantomimes comprehended the whole cycle of Greek and Roman mythology, the stories of Medea and Jason, Tereus and Philomela, Perseus and Andromeda, etc. etc. Sidonius Apollinaris fills twenty-six lines with these enumerations.

the *opéras bouffes* of Offenbach and to the burlesques and extravaganzas of our own stage. In such exhibitions as these Roman ladies of birth and fashion did not shrink from taking a part, and we may gather from the varied information which is incorporated in the pages of Friedlander, that they occasionally paid theatrical managers large sums in consideration of being allowed the privilege of publicly appearing behind the footlights. A misguided taste, it is true, but one which we may as well recollect is not unknown in some eminently respectable circles of English society; while if English theatrical managers were to consent to sacrifice the sums which they are said to receive from *débutantes* and their friends, on the occasion of "first nights," they would forego one of the most profitable sources of their revenue.

Roman pantomimes might not always be so innocent as that described by Apuleius; but, judged by the standard of the general morality and sentiment of the two ages, it cannot be said that the Pagano-Christian public of fifth-century Rome exhibited a greater degree of indifference to theatrical decorum than the wholly Christian public of nineteenth-century London, in the eagerness with which it flocks to see Schneider in the "Grande Duchesse," to witness the unlovely motions of the can-can, or to contemplate the last edition of a very questionable ballet dance newly imported from the Porte St. Martin. Barbarous and brutal enough the gladiatorial *spectacula* in the amphitheatres were, as any one who had seen the pictures of Gerome will feel with a little shudder. Still, when it is remembered that the multitudes who thronged to see these were the descendants of a people who had been assiduously taught during successive generations 'to hold bloodshed as nothing by the side of patriotism; when it is considered that in the brute courage and bull-dog resolution with which those brawny figures met death in the arena below, the crowd which cheered to madness saw the exaltation of the national ideal of excellence—it may be doubted whether a grosser sentiment of cruelty was appealed to than that which thrills an English mob at the sight of the hazardous feats of the flying trapeze, or the more select circles who gather at Hurlingham to witness the "tournament of doves," or which animates Admiral Rous in his defence of cockfighting!*

The chief interest in the study of the period on which we have dwelt, arises from its prophetic presentment of the spirit and the circumstances of a later generation. Christianity in its infancy is not unmarked by those features of sectarian strife which are visible in its maturity. The intellectual keynote

* To class the public spectacles of Rome at this period under their different heads, they must be divided as follows: (1) Gymnastic Games (our own Athletic Sports); (2) The Plautine and Terentian Drama (Legitimate Drama); (3) Mimes (Burlesque); (4) The Sports of the Amphitheatre (with which compare the trapeze, Hurlingham, and, if it exists anywhere still, the Prize Ring); (5) Chariot Races—an institution which corresponds exactly to our own "Turf."

of the two ages gives forth a nearly identical sound. In the Rome of Ammianus Marcellinus, one system of thought and religion had decayed without another having yet completely taken its place. It was a period of transition, and like all periods of transition it was one in which conviction was weak, and superstition and scepticism strong. "There are many," says Ammianus, speaking of the Roman nobles, "who do not presume either to bathe, or to dine, or to appear in public till they have diligently consulted, according to the rules of astrology, the situation of Mercury and the aspect of the moon. It is singular enough that this vain credulity may often be discovered among the profane sceptics who impiously doubt or deny the existence of a celestial power." St. Augustine's testimony is of similar significance. "There are," he tells us, "men who, though they act as if they believed not in God, yet when seized with fear, suddenly cross themselves."

We may smile at the traits of heathen superstition mentioned by Ammianus, but we may as well recollect that we ourselves live in the time when the spirits of the departed are believed by not a few to embody themselves in the panels of oak sideboards, and to take up their temporary habitation in the legs of mahogany tables. Gibbon fills page after page with instances of the power and charm which the miraculous had already begun to exercise with the children of the Christian Church. Relics of inestimable value and sanctity were perpetually being discovered: "The bones of martyrs, their blood, their garments, were supposed to contain a healing power; and their preternatural influence was communicated to the most distant objects without losing any part of its virtue."* Pilgrimages had already begun to be undertaken by members of fashionable Rome to shrines and sepulchres; and the follies of the Roman season were considered to be amply atoned for by one of these pious progresses. In the fifth century the expeditions were performed on foot; in the nineteenth the pilgrims travel first-class express. That is the chief extent of the difference.

But fashionable and popular as Christianity had become, it was scarcely yet a nationally animating power. Its doctrines created a vivid superficial enthusiasm; they sank in few cases to the depth of a profound moral conviction. Rome has not yet had time to recover from the pernicious effects created by the juxtaposition of the multitudinous worships that had asserted themselves in the time of Augustus, and that had "effected," as Mr. Lecky justly remarks,† " what could not have been effected by the most sceptical literature or the most audacious philosophy:" the complete annihilation of the moral influence of religion. Stoicism was still the gospel of a majority of the intellectual men at Rome, even though, in deference to the feelings of their wives and daughters, they professed themselves believers in the Galilean revela-

---
* "Decline and Fall," chap. xxvii.
† "History of European Morals," vol. i. chap. ii. p. 178.

tion. The teachings of Epicurus obtained the sympathies of the mass, and Epicureanism was nothing less than the principle of national disintegration. The wealth acquired by the middle classes, combined with the supineness of the aristocratic order, had effectually removed the impassable social barrier which had till then existed between the two.

Rome had taken its rank as Cosmopolis; the cosmopolitan spirit had supplanted the national; the entire community were steeped to the lips in national as well as in political indifferentism; patriotism had expired; and a *régime* of public greatness and grandeur had been succeeded by one of ambitious luxury. It was to no purpose that Christian preachers endeavoured to awake the public mind to a sense of the inevitable catastrophe in store. A Jerome or a Chrysostom might crown his denunciations of the sins and the apathy of the time by telling his audience that the Goths were at their gates. They were. In less than eight years after the occasion on which fashionable piety gave St. Melania so superb a welcome on the Appian Way, Roman civilisation received its death-blow from the hands of Attila and his hosts.

If in all this there is nothing that is strictly analogous to our own national conditions, is there nothing which appeals to us in accents of salutary warning? The foundations of social order may be fixed too deep in England to render us apprehensive of social dissolution. It was the absolute supremacy of the Roman empire—the absence of all competition with its resources and prestige in the lists of the world—which paved the way for its fall. It perished of its own security, and was buried beneath the monument of its own greatness. From this danger we are happily free. We have rivals abroad; we have at home men marked out by the combined qualifications of birth, character, and position as the natural leaders of the people, who are able and ready to play their part in the national history. This was a boon never vouchsafed to Pagano-Christian Rome. Nevertheless, are we not, too, passing through a period of transition—of transition political, social, religious, philosophical? Is not our lot cast also amid the conflict of creeds and the fierce antagonism of ideas? Are we beset by no perils of political infidelity and national selfishness? If this is the case, then the contrast which in these pages it has been attempted to draw cannot be otherwise than seasonable and suggestive.

VI.

JOHN BRIGHT.

It is seldom that men who have taken a prominent part in the history of their time are able to anticipate with calmness and confidence the verdict of posterity upon their character and their achievements. For the most part they have commenced enterprises, and been associated with movements, the true merits of which must be judged by slow results. Years may conclusively prove the soundness of their judgment and the accuracy of their prevision, but are, perhaps, just as likely to show that the measures which they laboured to advance were crudely formed and pressed forward in ignorance of the difficulties and complications which posterity is quick to see in their development. It would be confessedly premature to attempt to define the place which Lord Beaconsfield will permanently fill in the gallery of English statesmen. It would be yet more difficult to forecast the final award of political and national criticism in the case of Mr. Gladstone.

But with Mr. Bright there is none of this uncertainty. The foundations of his fame are not laid more securely than its quality is decided, irreversible. He is already an illustrious figure of the past. His voice is still listened to wherever it is heard; the familiar presence is gazed at with admiration wherever it is seen. But alike as statesman and orator, reformer and partisan, John Bright belongs to a bygone generation, and his fellow-countrymen have long since come to an agreement as to the measure and kind of distinction that is his due. It is not that he has outlived his powers, or has worn away to the shadow of his former self. His parliamentary eloquence is still occasionally impressive. He can hold vast audiences in the country spell-bound by the rhetoric which is always more or less autobiographical; his intellect is yet clear and powerful; his memory is undimmed, and his faculty of appreciation and enjoyment of existence is singularly keen. But the cause for which he battled was long ago definitely won; the strongholds of exclusiveness, privilege, and monopoly which he entered public life to attack have all surrendered; the fruits of his service to political progress and popular enlightenment have been gathered into the storehouse of history, and weighed in an unerring balance; the questions which were open in his early, and even in his mature, manhood are closed; the principles for which he first contended, and which were denounced by those who differed from him as involving consequences disastrous to English trade and industry, to the whole structure of

English society, and to the British empire itself, have become the postulates and commonplaces of politicians of every school.

Free Trade, parliamentary reform, religious equality, the assimilation—gradual and qualified though it be—of the government of Ireland to that of England; the removal of Irish grievances; the avoidance by every legitimate expedient of friction between England and Ireland; these are the objects round. which Mr. Bright's activities chiefly centred at successive stages of his career, which incurred for him an amount of personal obloquy and bitterness proportionate, perhaps, to the vehemence of his own attacks, and which are now regarded as nothing more than reasonable and right. Periodically feeble attempts are made to propose Fair Trade as an alternative for Free Trade, to check the political enfranchisement of whole classes of the population, and to revert in other matters to the policy of an extinct period. But every serious politician in England knows that it would be just as possible to rebel against Free Trade as to mutiny against the law of gravitation, and that whenever the question of a further enlargement of the electoral suffrage is raised, it will not be dropped till it has been settled in the affirmative.

In other matters than these, John Bright is to the English public to-day what he will be to the English public a century hence. He is not known, and he never will be known, as a great administrator, as a great legislator, or as a great master of parliamentary detail. He cannot even be considered a debater of the first order. He is a man, however, just as indispensable to the legislation which has been accomplished during his career as the Minister who conducts a Bill through Parliament. As an orator he has acquired an equal renown in the House of Commons and on popular platforms. Such are the power and fervour of his eloquence that it has always constituted a force with which responsible statesmen have been compelled to reckon. Disraeli once said of Cobden that, "he was the greatest politician that the upper middle class of England had produced, and that he was not only an ornament to the House of Commons, but an honour to his country." It may be asserted of Mr. Bright that he has surpassed all his contemporaries in the art of giving simple and weighty expression to the views and aspirations of the English multitude. He has been called a demagogue. As a matter of fact, no man was ever less of a demagogue. Had he been capable of pandering to the popular sentiment of the hour, he would not have resisted the Ten Hours Bill, nor would he have lost his seat for Manchester twenty-seven years ago by denouncing the foreign policy of Lord Palmerston in China and in Russia. It would be unjust to say of him that he was ever the mere mouthpiece of public feeling. He has acted as the champion of the popular cause just so far as he could identify that cause with, and vindicate it by reference to, what have seemed to him the eternal laws of justice and right.

There were Radicals before Mr. John Bright. There are, and will continue to be, Radicals after him. But as he had little in common with many of those who were spoken of as his allies at the beginning of his public life, so he has slight sympathy with the most powerful and representative Radicals whom he sees round him as the shadows of his life begin to lengthen. The Radicalism of Roebuck and of the hard-headed political economists of *The Westminster Review* was as different from the Radicalism of Mr. Bright as is that of Sir Charles Dilke and Mr. Chamberlain. The political convictions and aims of Cobden's friend were traversed by a vein partly of deep sentiment, partly of moral indignation peculiar to himself and to his era. What impressed his mind was not merely the need of giving unfettered play to the law of supply and demand, or of removing purely political inequalities. He looked and he saw around him a great mass of men and women whose daily lot was one of want and misery, attributable to the operation of unjust laws. He would never have wielded so mighty an instrument in the work of political reform if he had not possessed so large a share of the fiery spirit of a moral reformer. A sense of righteous resentment against the state of things under which oppressive taxes were levied, and poverty stood in the place where plenty and happiness ought to be,

L

animated him in his first political efforts. The gift of oratory was innate in him; but over and above that, he possessed something of the old Israelite—something of the old Puritan-spirit, which impelled him to assail secular abuses and political wrongs with an ardour greater than ordinary political passion could generate.

The secret of this must be largely found in the conditions of his birth and the associations of his childhood. The tale of civil and religious oppression was the first to which the second son of Martha and Jacob Bright, born on the 16th November, 1811, ever listened. His father, as a staunch Quaker, persistently refused to pay Church rates. These were at that time legal and compulsory, and Mr. Bright, senior, was therefore the victim of habitual distress warrants, which were satisfied not in cash, but in kind. Cotton twist was the principal article seized upon, but on several occasions cotton shirting to the value of four or five pounds was taken. Is it surprising if the hardship and humiliation of these exactions produced an abiding effect on the mind of so quick and sensitive a child as John Bright was? Nor were the circumstances of his boyhood less stirring in other respects. Rochdale, where his earlier years were spent, was the head-quarters of a chronic agitation in favour of parliamentary reform. Collisions between the popular meetings held and the military were frequent.

The young John Bright, if not an actual spectator

of the Peterloo massacre, had drunk in with eager ears all the local narratives of it. It is not so long ago that in a speech delivered at Birmingham he stated that some articles published in a Lancashire journal had a very great effect on his mind. "I must," he continued, "say that I date some portion of my political activity to the influence of that paper over me in those days." Before he was twenty-one years of age he had seen the Reform Bill of 1832 become law, the Test and Corporation Acts repealed, Catholic emancipation carried, and a French sovereign driven by revolution to the shores of England. Moreover, the value of goods taken from his father's premises under warrants for Church rates amounted during this period to only a little less than a hundred and ten pounds. Whatever of deep and inspiring sentiment the events of this epoch could excite, communicated itself to John Bright. A literary and philosophical society was formed in Rochdale, and the weekly discussions held by its members provided him with his first opportunities for the display of his oratorical power. He was an indefatigable reader, and soon knew many of the most famous passages in Milton's "Paradise Lost" by heart.

A visit which he paid to Jerusalem in his twenty-sixth year marked an epoch in his intellectual development. It was about this time, too, that he formed the acquaintance of Mr. Cobden, and in 1839 he took part in an open-air Anti-Corn Law meeting. "The question," he said, "lay between the working millions and the aristocracy." But the Church rate controversy was not yet at an end, and Mr. Bright, who had now become a celebrity in his neighbourhood, delivered a series of powerful and characteristic speeches against the rate. With the Church itself, he had, he protested, no quarrel. "I would," he exclaimed, in a passage curiously prophetic of some of his subsequent oratorical triumphs, "that that venerable fabric"—and here he pointed to the parish church of Rochdale—"were the representative of a Church really reformed; of a Church separated from the foul connection with the State; of a Church depending upon her own resources, upon the zeal of her people, upon the truth of her principles, and upon the blessings of her spiritual head."

Meanwhile, an event that was to have a more decisive influence upon Mr. Bright's career than any which had yet happened was at hand. Two years after his marriage—in September, 1841—his wife died. Cobden called upon him the next day, and, finding him prostrated by the blow, said: "Do not allow this grief, great as it is, to weigh you down too much. There are at this moment in thousands of homes in England wives and children who are dying of hunger made by the law. If you will come with me, we will never rest till we have got rid of the Corn Law." These words have been often quoted, but, like the circumstances under which they were uttered, they are important, because they indicate the state of mind in which, together with Cobden, Bright entered upon the great labour of his life. As, years earlier, it was the consciousness of domestic suffering that inspired him with hatred of the Church rate, and of the physical maltreatment of the Peterloo mob that gave him his first bias in the direction of parliamentary reform, so it was the sense of personal bereavement—the loss of a young wife in childbed—that sent him forth against the upholders of monopoly. In each instance anguish of soul was transformed into political vigour, and the keynote of Mr. Bright's public character and career will be missed if this fact is not borne in mind.

The experiences encountered by him during the next few years, painful and agonising as they often were, of the evils and suffering involved in the operation of the Corn Laws, account not only for much of the passion he infused into his crusade, but for what has often seemed to the public the exaggerated self-satisfaction with which he has since been in the habit of recounting the story of his triumph. He addressed himself to the enterprise as a social reformer and philanthropist rather than as a political agitator, and it is not too much to say that neither then nor afterward did he magnify his apostleship on political, still less on partisan, grounds. One of the first important incidents in his Anti-Corn Law campaign was his earliest meeting with Mr. Gladstone, who, with Lord Ripon as his chief, was Vice-President of the Board of Trade in 1842, when Mr. Bright was one of a deputation sent to London on the subject of Free Trade. Commenting upon Bright's statement that the Lancashire operatives who could raise enough money invariably emigrated to America, Lord Ripon remarked that the Americans themselves had a law against the admission of Canadian wheat. "Yes," was the immediate rejoinder, "and the carriers of that measure quoted your example as a precedent."

Mr. Gladstone, without volunteering an opinion on the matter, asked if there was any symptom of improvement in trade, and was informed that, on the contrary, distress was greatly aggravated. The American tariff of 1828 exercised the most disastrous influence on the flannel trade of Rochdale, one-third of which had been previously done with the United States. In 1831 wages in Lancashire were forty per cent. below the average of 1828. In 1840 the decrease was fifty per cent. On the 13th of December, 1841, the local medical men testified that, "owing to the high price of food, and the want of employment, the labouring classes in the borough of Rochdale and its neighbourhood are suffering appalling privations." "Misery," was Mr. Bright's comment, "is to be seen in the house of every poor man. Haggard destitution and extreme poverty are the most prominent things in the family. The consequence is that discontent has so pervaded the country that scarcely any working man will lift a finger in defence of those institutions which Englishmen were wont to be proud of. Neither the monarch nor the aristocracy is safe under a state of things that would blast the fairest prospects, and destroy the most powerful nation that ever existed."

Chartism was rampant, and Bright did his utmost to divert into a healthier channel the energies which Chartism enlisted by pursuing the Anti-Corn Law agitation. Throughout the whole of the north of England immense Free-Trade meetings were held. In March, 1843, Drury Lane Theatre, London, was the scene of a huge demonstration, at which Mr. Bright was the first speaker. "There is," he said, amid tremendous applause, "no institution of this country, the monarchy, aristocracy, Church, or any other whatever, of which I will hesitate to say, attach it to the Corn Laws, and I will predict its fate." Presently he quoted the couplet:

> There's yet on earth a far auguster thing,
> Small though it be, than Parliament or King.

John Bright, indeed, was fast becoming a power in the country. He was invaluable to Cobden, and the two worked together upon a regular system. First, at any great public gathering, Cobden would deliver a speech, defining the area of dispute, bristling with statistics, facts, and figures. Bright spoke last, summing up and embellishing with his eloquence all that had been said by those who had preceded him, and finally dismissing his audience in a state of rapturous enthusiasm. In the summer of 1843 he was elected Member for Durham; on the 7th of August he delivered his maiden speech in the House of Commons in support of Mr. Ewart's motion for the reduction of import duties. The effort, if not a striking success, was far from being a failure. He was a little nervous at first, and in his trepidation did injustice to his voice. But the parts of his discourse were so admirably arranged, he so soon recovered his self-possession, there was so transparent a depth of moral earnestness in his pleadings, above all his language was so happily chosen and simple, that he commanded the attention of his hearers, and great things were at once prophesied for him.

It is probable that but for the exceptionally bountiful harvest of 1844 the repeal of the Corn Laws would not have been delayed by two years. The Protectionists began to be sanguine as to their power ultimately to repel the attack made upon them. Mr. Bright replied that "though Providence might send one or two good harvests more, the course of the seasons could not be changed to suit the caprice, the folly, or the criminality of human legislation." Nor, as a matter of fact, did the movement ever flag. Tens of thousands of pounds poured in from every side. Tracts were circulated by millions. Free Trade had its bard in Ebenezer Elliott; skilled lecturers visited every town and village in the kingdom. Sir Robert Peel had already somewhat modified the duties on corn, and now proceeded to reduce or abolish duties on seven hundred and fifty other articles. A year later famine in Ireland forced his hand. He proposed the total repeal of the Corn

Laws, and carried it by a majority of forty-seven. It is needless to dwell upon the parliamentary incidents of this memorable period; on Mr. Disraeli's famous attacks on the Conservative Premier for his desertion of Protectionist principles and betrayal of his political friends. But it may be mentioned that on the last night of the debate, Mr. Bright eulogised Sir Robert Peel's conduct in words that brought tears to the eyes of a statesman usually immovable and cold. Of the speech which the Prime Minister had delivered on the preceding evening, he said : " It has circulated by scores of thousands throughout the kingdom and throughout the world, and wherever a man is to be found who loves justice, and a labourer whom you have trampled under foot, it will bring joy to the heart of the one and hope to the breast of the other."

This is not the place in which to enumerate all the social and industrial results of Free Trade. Speaking some twenty years after the Corn Laws had been repealed, Mr. Bright was able to say that nearly 500,000,000 pounds' worth of food which that law was intended to prohibit, had, since 1846, been imported into England, and that, notwithstanding the diminution in the actual production of each worker, wages had increased from thirty to forty per cent. In 1846 the whole foreign commerce of the United Kingdom did not exceed £134,000,000. In 1876 it had risen to the total of £665,000,000. In that same year John Bright, quoting from

Scripture the words, "The earth is the Lord's and the fulness thereof," was able to say : " We have put Holy Writ into an Act of Parliament, and since then—since, that is, 1846—of that fulness every man and woman and little child in this country may freely and abundantly partake." As has been already said, the same principles on which Mr. Bright collaborated with Cobden on the abolition of the Corn Laws seemed to him to justify, or rather demand, opposition to the Bill introduced for compulsorily limiting the hours of labour in factories. He believed it would be better for working-men to labour ten hours than twelve; but he objected to the rigid system of Protection, and as he was careful to say, he used the word in the same sense in which it had been used by all who were in favour of monopolies. He has often been taunted since with his action in this matter; but that it was approved by the public, and especially the industrial opinion of the period, may be judged from the fact that in the next year, on the 29th of July, 1847, Mr. Bright was elected Member for Manchester.

We may now consider that Bright had entered upon the second great stage of his public career. He had accomplished the first supreme object which he proposed to himself. The Corn Laws were abolished. He now rested on his oars for a little, or, as it would perhaps be more correct to say, he proceeded to strengthen and broaden the foundations of an oratorical fame and excellence already securely established and generally confessed. During the next two decades John Bright was nearly the most impressive figure in English history. He had entered Parliament ten years later than Mr. Gladstone or Disraeli, and he and Cobden were among the very few great speakers of the Victorian era who had not a seat in the first House of Commons constituted after the accession of her present Majesty to the throne. It is enough to glance at him in some of the best-known aspects of his career between 1847 and the year in which he became a responsible Minister of the Crown. In English politics this period was principally remarkable for the sustained ascendency of Palmerston. Although Mr. Bright gave a general support to the various Russell and Palmerston Governments, he had little or no sympathy with the spirit which animated Palmerston or Russell in his foreign policy. Both of these statesmen, and in a special degree the former, seemed to Bright the exponents of what he might have called the purely pagan idea in politics.

No one can doubt that the illustrious subject of this sketch honestly endeavoured to introduce into politics the canons of Christianity and the standards of Scriptural religion. It was no narrow sectarian bigotry which prompted him to condemn the Crimean war and to inveigh against the aggressive militarism with which he regarded that war as identical. From the first he protested that it was avoidable, and the impartial verdict of history has confirmed his judgment. He knew well enough that he was out of harmony with the general feeling of his countrymen. He felt and he spoke as one who was conscious of belonging to a small minority, but who was strong and bold in the conviction that in the eyes of Heaven he was right. No man, whatever his genius for eloquence, unless animated by such a belief as this, could have delivered the oratorical masterpieces with which Bright's name will ever be associated in the House of Commons: first, when we were on the eve of war with Russia; secondly, when the war was in progress. He had no formal connection with the Peace Society which sent out a deputation to the Czar to deprecate, and if possible to prevent, the violation of the peace of Europe. But he believed war to be an evil generally, and the Crimean war in particular to be a preventable evil. He denounced it, therefore, in a series of harangues that have already attained the dignity of parliamentary classics, and that for sublimity and simplicity, pathos and power, are the most marvellous compositions contained in the book of Hansard. He held Parliament spell-bound, and when it was known he was upon his legs not a bench was empty. His doctrines, indeed, did not commend themselves to the judgment of the English people or to their representatives; but who could resist their charm, or be blind to the beauty of those superb descriptions of the horrors of battle, of the misery and havoc which war meant to private households and to peoples; of the picture drawn by the orator of the angel of death, "the beating of whose wings," he said, "he could almost hear!"

At this juncture of his career Bright spoke less to convince men than because he was convinced himself. More than once he confessed his distrust of the temper of the English democracy. The war, as the result showed, saturated the country with the leaven of militarism; and when a little later Lord Palmerston appealed to the constituencies, asking them to sustain him in his Chinese policy, and to sanction his chastisement of the "insolent barbarian who, wielding authority at Canton, had violated the British flag, broken the engagements of treaties, offered rewards for the heads of British subjects, and planned their destruction by murder, assassination, and poison," the English people rallied to the summons, and Bright and Cobden, together with Milner Gibson, W. J. Fox, Layard, and many others, lost their seats. Within six months Bright was returned for Birmingham, and, though for nearly two years his health prevented him from taking an active part in parliamentary warfare, he was not forgotten by his countrymen; nor was it till he had earnestly ranged himself on the side of the reformers that a fresh instalment of parliamentary reform became an effective political cry.

The commercial treaty between England and France was negotiated and effected in 1860 by the joint efforts of Cobden and Bright. It was Cobden who first suggested the idea of an interview with

Napoleon III.; it was Bright who had taken the initiative with regard to the new international compact. With two other great public questions John Bright's name was soon prominently coupled—the repeal of the paper duties, which made the penny newspaper press in England possible; and the American civil war. Cobden, like Bright and all the survivors of the Manchester school, was the champion of the North. Before this he had incurred much unpopularity by the line of argument he adopted in the *Alabama* debate, and had elicited from Mr. Laird, who was responsible for the construction and putting to sea of that cruiser, the taunt that he "would rather be known as the builder of a dozen *Alabamas* than be a man who, like Mr. Bright, had set class against class."

Ireland, and especially the Irish Church, were also subjects on which Mr. Bright delivered several famous speeches during this period of his career. He pleaded vehemently for a relaxation of the punishment meted out to those who had taken part in the Fenian rising of 1867, and he denounced the Irish religious establishment in language which heralded its doom. Difficulties of the gravest nature, he admitted, were yet in the way; but he reminded the House of Commons, in tones which will never be forgotten by any of those who heard them, that "to the upright there ariseth light in darkness."

Mr. Bright had now obtained a position amongst his countrymen as commanding as the power instrumental in securing it for him was unique. There was no great popular movement of his time which, by his eloquence and by the intensity of the moral zeal underlying his eloquence, he had not helped forward. The Tories, under Mr. Disraeli, had carried reform; but it was Bright, more than any of his contemporaries, who had rendered that consummation possible, and who, by the unflagging zeal of his advocacy, had kept the fire of reform alive. In the same way Mr. Gladstone recognised the fact that his old friend's harangues on the condition of the Sister Island had more than anything else contributed to bring the disestablishment and disendowment of the Anglican Church on the other side of St. George's Channel within the limits of practical statesmanship. When, therefore, Mr. Gladstone was called upon in 1868 to form his first Cabinet, it was natural, and it was right for two reasons, that he should press Mr. Bright to occupy a place in it. First, Mr. Bright enjoyed a larger share of the confidence of the Liberal party in the English constituencies, and especially of the Nonconformist section of it, than any other public man, Mr. Gladstone himself not excepted. Secondly, it is a wholesome doctrine that responsibility should be the accompaniment of power, and that a statesman and orator who has wielded at will the British democracy should, when the time comes, submit to the test his capacity for moulding the legislation that he has encouraged it to expect. Mr. Bright recognised the force of both these considerations, and, after having told the electors of Birmingham that for his part he had no ambition for office, but would be well content, like the Shunamite woman, to live amongst his own people, accepted the Presidency of the Board of Trade. Office had, from the point of view taken by the English people, become inevitable to him, and the fact that he did not prove a great administrator cannot be cited as an argument which would have justified his refusal of it.

In one sense, however, his political career, so far as achievement is concerned, was as much at an end in 1868 as in 1874. His health once more showed signs of failing, his absences from the House of Commons were frequent, and he entered but seldom into the war of parliamentary debate. Yet his speech on the Irish Church Bill, on the Ballot Bill, on the indirect *Alabama* claims, and on other matters, were as fine and as effective as any he had ever delivered. At the Board of Trade he continued till 1873, when, a redistribution of Cabinet offices taking place, he was appointed to the Duchy of Lancaster. This office he again occupied, when, after an interval of six years, during which the Conservatives, under Lord Beaconsfield, were in power, the constituencies once more declared for Liberalism. He resigned it only in 1882 because, like not a few other members of his party, he disapproved of the Egyptian policy of the Government, which for the time—it has gone through many critical developments since then—culminated in the bombardment of Alexandria. During the past two years (1883-4) Mr. Bright has addressed the House of Commons and popular audiences upon several occasions in his old manner; but it is no disparagement to his fame, and to the great work which he has accomplished in the past, to say that he has ceased to be an elemental force in politics, or that he receives the admiration and homage of his countrymen less on the ground of present performances than of past services.

"There are some men," said Mr. Disraeli, in a speech (from which a brief extract has been already given) in the House of Commons on the day of Cobden's death, "who, although they are not present, are still members of this House, independent of dissolution or the caprice of constituencies, and even of the course of time. I think that Mr. Cobden is one of these men." Mr. Bright, one may venture to say, is another. If a perfect mastery of the art of parliamentary debating is an essential element in the fame of a great orator, then Bright has several equals and one or two superiors, notably Mr. Gladstone himself. But if it is the cardinal condition of oratory of the first rank to produce with the simplest instruments magnificent effects; to strike right home to the hearts of hearers with words that come even more from the heart than from the head; to combine with the most perfect propriety of phrase the most studied absence of theatrical declamation; to know intuitively how wit and humour may be made to serve the same purpose as, and to work in unison with, tragedy and pathos; to display, as, according to Tennyson, it is the mission of the poet to display, the "hate of hate, the scorn of scorn;" to run in half-a-dozen sentences the whole gamut of human feeling; to say the aptest things in the aptest voice, now full and resonant, now low and clear, but always pitched in the key precisely consonant to the sentiment conveyed, and exactly calculated to impress those who listen with the emotion of him who speaks;—then, unquestionably, John Bright is the greatest orator that our age has beheld.

Nature has denied him none of the attributes necessary to so exalted a reputation. "There came up a lion out of Judah," was Charlotte Brontë's exclamation when she was present at one of Thackeray's lectures. The same remark will have suggested itself to many persons who have witnessed John Bright on the occasion of one of his great oratorical efforts. The massive, well-set head, the lofty brow, the clear blue eye, as Saxon in its expression as the language of the speaker, have immediately arrested the attention of all spectators. Yet, in the House of Commons, the visitor may have failed to recognise immediately the voice and the presence of its greatest orator. Slow, low, and distinct in his commencement, he has appeared to be suffering from a nervous hesitation which those who have never heard him previously might doubt whether he would succeed in overcoming. But in five minutes all apprehensions on this score have disappeared. The popular chamber is crowded, for, with the speed of electricity, the news that "Bright is up" has run the round of lobbies, library, and smoking-room. Never has there been associated in the same speaker and in the same speech merit so sustained with excellence so rare. Mr. Bright has spoken, no doubt, not infrequently below himself; but when he has spoken at his best, or at anything like his best, he has been at his best throughout. His eloquence may be compared to the glow of a clear fire steadily burning almost at a white heat. There is nothing fitful or spasmodic about it. The solemn and the sportive are interwoven as naturally as the serious and comic scenes in one of Shakespeare's masterpieces. Mr. Bright has probably coined as many concise and adhesive phrases as Disraeli himself. It is he who invented the words "fancy franchise," who first employed "the Cave of Adullam" as a metaphor for the refuge of the disaffected, and who compared the Adullamites themselves to the Scotch terrier of which it was difficult to say what portion formed the head and what the tail.

His humour has always been of the quiet, cutting, and sarcastic style. He likened Mr. Disraeli to "the man who was not a Cabinet Minister, but only a mountebank, and who set up a stall and offered the country people pills that were very good against earthquakes." He likened Lord Derby's professions about reform to "the sort of feast that a Spanish host sets before his guest, consisting of a little meat and a great deal of table-cloth." The remark of a peer, when Mr. Bright was once absent from Parliament through illness, that "Providence, in punishment of the manner in which he had abused his talents, had inflicted upon him a disease of the brain," elicited from him on his return to the House of Commons the retort, "It may be so, but in any case it will be some consolation to the friends and the family of the noble lord to know that the disease is one which even Providence could not inflict upon him." Nor could anything be better than his criticism of Sir Charles Adderley, now Lord Norton, when that gentleman had made some statement from which Mr. Bright dissented: "I hope he thought he was speaking the truth; but he is rather a dull man and liable to make blunders." One instance more. During the American war, when the cotton supply failed, it was attempted to keep the mill hands employed with an Indian cotton known as Surat, which was exceedingly difficult to work. One Sunday morning a minister of some religious denomination was praying that Heaven would send a plentiful supply of cotton. According to Mr. Bright, a spinner in the congregation cried out, "Yea, Lord, but not Surat."

As Mr. Bright has lived to witness the completion of all the great political movements to which he ever put his hand, he has lived to witness also a curious revulsion in the sentiment even of the privileged classes about himself. A quarter of a century ago he was spoken of as the tribune of the people, a latter-day edition of Jack Cade, a demagogue—though, as we have seen, he was never in reality a demagogue at all. Now, as for years past, he is regarded by his political opponents as a moderator and controller of popular passions, and is esteemed, in comparison with Mr. Gladstone or Mr. Chamberlain, a "safe man." It was only the other day that he himself declared he could not lay claim to the title of Radical, as that word is now understood. Mr. Bright's Liberalism or Radicalism, by whichever name it may be called, has never failed to reflect the national temper and the political genius of the English people. In other words, it has always been largely tinged by Conservatism. The reforms for which he has struggled, and whose triumph he has beheld, have been demanded by him not for reasons of abstract political perfection, but because so long as they were denied a gross moral and political scandal was, in his opinion, perpetuated.

When, therefore, the offence against natural equity —the inalienable rights of man—has been removed, the fire of the political reformer has, in the case of Mr. Bright, subsided. He has absolutely nothing of the revolutionary temperament about him. He has nothing either of the sympathy possessed by some English politicians—but in its origin French rather than English—with vague doctrines of political evolution. He has called the Conservatives "the stupid party," and, as in a letter addressed to a Birmingham meeting, when it was considered likely that the Lords would throw out the Irish Church Bill, has admonished the peers that "by throwing themselves athwart the national course, they might meet with accidents not pleasant for them to think of." But Mr. W. E. Forster used, three or four years ago, much stronger language than this in speaking of the same assembly.

His own native good sense has ever kept Mr. Bright from extravagance. In 1872, when certain signs of Republican feeling asserted themselves in England, and a correspondent wrote to Bright on the subject, he replied that "as to views on the question of Monarchy or Republicanism, I hope and believe it will be a long time before we are asked to give an opinion. Our ancestors decided the matter a good while since, and I would suggest that you and I should leave any further decision to our posterity." Mr. Bright never wrote or said anything more characteristic than this. At no period of his career has he failed to show himself in words as well as action the loyal subject of the English crown. To the Sovereign herself he has been and is personally attached, and it is the fact that the beginning of his personal estrangement from Mr. Disraeli was not, as has sometimes been supposed, his exposure of the sentiments favourable to regicide which the Conservative statesman had expressed in his now forgotten "Revolutionary Epic," but the manner in which Mr. Disraeli upon more than one occasion introduced the Queen's name into parliamentary debates. "The right honourable gentleman," he said, when Mr. Gladstone's Irish Church resolutions were being discussed, "talked, the other night, sometimes with pompousness and sometimes with servility, of the interviews he had with his Sovereign. I venture to say that a Minister who deceives his Sovereign is as guilty as the conspirator who would dethrone her."

Another evidence of Mr. Bright's innate Conservatism may be seen in the difference of opinion formed by Cobden and himself on the Reform Act of 1832. Cobden was never satisfied with that measure because, he said, it did nothing more, as was undoubtedly the case, than enfranchise the middle classes. But with that, for the time, Mr. Bright was content. He was, indeed, less advanced in his views of the political rights of the English people than was Mr. Disraeli himself, who objected to the Whig Reform Bill on precisely the same grounds as Cobden. It may therefore well seem surprising that when, in 1859, Lord Palmerston was engaged in the formation of a Government, he offered Cobden a seat in the Cabinet, but declined to make the same offer to Bright on account of the political violence of the latter. The fact is that just as Lord Durham in 1832, and again some years later, was desirous of going a good deal further in the direction of Radicalism than Bright, so Cobden was always much more advanced and aggressive in his ideas than his colleague. That this did not appear to be the case was due to diversity of temperament. Bright always spoke, and seemed to feel, as strongly as, and more bitterly than, he actually felt. His nature was full of the indignation which Juvenal declared was the inspiration of his verse. Although he has been and is popular in society, Mr. Bright has never been famous for urbanity of manner. He has rather taken a pleasure in displaying his angularities and a certain irreconcilability of antagonism, superficial often rather than real, to the convictions and prejudices of others. Cobden, on the contrary, was full of natural *bonhomie*. If he was as earnest as Bright, his earnestness was never so militant, and the opposition he provoked was never so persistent.

For these reasons English society may have before now misunderstood Mr. Bright, but it has long since discovered its error. Indeed, it may be doubted whether, even when he was in the habit of applying his most passionate and vituperative language to objects and to individuals whom he disapproved, he ever concentrated upon himself the same sentiments of personal bitterness as other living statesmen have elicited. Whatever his faults, and however dangerous have seemed his machinations against the privileged classes, who were once taught to see in him their most uncompromising foe, there has never been anything subtle or sinister in his way of dealing with them, of which they could complain. He has dubbed spiritual peers "creatures of monstrous, nay, even of adulterous birth." He has spoken of "this regard for the liberties of Europe, this excessive love for the balance of power," as "neither more nor less than a gigantic system of out-door relief for the aristocracy of Great Britain." But as, when Lord Shaftesbury declared "Ecce Homo" to be the vilest book ever vomited from the jaws of hell, he meant nothing more than that he disapproved of its teachings, so it has always been known that Mr. Bright only wished to express, however vehement his anathemas, his dissent from his opponents in an emphatic fashion.

Thus it is that, not only in the House of Commons but in general society, he has always been personally acceptable. "If you will come down to the House," remarks one of the scions of the nobility to Lothair, in what is nearly Lord Beaconsfield's worst novel, "I will take you into the tea-room and introduce you to Bright." There is a degree of social truth in this casual comment which invests it with a real historical value. At the present moment Mr. Bright is much sought after in London drawing-rooms and dining-rooms, whatever the political views of their proprietors. Nor is there anything new to him in such an experience. All the memoirs recently published, which throw any light upon the social or political history of the last three decades, especially the biography of the late Bishop Wilberforce, contain numerous references to John Bright. Anecdotes are told in every chapter of the good things he said upon certain occasions, of the pleasant little snubs he administered to indiscreet intruders into select companies, of the freshness which his remarks ever carried with them, and of his far-reaching interest in a thousand matters that have nothing whatever to do with his political creed. If Mr. Bright were ever to write or to publish his autobiography, it would be found more valuable as a contribution to the social than to—since upon that point he has said in his speeches all there is to say—the political history of the age. Unfortunately Mr. Bright is not particularly fond of literary composition. Though he has always prepared his speeches most carefully, he has never written them out at length; and though he was popularly reputed to contribute leading articles to *The Morning Star*, which was once the recognised exponent of his views, there exists the best authority for saying that he never penned an editorial in his life.

The commanding position which Mr. Bright has achieved in England is, it may be said in conclusion, due, next to his genius, to the fact that he is an eminently faithful representative of the English character. If he has seemed to some of us in these latter days to have grown too autobiographical in his speeches, too prone to dwell at inordinate length upon the triumphs he has won, it must never be forgotten that he devoted to the labour which secured these not merely enormous energy, courage, and patience, but intellectual gifts and literary power of a sort that had never before been expended upon similar or analogous objects. It is no exaggeration to say that the marvellously delicate graces of his always robust rhetoric have proved instrumental in investing with a spiritual charm the hard and rugged features of nineteenth-century Radicalism.

John Bright is a speaker whom in some respects it is difficult to compare with any of his contemporaries. He has not passed through the ordinary scholastic and academic curriculum of English politicians. His mind, unlike that of Mr. Gladstone, of Canning, Pitt, Fox, and a host of others, was free from all associations of classical literature. He has studied English, and English alone. The diction of the English Bible and Milton has become part of his intellectual texture — colours his diction like the varying yet dominant hue in shot silk. He is the first English orator who has shown his countrymen what may be accomplished with the unaided resources of the Anglo-Saxon tongue, and in after ages there can be little doubt that his achievements will be cited as illustrating the finest possibilities of our language. A man who has done all this; who in addition has witnessed the assured triumph of the great public causes which he has advocated; who, sated with victory, has in a manner detached himself from the strife of parties, is able to enjoy in his own lifetime a foretaste of the fame which must to others, not less gifted perhaps than John Bright, be a vision or a hope.

VII.

A CHILD'S AUTOBIOGRAPHY.

A DULL, bleak level of depressing dreary monotony, yet not altogether ungladdened by fitful and too transient bursts of sunshine, not entirely unbroken by brief incidents of petty joy—that is the retrospect which meets the eye as it glances leisurely down the lengthened vista of the past years. The child, indeed, knew, like his elders, occasional intervals of positive happiness and gladness. But the prevailing colour worn by the period of his infancy was a sombre chilling gray; his reminiscences of the epoch are those of one of the dull, dead, soundless days of autumn. Yet it was not to intentional cruelty and deliberate wrong that he was subjected. There was no consciousness of oppression or harshness on the part of those who were responsible for the gloom amid which his existence began. They in their turn had perhaps known the same dark, overclouded time; and thus the memory of the parent became the experience of the child.

Such things are as traditions in families. In some,

from generation to generation, it is esteemed a part of the domestic religion that where the infancy of the father has been subjected to severely repressive influences, that of the son shall be confined within the same sad atmosphere. Subjection, coercion, the checking of all those harmless impulses whose wise indulgence makes childish happiness, are a law of the house. As the sire was not allowed to laugh too loudly, or to say too much in the presence of his elders, so the son is prohibited, under penalties, from the too public display of all those emotions of hope and fear and mirth of which childhood largely consists. In other cases the ancestral law of the house is one of infantile happiness. Here you will see portraits of daughters smiling at their mothers' knees, of chubby-faced boys whose eyes sparkle and brim over with the quintessence of pure delight. It is the *cachet* of the race that the son shall find an elder brother in the father, and the daughter an elder sister in the mother. All our moral and all our political ideas come, we are told, from the development of the family. Different families, it may be said with at least equal truth, are the types and reflections of different political systems. You have the democratic theory illustrated beneath the domestic roof-tree, as well as the monarchical; and you may as readily expect to find the fresh elastic liberty of a republic under the sway of an iron despotism, as happy childhood in those homes where coercion is the hereditary *régime*.

The child now spoken of perceives, as he looks back upon that desolate and forlorn era, that he was brought up in such a way and upon such principles as to acquire the ever-growing, ever-strengthening conviction that life was a necessary evil. It was as if the lullaby whispered in his ear at the very earliest stages of his existence had been the favourite refrain of a Greek tragic chorus: "Best of all things is it not to be born; and next best, when one has been born, to quit the stage of life as swiftly as possible." The gradual unfolding of events, the successive growth of circumstance, caused this melancholy aphorism to become a kind of fixed idea in the child's mind. The whisper of mortality was ever audible to him, was ever destroying, with its still small voice, his peace of spirit. He was taught to note the fall of the leaf, and not its budding growth. He was bidden to fix his attention rather upon the decay of autumn than the hopeful lessons of spring. The summer suns might be bright, and the summer skies one wide overarching vault of unfathomable cloudless blue; but there were clouds which were sure to rise, and pitiless rains were ever being drawn up from the seas into heaven.

Thus it was that imperceptibly the entire life of the child became overhung by the shadow of some coming eclipse. A vague presentiment of calamity, of total darkness that might at any moment descend upon the earth and cover all, a chronic state of mute, mournful, passive acquiescence in a grim and tyrannical dispensation, were the outcome of the influences by which he was surrounded. The future never suggested itself as an infinite succession of glad possibilities. It seemed rather to shape itself to the childish and most fearful imagination as a narrow sunless path, never once turning to right or left; stretching on, on, on, for weary mile after weary mile, till it became lost in blinded mists and rain, beyond which were fiery terrors and the torture-house of implacable Fate.

Some relief to this ordeal, which was really one of agony and prostration of spirit, the heavily-passing days brought with them; but it was the relief, not which came from the essential condition of the child's home, but either from events external in origin to his home, or else from the child's own inner resources. It was vain to expect that an infant taught to take this view of the universe, and to recognise in the Divine Providence a mode of diffusing misery, which, under pain of endless punishment, mankind were compelled to accept as happiness, and hypocritically to speak of as such; taught to recognise in his earthly parents the symbols of a relentless power who observed all and punished all—it was vain to expect that such a one should pour the record of his secret sufferings into father's or mother's ear. It is love which encourages confidence; and the only love which a child understands is that whose expression is tenderness.

To impress upon the child's mind the doctrine of

the Calvinistic God, to declare that the Being of whom the child is told thus to conceive is one of infinite mercy and all-abounding love, is to use language which is sure to terrify him, but which he cannot understand. Further, to impress upon him that father or mother is, in a minor degree, what the Supreme Ruler of the world is on a scale of measureless magnitude, is to raise between parent and offspring a cold, impassable barrier. Under such circumstances, the idea of home, as home ought to be, cannot be realised. Home may be a place where meals are eaten, where unhappiness departs at nighttime in the blessed oblivion of sleep, where lessons are learned and unending sermons are preached. But it is only on the escape from home, the partial or complete throwing off of home associations, that an approach to happiness can be found.

So was it with this child. It was a relief to him to speed away from that joyless roof, from the eternal round of spiritual precepts and ghostly monitions, into the fresh life of Nature. He dared even at times to face the certainty of parental chastisement, and, as he was taught, of the fiercest manifestation of Divine displeasure; and lying hid in the long summer grass, or sheltered by the umbrageous shrubs, which favoured his iniquitous design, he gave the party of churchgoers the slip. It was a dearly-purchased gratification; for the act meant close confinement for twenty-four hours when caught, and the necessity of learning by heart three extra collects, epistles, and gospels—a sufficiently severe penalty for an anti-Sabbatarian infant of seven. Yet even this was something to break the dreary, chilling round.

The child on these occasions seldom had playmates. But solitude with Nature was better than society at home. At least, as he wandered through the fields, basking in the June sunshine, he could hear the lark carolling high in heaven; could listen to the buzz of multitudinous insects in the hot air; could watch the shadows chase each other over the distant hills; could see the trout darting to and fro in the clear flowing stream. It was something to feel that, for a few minutes at least, he was beyond the reach of lessons, and sermons, and prayers, and parental homilies; and that he was certain of a short interval of leisure and pleasure before a stern voice would tell him to commit to heart so many verses of the Hundredth Psalm, so many hymns, or such and such passages from Cowper's "Task." At such moment the child had two chief wishes—to pass away altogether; to become an insentient thing; or if not, and better than that, to become transformed into some creature, who might revel at will in the warm breezes of summer; shelter himself as he best might from the winter colds, and hear never a word again of lessons, and religion, and parents, and heaven. Then, too, there were the long, lonely rambles on the shingle of the sea-shore; the tranquil enjoyment of the music of the rippling waves as they touched the pebbly ridge, and then shrank back as if they had done a rash thing; and the occasional excitement of the spectacle of the mackerel-fishing—a dark speck suddenly appearing in the offing, the sure sign of the presence of a shoal; the speck growing larger and larger, the sudden descent of fishers from the cliff to the beach, the launching of the boats, the hauling out of the nets; then the slow tugging in of the long coils of seine, till at last, amid speechless excitement, its deep bosom touched the shore; and there, before the admiring multitude, were masses of live fish, leaping and tumbling about, and sparkling with silver and emerald.

There were bands of unregenerate fishers in these parts, who declined to be bound by Sabbath ordinances. Church they eschewed; and all the Sunday long would stand silent, but seldom pipeless, leaning against rails or posts, on the low cliff confronting the sea. Then, when the shout was raised that the mackerel had come, they would rush down, regardless of the sanctity of the day, and hurry off in their boats to sea. These men were the secret heroes of the child's mind. He indeed at first expected to witness the fiery vengeance of Heaven suddenly descend upon them. It was a mystery to him that the waves, whose Sabbath sanctity was thus outraged, did not swallow up the impious fishers. When he perceived that none of these things came upon them, he recognised in them, not so much sacrilegious wretches, as the champions of the principle of human liberty. It was the earliest instance of organised revolt against church-going authority which the juvenile observer had ever beheld ; and he was gratified to know that such a revolt might be successfully conducted. It gave him hope.

There were more exciting pleasures than these which he was sometimes permitted to know. In this age of infinitely extended locomotion — when the arrival of a visitor by the train is no more matter of surprise than a shower of rain on an April day—there may be a difficulty in remembering—or in imagining, if the facts of memory do not exist—the emotions caused by the arrival of the stranger who travelled by road. To the child, situated and trained as the one of whom I am now speaking, these events were the revelations of another order of existence. He was supposed to be too much busied about spiritual matters to be forewarned of such trivial occurrences ; and there was always a delightful uncertainty whether, in the course of half-an-hour after the time at which he knew the mail-coach was due at the village, some visitor might not present himself, or whether at any moment some traveller by postchaise might not appear on the scene. Friends now drop in on us suddenly, but their arrival is a commonplace and prosaic affair. It is doubtful whether even the childish mind would have been impressed by these advents in the same way that he was by those which were heralded by the long rumble of wheels, and the approach of a carriage-and-pair, conducted by a red-faced postilion up the gravel-drive. There was room for so much interesting conjecture as to whom the equipage might prove to contain; and, above all things, there was the charm of a presence fresh from the outer world. For, to the child, the visitor was a messenger from another universe. He conversed about every subject, and brought tidings about many things. Strange that he could say so much, and yet say nothing about religion or duty; that he could even talk to the child for half-an-hour together, or take him out for a long walk, without once asking him who lived in the heaven and what became of the unconverted sinner; whether he committed his Bible verses accurately to memory, and how often he said his prayers. Not less surprising did it seem that even his parents should discuss with the new-comer other themes than were connected with their souls' salvation—that they, too, to judge from their words, were aware of the existence of a world which had not the sanction of the Gospel according to Calvin; that they had even been in this world, and that they could talk of it and its doings with interest, and occasionally with merriment.

That was one of the earliest circumstances which produced a profound impression on the child's mind. Could it be that his parents had one voice and face for him, and another for their friends? If so, how far was he to trust and believe them? The seeds of hatred of the discipline of infancy had long since been sown; there now began to suggest themselves grave questionings as to the sincerity of that discipline.

Contact with the real facts of existence, and experience of the world, in however limited a shape, were now beginning to be felt, and there commenced a long and quick succession of anxious self-questionings. One of these visitors once insisted, not merely on bathing in the sea, but in rowing in a boat, on the Sabbath. Here was a plain act of defiance of the most solemn laws of Heaven, which surely called for some emphatic exercise of Divine interposition. It was true that the irreverent fishers already mentioned had committed much the same crime and had been unpunished. This was explained to the child partly by the circumstance that they did not know better; secondly, by the assurance that they would be punished all the more severely hereafter. It was a very different thing when a guest who was staying under the parental roof audaciously infringed a celestial ordinance, and was not only not immediately annihilated, but on his return home was greeted with the expression of a hope that he had enjoyed himself.

Other forces than these were at work in the expansion and instruction of the child's mind. Of the great festivals of the year he had never been permitted to know anything but their most rigidly unbending religious significance. Easter was a season of exceptionally frequent church-going, and painfully numerous collects, epistles, and gospels. Christmas was associated, indeed, with holly, mistletoe, even with plum-pudding, turkey, and mince-pies; but there was still severely operative the inexorable law of attendance at Divine worship, and there was no cessation in the round of scriptural lessons to be learned. But the child was already tasting of the fruit of the tree of the knowledge of good and evil; and he had learned from books that there was another Christmas at once less harmful and more mirthful than the Christmas of the Puritanical household. He came in this manner to know of the Christmastides of Dickens, of the pastimes on the ice after morning service, of Christmas games and smiling firesides. He extended his studies of this good genius of fiction. He gradually formed a conception of a world in which the path of duty was not necessarily the path of suffering and tears. He was, by degrees, creating an existence for himself in which a kind imagination enabled him to find an opportune relief.

The dual life, which sooner or later we most of us lead, had begun for him, spite of his tender years. There was, on the one hand, the austere external life, full of terrors, impregnated with pharisaism and hypocrisy; there was, on the other hand, the inner life, the outcome partly of a joyous literature working on a childish imagination, partly of the stray experiences of happiness projected into the months as they passed away, which alone rendered the burden of living supportable. As time wore on, the attempt was made to despoil him of even that glad and innocent possession which was the solace of his sombre hours. He was considered to be old enough to recognise the mercies of Providence in Nature; and he was not permitted to take his walks by the cliff or in the woods without hearing homilies on the glories of creation, and being called upon to quote scriptural texts illustrative of them. Soon Science added her horrors to those of Theology. The primrose by the river's brim was no longer suffered to be to him simply the yellow primrose, and nothing more. It was a factor in a vegetable system. He had been delivered from the persecuting Puritanism of his earlier days to friends, relatives, and preceptors with a taste for botany. He was now admonished to see, not only God in Nature, but Linnæus. He was compelled to spend hours grubbing in hedgerows for roots and plants, in order that he might listen afterwards to a lecture on their economy.

Nor did his troubles end here. It was discovered that as he was deplorably wanting in the elements of botanical taste, and indeed with as little aptitude for natural science generally as for dogmatic theology, so he was a poor, nervous, irritable, sensitive urchin. The time was now approaching when he would have to leave home for school. It was necessary that he should have some preliminary experience of what that stern ordeal would prove. So he was delivered over to the tormentors in the shape of cousins, as playmates, of maturer years than his own. Boys, he was told, had no business to be sensitive, irritable, or nervous. Their Heavenly Father had never intended them to be so, and if they would not cease being so of their own accord, they must be laughed, and if necessary beaten, out of it. It was the will of Providence that he should unlearn these silly ways, and the instruments whom Providence had selected were these impish relatives.

The child was now fairly scared. Above him there was an angry Deity; around him and on every side of him were frowning elders or younger companions, the refinements of whose cruelty seemed to have about it something that was diabolical. The boy's existence was one of prolonged and unendurable misery. He was like a hunted creature. He could not follow the instruction of his teachers; he cowered before the glance of those who were pleasantly called his playfellows. He knew no happiness save when he was asleep; and when he said his prayers he supplicated Heaven to remove him from his childish, but most real, woes. He began to pine, and to look ill; his parents shook their heads, and informed him that he was possessed by a devil. Yet there was no conscious barbarity in these excellent people. They were both God-fearing, and they never wearied of Bible and sermon. The truth is they lacked imagination. It never occurred to them to ask what the effect of this hideously unnatural, detestably coercive *régime* was calculated to be. They had, as they conceived, the certain warrant of Scripture for it, and that was, or ought to be, enough. They were not even intentionally unkind; but the inhumanising superstition of their faith placed sympathy with the hopes, fears, and thoughts of a child out of the question.

In time there came something like deliverance. The child was decided to be of ripe age for a boarding-school, and thither he was sent. He wept no tears on his departure, and his dry eyes were said to be the sign of an incorrigibly hardened heart. He had not been a week away from home before he found that he was in a new world, and that he was himself a new creature. The life of the place was a reality, and not a sham. He felt that the advice given him had some relation to the actualities by which he was surrounded. There were a freedom and an elasticity in the existence which he had never yet known. It was something not to be told that he was already in Satan's hands, and to be menaced with sulphureous terrors because his memory gave way beneath an unnatural strain. It was something to be in the company of boys, who, if sometimes combatant, were not, for the most part, persecutors. In a word, school was the salvation of the child's character. And as it was with him whose experiences are here recited, so has it doubtless been with many others. It is well that one should be able to speak of these things in the past tense. It is well that one should be able to think that the darkness of the worst form of superstition, and the thousand inhumanities which these involve, are seldom to be found in the training of the children of to-day.

Happily, even at the period above referred to, there were forthcoming, in the majority of instances, the experiences of school to correct the baneful and mistaken teachings of home; and those who, under such a home system, have grown up to be honourable, bold, good men—and not cravens, hypocrites, and pharisees—have done so, not as a result of, but in spite of, such a system. But who shall say how many a character has been incurably dwarfed and irreparably spoiled by the ill-starred regimen? It is the parents, and not the schoolmasters, who should shape, and who are primarily responsible for shaping, the disposition of the son; and that they can only do, and can only have done, as they frame their teachings by direct reference to the conditions of life which will confront him hereafter. The object of the education of childhood is to equip the child in the manner best calculated to help him to acquit himself honourably, and it may be successfully, in the world into which he is born. It is not necessary on this account to exclude the religious element, without which experience shows that all early education is radically imperfect. But it is necessary so to regulate this that the moral and intellectual fibre shall not be debased and weakened; and it is also necessary for parents to cultivate those relations of equal friendship with their children which may cause the latter to listen with real affection to the teachings of experience, and may provide some kind of guarantee that the wholesome monitions of age will not be given in vain.

VIII.

MR. HAYWARD.

THE morning newspapers of the 7th of February, 1885, contained the account of a funeral ceremony held the previous day in St. James's Church, Piccadilly, which must have caused many readers no little surprise. The name of the man round whose bier the mourners were gathered was probably unknown to the large proportion of the provincial public, and would have been strange to a far larger, had not *The Times* of the preceding Monday devoted two columns of big type to his life, and summed up his character and career in a leading article. But the company collected to pay the last token of respect and regard to his memory within the church, from which the din of the most bustling of West End thoroughfares is audible, comprised men distinguished in various walks of life, known and honoured by all their countrymen. The Prime Minister placed a wreath of snowdrops, fresh from the woods of Hawarden, upon the pall. Near him stood one or two of his colleagues in the Cabinet; stood two or three ex-Cabinet Ministers; stood also men famous in diplomacy, in law, as well as in statesmanship and letters—the ornaments and representatives of what is called society. It is impossible to conceive of a more typical gathering, and Mr. Hayward could have desired no more significant tribute to the position he had achieved long ago, and the kind of ascendency he had held. Those to whom his patronymic either conveyed no idea at all, or little else than a dim impression of some powerful reviewer whose writings they could not well indicate, must have been at a loss to account for the attention paid to him by men who are already part of English history. I propose briefly, and, as it cannot but be, most inadequately, to give some explanation of this phenomenon; hereafter I trust there may be published in the pages of *The Fortnightly Review*, a more finished and worthy study of Hayward's life and labours.

Nothing can be more misleading than many of the estimates of Mr. Hayward which have already appeared in print. He has been represented as a professional diner-out, a *raconteur*, a trifler, a cynic, a mere wielder of flippant *persiflage*. If he had been only one of these persons, or if he had been all of them combined, he would have failed to acquire the influence and distinction which belonged to him. English society, whatever its follies and frivolities, is essentially serious. The wits and wags, the *farceurs* and light comedians of the dinner-table, make a transient reputation, but they never reach the place which, willingly or unwillingly, was accorded to Hayward. He had his angularities; he had his faults; but the estimate in which he was held and the authority which he had won were, on the whole, not more creditable to himself than to the society from which he derived his power. If he had been less passionate in his love of truth, less eager in his pursuit of it, less intrepid in his championship of friends and in his denunciation of foes, he would never have come to eminence and even autocracy.

Endowed with a legal and thoroughly logical mind, with accurate and abundant knowledge, with prodigious energy, with a rare power of argumentative speech of the kind one may call overbearing, he still will not be remembered as a great lawyer. He produced no independent work of large dimensions, and he was not, in the sense in which that expression might be applied to some of his contemporaries, a great writer. His essays, indeed, which fill five or six stout volumes, may be described as a thesaurus of miscellaneous information, not more curious for its comprehensiveness than admirable for its accuracy and precision. It is no exaggeration to say that any person who had assimilated a tenth part of the knowledge contained in Hayward's occasional pieces would be unusually well informed. The literary merit of these compositions is considerable; but it was as little in his capacity of littérateur as of lawyer, anecdotist, and critic, that Hayward took the most powerful and brilliant portion of the English public by storm, and, once having captured it, held it in fee. The qualities which were the instruments and guarantees of his success were his thorough genuineness, his intensity, his abhorrence of falsehood and sham, of trickery and imposture, his dauntless and fiery determination to arrive in every case at facts, to prevent others being misled by phrases, and, in the words of Figaro, to "whip hypocrisy." Attributes of this kind generate a moral atmosphere. They may often offend, but they never fail to attract.

When Johnson asked Boswell his impressions of the conversation over night, the faithful satellite replied to his master, " Well, sir, you gorged and trampled on a good many people." These words exactly describe Hayward's attitude to every species of falsehood, inaccuracy, or cant. One can understand how a young lady, on being told that Hayward was the sort of man who would do vehement justice to her if she were wrongly assailed, but would bring any slip she might make into prominent relief, had the *naïveté* to say, " What a horrid man !" And it was in the nature of things impossible for such a fierce hunter after truth to be extensively popular. People observing from without his distinguished position in society sat down at their desks and deliberately ascribed his elevation to a cause the reverse of the truth. Samuel Warren attempted to assail him in "Ten Thousand a Year" as Mr. Venom Tuft. Lord Beaconsfield, who often worked hard against him by manipulating the hogshead of abuse which his followers brought him and distilling it into three drops, was supposed, by many persons, to have lampooned him as Mr. St. Barbe in "Endymion." The original of that character, it is now known, was Thackeray, whom Lord Beaconsfield disliked for the same kind of reason that he disliked Hayward. As he resented Thackeray's burlesque of his literary style in "Codlingsby," so he resented Hayward's exposure of his plagiarism from Thiers' funeral panegyric on St. Cyr. Hayward had convicted him of a twofold rhetorical dishonesty: first, his appropriation of Thiers' masterly composition, ideas, words, and all; secondly, his appropriation of the language in which it was first placed before the English public by *The Morning Chronicle*.

But, independently of this incident, there was a natural antipathy between the two men which could not have failed to breed a reciprocity of dislike. To Hayward, Disraeli's character seemed essentially false; and the very reasons which made him, during the latter years of his life, so warm an admirer of Mr. Gladstone, prevented his ever being a sympathetic critic of Mr. Gladstone's great opponent. The reason of Hayward's unpopularity during the earlier stage of his career were, on the part of those who knew him, impetuous aggressiveness; and on the part of those who did not, a mistaken estimate of him. No man ever less merited the surname bestowed upon him by Warren; no man was ever less of a parasite, a toady, or a tuft. He performed no acts of unworthy or interested homage. Where others won by blandishments, he succeeded with frowns and reprimands. If the number of those who entertained towards him any warm sentiment of friendship or affection was small, it was larger than falls to the lot of most of us, and few men have ever received on their death-bed such marks of patient and tender devotion from those outside the pale of their own kindred.

Hayward, indeed, had outlived his unpopularity. He ceased to be unpopular when he became privileged. The vast legion of his acquaintances did not measure him by the standard which is usually applied as a gauge of social amenity. He occupied a position of his own, apart from others, and he was not expected to conform to any conventional canons. If these traits in his character had not been accompanied by sterling and rare merits, society would not have tolerated and have smiled upon him. In addition to his truthfulness and thoroughness, he was absolutely loyal to his friends, not only doing justice to them in his talk, but, when necessary, and often when unnecessary, doing fierce battle in their behalf. He was, moreover, of great practical assistance on more than one occasion to some of those friends when they were entrusted with the administration of the nation's affairs. He was never the depository of State secrets, for it was his way when anything had been told him which interested him to talk about it everywhere. Hayward's relations to statesmen and to Governments will be correctly indicated, if it is said that before passing into action irrevocably, Ministers found it occasionally convenient to try the strength of their case before him. When a Liberal Cabinet was preparing to deliberate on any measure, some of its members instinctively liked, before confronting the public, to "talk it over with Hayward." This "private trial," as racing men might call it, was of infinite service to Ministers adventuring on new ground; for they learned what could be effectively said both against their project and for it. If once brought to approve the design, Hayward never failed to become its strong partisan.

It may be convenient here briefly to glance at such stages and aspects of Hayward's life as are necessary for a correct understanding of the place he filled, and his connection with the politics and politicians of his time. He came of a good Wiltshire stock, descending from the Haywards of Hillcott, a family owning landed estates which, along with high moral characters, entitled them to the envied privilege of entering church before all the other parishioners. Hayward was indebted for his baptismal name to an uncle who lived at Taunton, with whom his nephew frequently stayed, and who was much shocked when, on calling on Hayward in his chambers in the Temple, he found him in the company, not of a future Lord Chancellor, but of one whom, in an angry letter still extant, he called an adventurer—the future Napoleon III. In point of property his family encountered vicissitudes, sometimes in the downward, sometimes in the happy direction. He was educated at Blundell's school at Tiverton, then a West-country Winchester. The discipline was harsh, the diet meagre, and his family believed that the lad's health was permanently injured by the rough life and the scanty fare.

On leaving school he went to a private tutor, and learned German. He was articled to a solicitor at Ilchester, who had little business, but an excellent library of the orthodox English classics, on which Hayward feasted at leisure, and acquired much of the varied and profound knowledge of English literature that appears on every page of his writings. Before he was twenty he began to keep his terms in the Temple. His means were at this period exceedingly slender. His chief pleasure, and, as it proved, a most valuable portion of his education, was to attend the debates of the House of Commons, admission to which was then to a large extent gained by favour of the door-keepers, who were entitled to charge half-a-crown, and to whom consequently many of Hayward's spare half-crowns went. While he was yet a law student he joined the London Debating Society. This event had a great influence on his life, and constituted a turning point in his career. Roebuck was the leader on the Liberal side. Hayward quickly stepped into the place of Conservative chief; and, among all the ardent young members of the society, there were none who pursued the pith of the argument with more closeness than the Blundell scholar. On being called to the Bar, and finding practice slow in coming, he established *The Law Magazine*, which was devoted largely to the philosophy of jurisprudence, and which brought him into connection with George Cornewall Lewis and John Austin, as well as some of the chief German authorities of the period on legal science. In 1832 Hayward paid a visit to Germany. He did not meet when there, as has been incorrectly said, Goethe, but he made the acquaintance of Savigny the jurist and the father of the subsequent Prussian Minister. He was thrown into the society of Tieck, and frequented the *salon* of the Countess Hahn-Hahn, whose acquaintance and friendship he retained during several years, and with whom he maintained a correspondence even after she had retired into a convent at Mayence.

Few Englishmen, indeed, have had a larger personal acquaintance on the Continent. Few knew the character of France and Germany better, or had a juster appreciation and a deeper insight into the spirit of their literature. Hayward's visits to Paris were frequent; and to the end of his life he seldom crossed the Channel less than once a year. He was on intimate terms with Thiers, Broglie, Dumas, and many others. He introduced more than one French writer for the first time into England. One of his most interesting essays is devoted to Madame Mohl, at whose house he was a frequent guest. When Thiers, in his futile quest for an alliance, visited this country just before the investment of Paris in 1870, the first person whom he saw on his arrival was Hayward. He sounded his old friend as to the possibility of the English Government giving France its support. Hayward at once said the idea was hopeless. Thiers then began to argue his case, and to show that in the interests of the balance of power it was the duty of England to support his country· "My friend," broke in Hayward abruptly, "put all that stuff out of your head. We care for none of these things."

The achievement in literature which firmly laid the foundation of his literary reputation, as the London Debating Society had done of his political and oratorical reputation, was his translation of "Faust." Society now commenced to welcome him; and when, in the year following the Reform Bill, a hundred members were added to the Carlton Club, he was included in the list. At the same time he was elected by the committee of the Athenæum, under the operation of Rule 2, providing for the admission of men distinguished in literature or science. Nor was he by any means a briefless barrister. Though a junior, he was entrusted with the lead in the great Lyme Pathway case, which he conducted with extraordinary energy, carrying everything before him, and bringing his local knowledge, as well as his legal acumen and forensic power, to bear upon his adversaries with an effect that achieved complete victory at every stage. Taking silk in 1845, he seemed "to have the ball at his feet;" but at that very moment he abandoned all thought of "the ball" in order to fight out a battle. He had years before quarrelled with Roebuck, who now excluded Hayward from the Benchers of the Temple, entrance to whose body was an honour that would have come to him in the natural course of things, on his promotion to the dignity of a Queen's Counsel. Hayward engaged in the business of redressing this wrong with characteristic vehemence. He brought the matter before the judges, and so far succeeded that they recommended the Benchers to revoke the decision. The recommendation was not acted upon, and Hayward, in the din of his fight with the Benchers, lost or rather abandoned the opportunity of acquiring a considerable legal practice.

But an eventful, and, as it afterwards proved to be, an auspicious epoch was at hand for him. He entered into the political controversies of 1846 with immense spirit, and, throwing over the Protectionists, worked night and day for Peel and his followers. This schism between the Protectionists and the newly-converted Free-Traders caused angry dissensions in the Carlton Club, and, together with his Peelite friends, Hayward ceased to frequent it. *The Morning Chronicle* was next started, Mr. Sidney Herbert putting then and afterwards into the paper £120,000, while the Duke of Newcastle contributed £20,000. In conjunction with his friend George Smythe, afterwards Lord Strangford, Hayward took a very active part as a leader writer, and one of his achievements in this capacity was to finish an article in the House of Lords with his pencil on his knees while Lord Derby was delivering his famous speech on the Navigation Laws, answering the chief arguments of the speaker. In 1852 the first Derby Government was formed, and Hayward addressed a letter to Lord Lansdowne asking him whether there would, in his opinion, be anything dishonourable in a union between the Peelites and the Whigs.

The reply, which exists among Hayward's papers, came speedily—to the effect that, so far from Lord Lansdowne's seeing anything dishonourable in such an arrangement, he considered it a political duty. Hayward's Temple chambers now became the scene of events of great political interest. The formation of a Coalition Government was preceded by a dinner in them, at which Lord Lansdowne, Mr. Sidney Herbert, the Duke of Newcastle, and Sir James Graham were among the guests. Hayward himself would probably have gone into the House of Commons but for his disagreement with popular feeling on the question of Maynooth. As it was, the Government did not ignore their obligations, and they resolved to secure him permanent employment under the Crown. Before this, it should be said, Hayward had had some experience of the public service. Shortly after he was called to the Bar he had been appointed a revising barrister in the West of England, and at a later date he had been dispatched to Ireland as one of the

Commissioners for the readjustment of the municipal boundaries of Dublin. He brought back with him to England a host of good stories from the other side of St. George's Channel. In 1852 it was arranged that Hayward should have a place, and Lord Aberdeen actually wrote a letter promising him one. The press condemned his contemplated promotion and scented a job. The courage of Ministers waned, Hayward never obtained the merited reward of his services, and the late Mr. Fleming was appointed in his stead. His conduct throughout the whole of this incident was admirable. He showed great magnanimity. He insisted on no claim, he bore no grudge, nor did he solicit place at any later period. Independence in such matters as these was one of the notes of his character.

A single anecdote will suffice to show the quality of the political influence exercised by Hayward, and the degree of political authority he occasionally exercised. In 1864 Palmerston and Russell were both bent on going to war with Denmark. The newspapers applauded their resolution. It gradually became known that some of their colleagues in the Cabinet dissented from this view, and that it was thoroughly unpopular with the rank and file of the Liberal party. When the tide of popular feeling was decisively setting against the war policy, inside and outside the House of Commons, Hayward called at Cambridge House. After some conversation with Lady Palmerston, to whom he represented the realities of the position, Lord Palmerston entered, fresh from a Cabinet, looking unusually tired, and Hayward left. He had scarcely descended the stairs when Palmerston came out of the room, and, leaning over the banisters, exclaimed: "Hayward, Hayward, come back!" The summons was obeyed, and the Minister at once asked what all this meant? Palmerston was nettled, and with some impatience proceeded to demonstrate the unreasonableness of the antagonism to his own and Russell's policy. Hayward, in his turn, was put upon his mettle, justified his opinion by explaining the structure of the political groups which were forming against the war, said: "Ask Brand," and roundly told him that unless he executed a change of front he would be out in a week. Palmerston rejoined: "I ought to have been told of all this." On the following Monday, Palmerston went down to the House of Commons and announced the right-about-face.

It will not be denied that the man who exercised such an authority as this with those high in power, merits the epithet remarkable. One of the secrets of Hayward's influence, as with Lord Palmerston, so with Mr. Gladstone, and many more of the public men whom he knew, was his singularly practical mind. Fond of speculation as he might be, Hayward was never dreamy or conjectural in his political judgments. He talked on these matters with authority, and not as the scribes; as a Cabinet Minister, and not as a publicist. Whenever his advice was asked or his opinion declared, he exhibited a sense of responsibility entirely foreign to the political quidnunc.

He did not say what he would wish to be done, but what in his view could be done and must be done at once. He dealt with an existing situation, and showed at every point the statesman-like instinct which prompted him to avoid barren inquiry into what might have been prevented in the past. He was a man of letters, but he was pre-eminently a man of affairs. In every business, great and small, which he undertook, he was supremely trustworthy. Lady Palmerston and Lady Waldegrave were of those who used habitually to consult him about the composition of their parties, and they both of them paid him the same compliment in very nearly the same words. " You have never brought me an unattractive woman or an undistinguished man," and, unless I mistake, another great lady, now happily living, has awarded him the same grateful praise.

Naturally, a counsellor who was as deeply in the confidence of these arbitresses of fashion was not unfrequently the object of gentle importunities at the hands of his fair friends. "Beauty parties" existed even in the days when there were no professional beauties, and Hayward received hints now and again that invitation cards would be welcome in particular directions; but the hint was never acted upon unless he considered that the aspirant guest came up to the prescribed standard of good looks and good company. Hayward's relations to women will constitute a very interesting chapter in his history. He won the favour of many ladies of consideration during his earliest years' experience of London society. He was the confidant and counsellor of other ladies than Viscountess Palmerston and the Countess Waldegrave as his life drew to a close. There is nothing which is not graceful, of which both he and they might not have been proud, in his friendship with those ladies whose good looks have familiarised the whole public with their photographs. They recognised in him a man of consummate knowledge and experience, and of no little kindliness. His advice was always trusted by them because it was always disinterested, and so it came to pass that when he was laid to his rest, beauty as well as power followed him to the grave. There is no reason why the fact should not be here recorded that when Mrs. Langtry made her private *début*, the late Mr. Chenery expressed his relief at discovering that Mr. Hayward possessed a ticket for the performance, and was willing to write a notice of it. The critique might not have been a masterpiece, but it struck the keynote which the press of two countries at once took up.

Whatever Hayward undertook to do he did exhaustively. He was ever on the crest of the social wave. No matter what might be the most prominent feature in the social life of the moment, he seized upon it, developed it, studied it, made it his own. In this way he brought his great and carefully trained intellectual powers to bear upon the smallest subjects. Let us suppose that some Ministerial crisis or some little, yet it may be, deeply instructive social incident is the topic discussed in a drawing-room. Hayward enters, and instinctively people say, "Here is Hayward, now we shall know the exact truth." He soon shows that he knows more of the subject than any of the gossips. He is not content with retailing the current comments of the hour or of expressing a few disjointed ideas on the topic. He delivers not an opinion but a judgment, and a judgment of a kind from which there is no appeal. Hayward has spoken; *causa finita est*. In society this was uniformly his way. Hayward bore down everything before him, and the polite world, finding that it could not resist him, that its protests against his vehemence were ineffectual, ended by doing him homage. He dragooned the society in which he moved, just as he commanded the waiters at the only club of which he was a member. He occupied the same portion of the dining-room at the Athenæum as tradition assigns to Theodore Hook, and it is not upon record that the instructions he issued upon any special occasion as to the disposition of places and tables at dinner were ever disregarded.

Seldom has there been such a combination of manly intellectual strength with feminine activity. It is no paradox to say that though Hayward was a confirmed bachelor, he was a born housekeeper. The qualities which made him a social king would have enabled him to organise and control the household affairs of any establishment, big or small. Guests and waiters, masters and servants, mistresses and maids, instinctively gave way to him. They were conscious of the presence of the dominant man, and if they occasionally reflected that his despotism was somewhat galling, they could no more resist him than they could the law of gravitation. Hayward has been described as an habitual diner-out. It would be more correct to say that he was a fastidious, and therefore a comparatively infrequent, diner-out. He chose the houses that he visited with great care, and not merely with a view to the *cuisine*, but to the company. Occasionally he went to houses where there was little on the part of the hosts to attract him, because he knew he would meet amusing people at the table.

I have already said that great as were Hayward's powers, and extraordinary as were his resources of anecdote, his social position was not won by his faculties in this direction. Indeed his skill and felicity as a *raconteur* were perhaps somewhat overrated. His admirable love of brevity caused his narratives to be wanting in embellishment and local colour, and as a sayer of good things and a narrator of interesting historiettes he had several superiors. He never, for instance, attained the happy art that nature has conferred upon Sir Henry Drummond Wolff in the description of incidents to which society is never weary of listening. He never acquired, as Sir Henry Wolff has always possessed, the capacity of accompanying the narrative of occurrences with a vein of meditative comment so ingenious and apt that it recalls the peculiar conversational felicity of Lord Melbourne. On the other hand, his conversation was invariably apposite and cogent, and those who listened to it across a dinner-table rose with the knowledge that they had heard everything it was possible to say, said in the best of all possible ways, upon the events of the hour. For these purposes Hayward of course required an appropriate audience. He could tolerate the presence of no rival, and if such an one, who was usually his inferior, asserted himself, he generally relapsed into silence. Above all things he disliked the loud man; and this was probably the reason why he could never arrange a social *modus vivendi* with one of the best and kindest friends I have ever been privileged to possess, the late Anthony Trollope.

In the same way, though having the truest regard and liking for Bernal Osborne, he never succeeded in overcoming his objection to Osborne's habit of talking across the dinner-table and silencing the rest of the guests. Between Bernal Osborne and himself there was indeed an utter want of intellectual affinity. Although a large purveyor of humorous and witty narratives, Hayward was neither a humorist nor a wit. He was, as has been said already, possessed of an overmastering, intellectual love of truth, and he regarded the badinage and cynicism, the quips and facetiæ of talkers like Osborne as impediments in the way of his favourite inquiry, and as calculated to distract conversation from its legitimate path. It must not, however, be supposed that Hayward's talk was invariably didactic and austere. On the contrary, he considered that an occasional laxity of tone, or, as he might have expressed it, a *grata protervitas*, was one of the conversational notes of the high-born gentleman, and he would have found little difficulty in defending the assertion that, as Bacon had declared there is no perfect beauty which hath not some strangeness in its proportions, so no talk can be perfectly high-bred which is without a certain *soupçon* of licence. Hayward's mind was essentially that of the littérateur, and, as such, it was unsympathetic with the scientific mind. He was, moreover, so passionately fond of ascertaining truth and verified certainty, that he could not simulate fondness for subjects or inquiries which did not admit of demonstration. He might have said of himself as Lord Derby did, that he was born and educated in a pre-scientific era. He had little knowledge and less appreciation of the Darwinian doctrine. He had not mastered the philosophy of evolution, and he disliked it. "About," to quote the exact language he used to a friend during his last illness, "a future state, we can know nothing, but there is something great." These words, as they appear in type, bear little meaning; their significance was derived from the tone in which they were uttered. In another conversation with one of his best and most illustrious friends, he said he had no fear of death, denied that he was a sceptic, and spoke with loving and tender reverence of the Lord's Prayer—though "he had talked sceptically," in which, he said, he found the most natural and frequent vent for his feelings.

As with Hayward his social occupations were part of the serious business of his life, so his literary business, whatever for the time it might happen to be, was manifest in the field of his social occupations. No person who met Hayward in society could fail to know what occupied him at the moment in his study. When he had exhausted a subject with his pen on paper, he would press it home to his audience of private friends with, if the metaphor be permissible, the bayonet point. No sooner had any article of his appeared than, especially if it happened to be of a controversial kind, he proceeded, to use his own phrase, to follow it up. His persistence was as intrepid as it was astounding. He gave his acquaintance no rest until they had not merely read what he had written, but assimilated it. He catechised the company in which he was at home upon it as a lecturer may catechise undergraduates with a view of discovering whether they have followed and understood his discourse.

This method, not unnaturally, frequently led him into animated discussions. He was intolerant of contradiction, and often went to invective against those who presumed to differ from him. But if he ventured more upon the licence which society accorded him than others might have done, and in doing so occasionally transgressed the limit of politeness, he was generally ready with the *amende*, and, once satisfied that he had been unjust or discourteous, he seldom failed to make an adequate apology. Nor was he unforgiving of casual wrongs. A friend once remarked, when he was in one of his most critical humours, that his translation of "Faust" was exceedingly—only a stronger adverb, or rather not an adverb at all, but a past participle, was employed—bad. He was very indignant at the moment, but he was soon conciliated, and he may well have found substantial satisfaction in the circumstance, generously communicated to him by the aggressor, that Carlyle, who was the chief theme of the conversation in question, declared of the nineteen translations of "Faust" extant, Hayward's was the best.

For some years past Hayward never exceeded and never fell short of four articles a year in *The Quarterly Review*. These were always looked forward to with the keenest expectation, and their author never failed to herald their advent in society. The income which he made from his pen was disproportionately, and, in comparison with the time he devoted to it, even ludicrously small. Most of his mornings were given to writing, and his way of work was this: Having collected all the books which told upon his subject, he would devour whatever was essential in their contents, and would then ascertain who were the persons living most likely to give him original and authentic information. He then worried his subject as a dog worries a bone, and when his mind was filled with all the necessary knowledge, he would concentrate every fact relevant to his theme into a focus, and display in his treatment of it an omniscience, combined with a lightness of touch, seldom, if ever, equalled in periodical literature. He did not produce the stately essay of Macaulay or Lockhart, but instead he gave the public a literary *macédoine*, in which the hand of the artist was apparent throughout. Such, then, in brief, was Abraham Hayward, the man and the writer. In society, in letters, and in politics, he has left a place vacant which will never be filled. His writings are already part of English literature. His rare personal qualities are sufficiently attested by the extraordinary devotion and affection which waited upon his last hours, and by the brilliant representative character of the mourners who met round his bier in St. James's Church, Piccadilly.

I have been favoured with this interesting reminiscence by one who knew Mr. Hayward well : "Naturally, like all men who have the courage of their opinions, Mr. Hayward possessed enemies, and I have heard it asserted by some of these that he never forgot a slight, even when the offender belonged to the weaker sex. From Hayward himself I received once some sort of confirmation of this. Years ago I was re-introduced to him, for he had known me when a child, one morning in the Park, by a lady who was a friend of us both. He seated himself by my side, and we talked, at first, about old times. By-and-by, in answer to some remark of mine, 'That reminds me,' said he, 'of the celebrated story of "Hymen."' But I could not at that moment take any interest in 'Hymen.' I had had an object in coming into the Park, which seemed to me, then, to be all-important. I was giving one of my first dinner-parties that very evening, to consist, so I had intended, of some twelve or fourteen congenial guests, and Fate was trying hard, as Fate generally *does* try, upon such occasions, to arrange that it should become a dinner of thirteen. I had come into the Park to look for a 'numéro quatorze.' Before the story was finished I broke away, and darted across the gravel walk to the railing which divided it from the ride. I had seen my 'numéro quatorze' upon a prancing steed, and to secure him was but the work of a moment. In that moment, however, Mr. Hayward had departed. He had risen abruptly, just after paying the chairman, my friend informed me, with a frown on his brow. 'He will never forgive you,' she said tragically, 'as long as you live!—you who wish to succeed in literature, have stupidly offended the severest critic of your time!' I was terrified, but made up my mind that when I next saw Mr. Hayward I would endeavour to atone. As it happened, however, owing to a combination of circumstances, it was nearly four years before I had an opportunity of doing so. Only quite lately I confessed to him what I had done—my supposed offence, my remorse and terror, my atonement. 'Would you really have been so hard and relentless?' I inquired; 'and unless I had asked you for the end of that story should I never have been forgiven?' 'I should have forgiven you, I dare say,' he answered, 'but perhaps I might have forgotten you too.' And he then read me a lecture upon the satisfaction which a man well-stricken in years may derive from perceiving that younger men—and more especially younger women—are anxious to avoid wounding their susceptibilities. It was this almost feminine sensitiveness, I think, which made him ever anxious to do a kind act or to say a kind word to a friend. He knew, from personal experience, the effect that only a word can produce, and I have known him to go out in bad weather and when every moment was precious, on purpose to tell some one something which he knew would give them pleasure to hear.

"VIOLET FANE."

IX.

SMALL TALK AND STATESMEN.*

It is not because they resemble each other either in literary merit or in historical importance that Lord Malmesbury's "Memoirs" and Mr. Greville's "Journals" may conveniently be placed side by side on the present occasion. It is indeed difficult to conceive of two books dealing with facts and circumstances of essentially the same kind more conspicuously dissimilar both in substance and in style. Lord Malmesbury's narrative becomes more full just where Mr. Greville's narrative altogether breaks off, and is continued from that period down to our own day. With the tone of Lord Malmesbury's "Memoirs," there is no fault to find. He says what he has to say in the spirit of a considerate and amiable gentleman. He is as free from malice as he is from wit; and never dissatisfied

---

* "The Greville Memoirs (second part): being a Journal of the Reign of Queen Victoria from 1837 to 1852." By the late Charles Cavendish F. Greville, Esq., Clerk of the Council. (3 vols. Longmans.) "Memoirs of an Ex-Minister." By the Earl of Malmesbury. (2 vols. Longmans.)

with himself, he is invariably tolerant of the rest of the world. On the other hand his pages are frequently dull, and, as a rule, they do not atone for their lack of vivacity by the value or novelty of the information they supply. Although Lord Malmesbury has been a member of three Cabinets, his conclusions, whether on men or society, are rarely very striking or profound. It is true that it used to be said of him, and not by his political opponents alone, that he was never less in place than when in place. But one might have imagined that his long and habitual association with some, at any rate of his former colleagues, would have had a visible effect in endowing him with a fair amount of the second-hand wisdom which women in particular often acquire from the men they are thrown with, and which in their case passes well enough for wisdom itself.

In one respect, however, it must in justice be allowed that Lord Malmesbury displays a certain amount of humour. He pretends to take himself in earnest as a statesman. It is possible, no doubt, that this may be merely a delusion on his part; but some of his readers will prefer to accept it as a joke. Lord Malmesbury attributes his appointment as Foreign Secretary to the influence of the stars, and in the days when people believed in judicial astrology this, no doubt, would have been received as a sufficient explanation of something otherwise unaccountable. But the story once current of this extraordinary event is that when the late Lord Derby was in process of forming his first Administration he accidentally met Lord Malmesbury in the street, and asking him half in earnest and half in jest, to whom he thought the department of Foreign Affairs would best be entrusted, received the unexpected and embarrassing reply that he himself would take it. In the face of Lord Malmesbury's own very different account of the matter, the truth of the anecdote cannot be insisted upon. It is, however, a problem of no great moment, and will not affect Lord Malmesbury's reputation with those "gentle historians" at least who, according to Burke, "judge of every man's capacity for office by the offices he has filled, and the more offices the more ability."

Before Lord Derby had invited Lord Malmesbury to become Foreign Secretary—a circumstance which Lord Malmesbury himself can be pardoned for not mentioning—he had applied to Lord Stratford de Redcliffe, who refused. It is not too much to say that Lord Malmesbury would never have been able to carry on the affairs of the Foreign Office even as he did, but for the circumstance that he enjoyed the invaluable assistance and instruction of Lord Cowley. Many inconvenient questions were not put to the Foreign Secretary in the House of Lords because of the inquirer's regard for our ambassador at Paris; many more were successfully answered by the Foreign Secretary, because Lord Cowley had previously communicated with him on the subject.

Still, on turning to Mr. Greville's "Journals," after wading through Lord Malmesbury's "Memoirs," it may be asked why it was not so ordered that Lord Malmesbury should have been Clerk of the Council and Mr. Greville successively Secretary of State and Lord Privy Seal. In the respectable routine of the Council Office, Lord Malmesbury, but for his rank and wealth, would have been furnished with a sphere of action exactly fitted for the exercise of his talents, while in the Cabinet Mr. Greville might have found an appropriate field for the practical development of his great and varied intellectual gifts. It is not too much to say that the publication of the earlier portion of Mr. Greville's "Journals" created in the public mind, if not an entirely false, at all events a distorted and insufficient, conception of his real character and powers.

When this instalment appeared ten or eleven years ago, it took the world by surprise. People were then unaccustomed to see the gossip and scandals of "society" in print. Nothing of the same sort had been presented to their notice since Horace Walpole and Sir Nathaniel Wraxall. At the latest it was the contemporaries of their grandfathers and grandmothers who were the subjects of the anecdotes with which they were familiar. Mr. Greville introduced them to the inner life of personages whom many of them had known themselves, and of whom almost all had heard from others who had known them. What was in effect a new dish was offered to his readers, and the vast majority fed upon it so greedily that they forgot the additional elements of the repast with which he supplied them. It was his gossip and scandal which they remembered, while by all but a select few the more solid and in every way more valuable parts of his work were either only slightly noticed or totally ignored.

In the course of the last decade circumstances have tended very much to moderate the popular craving for gossip and scandal. In the interval which has elapsed since the publication of the first and second instalments of Mr. Greville's "Journals," the opinion has gained ground and strength that he was something more and something better than an accomplished and entertaining *flâneur*. No doubt he was pre-eminently a man of news and conversation, as he was also a man of pleasure and of sport. But it is equally certain that he was as keen and shrewd an observer of public as he was of private life, that he was as good a judge of mankind as he was of horseflesh, and that notwithstanding the society in which he largely lived there were in him depths of seriousness and sagacity, of the existence of which, while he was yet with them, even his intimate friends may have been unaware. His frequent lamentations over his wasted time and neglected opportunities appear to be something far more pathetic than the complaints of peevishness or *ennui*.

It cannot be questioned that Mr. Greville was in every respect an abler man than his cousin, Lord George Bentinck. His judgment was sounder, his knowledge was wider and deeper, his connections were equally influential, and his attachment to the Turf was not more immoderate and notorious. Yet it is certain that if Lord George Bentinck had lived he would have been Prime Minister, while the position of Clerk to the Council was that to which, by the interest of his family, Mr. Greville was relegated in early life, and beyond which his ambition was never permitted to aspire. If a political career had been opened to him, the world would not have long been in doubt as to whether Westminster or Mayfair was the stage on which he was best qualified to shine. It is difficult to imagine anything more fitted to cramp the energies and dwarf the intellect of a young man than an easy and lucrative official post. What would Lord Beaconsfield, or Lord Melbourne, or Lord Derby have been if by any chance he could have been made Clerk of the Council at two or three and twenty? Assuredly the first would not have been less of a saunterer, the second would not have been less of an idler, and the third would not have been less of a turfite than Mr. Greville. But of these three Prime Ministers who can doubt that the writings of Lord Beaconsfield alone would have equalled his in excellence, acuteness, and vigour?

In one sense, however, Mr. Greville could not have been more fortunately and appropriately situated than he actually was. It was from the combined advantages of his birth and his official occupation that he derived the means of compiling the record of his own times on which his fame is founded not less surely and lastingly than that of Pepys or Boswell. As a man of society he was enabled to know all the men and women of his day whom anybody could care to know or to know about. As the Clerk of the Privy Council, although he was precluded from making history himself, he was brought into contact with everybody who was engaged in making history around him. While he was still a young man, the people of the Court and the people of fashion received the larger share of his attention. When he became older and wiser, they were gradually superseded in his regard by the people of affairs. In this respect his "Journal" under the reign of Queen Victoria contrasts very favourably with his "Journal" under the reigns of George IV. and William IV. It is far less of a *chronique scandaleuse* and far more of a *mémoire pour servir à l'histoire.* In his earlier volumes his political criticisms were always forcible and to the point; but they were not unfrequently hasty and inconsiderate.

In the present volumes Mr. Greville has been

more careful in forming and more cautious in expressing his opinions of contemporary politicians and statesmen. He has consequently had less occasion to modify by means of notes suggested by subsequent experience the often unmerited severity of his original text. But it must be allowed that the general tendency of his mind was to disparage rather than to appreciate the claims of rising talent and unrecognised superiority. The few allusions which he makes to Lord Beaconsfield and Mr. Gladstone, although both had been or were Cabinet Ministers when he refers to them, indicate no suspicion that they would ever attain to the eminence they were destined to achieve. Both of them were in the eyes of Mr. Greville, as they were in those of his contemporaries generally, quite inconsiderable personages. Whenever Dizzy—political nicknames are usually ominous of success, for they are at least an evidence of notoriety—is mentioned, it is in words which echo the current derision and suspicion of the day. It never seems to have occurred to Mr. Greville that a man who had not been at once crushed by the enormous weight of ridicule and obloquy heaped on him, but who, though assailed on all sides with hatred or contempt, contrived to fill year by year a larger and larger space in the notice of the public was certain sooner or later to make a great position for himself.

The leading statesmen of the period covered by Mr. Greville's "Journal" from 1837 to 1852 were six in number. Three of them died while it was being written, and three survived the date at which it comes to an end. All of them were Prime Ministers. One of them, the Duke of Wellington, seven years before 1837; four of them—Lord Melbourne, Sir Robert Peel, Lord Russell, and Lord Derby—between 1837 and 1852; and another of them, Lord Palmerston, three years after 1852. With each Mr. Greville was personally acquainted, and with two at least he was on terms of intimacy.

The Duke of Wellington was a disciple of the "stern and unbending" school of Toryism which was finally extinguished by the three great surrenders of Catholic Emancipation, Parliamentary Reform, and Free Trade. It was not the Toryism of Pitt, who was the advocate of Catholic Emancipation, who had conceded the principle of Parliamentary Reform, and who was too sound an economist to make it at all likely that he would have been opposed to Free Trade. It was the Toryism of Liverpool and Castlereagh. It consisted of the twofold conviction: first, that the Constitution in Church and State exactly as it then existed was the perfection of public reason; and secondly, that the Treaty of Vienna had effected a final and unalterable settlement of the European system. To the articles of this narrow creed Wellington adhered as firmly, and as unreservedly, as if they had been articles of religion or of war. It appeared to him to be "his duty" to believe in them, and "his duty" to maintain them. The wishes of the people, whether at home or abroad, who happened to be affected by them, entered at one time as little into his consideration as the wishes of the rank and file of his armies when he was planning his campaigns. It did not seem to him that the first were any better judges of the measures taken for their welfare than the second would have been of the measures taken for their safety. In his view policy, like strategy, was the business of those who command and not of those who are bound to obey. He was not ignorant of the state of popular feeling either in this country or on the Continent. But it did not occur to him that popular feeling was a thing to which, under ordinary circumstances, it was necessary to pay the slightest attention. No doubt the Duke's political temper was in large measure due to his military training and experience. Lord Beaconsfield, in a well-known passage in "Coningsby," attributes it almost entirely to them. In this conclusion Mr. Greville coincides. But it should not be forgotten that Wellington was an Irishman, and by birth and sympathy an Irishman of the dominant minority. Moreover his earliest political employment had been as secretary to the Lord Lieutenant, in some, at any rate, of the darkest days of Protestant ascendency.

His military habits naturally gave colour to his character. From the tone in which it was once customary to speak of him, one might imagine that his campaigns had affected his mind in much the same way that the siege of Namur had influenced Uncle Toby's, or that he was a sort of General Bombe, with a brace of pistols instead of a snuffbox in his pocket, ever and anon refreshing himself with the smell of powder on their discharge. It used to be asserted that his military genius had been developed at the expense of all his other intellectual powers. Even his colleagues are represented as conducting themselves towards him as if they were constantly running the risk of a trial by court-martial. But, after all, the Duke's character does not appear to have been influenced by his profession in any greater degree than that of most Lord Chancellors and most Archbishops is by their career as lawyers or clergymen. He was, as Mr. Greville says, by nature "hard;" he had "no tenderness in his disposition," he was not "an amiable man." With such defects, whether he had been or had not been a soldier, he could never have secured the affection, as distinguished from the respect, of his followers; and if he had entertained the most advanced opinions, he would still have been almost as far as he actually was from fulfilling the idea of a popular leader. It is, however, a mistake to suppose that he was so self-willed as to be incapable of listening to reason, and seeing when events had become too strong for him. When, on the retirement of Lord Liverpool, he refused to join the Canning Administration, there is no ground for supposing that he was actuated by personal hostility to Canning, or that he was insincere in his opposition to Catholic Emancipation.

He has been frequently accused indeed of an unworthy jealousy of Canning, and of having repudiated his advances because he wanted the premiership himself. There is some excuse for believing that this is partly true. But even if the Duke had held that he, rather than Canning, should have been entrusted with the formation of the Administration, there would have been nothing discreditable or extraordinary in the belief. They severally represented the two sections of the late Government and the Tory party, the one determined to resist, and the other ready to concede, the Catholic Claims. Canning was the most accomplished statesman of the day, and had in so many words asserted his right to the premiership by inheritance as the political heir of Pitt. Wellington was equally the most distinguished subject in the Empire. As Mr. Greville says, he was everywhere treated almost as a royal personage. He held undisputed sway in the House of Lords, and at that time the House of Lords controlled the House of Commons. There would thus have been nothing wonderful if he had entertained the opinion that if he was to be a Minister at all he ought to be the Prime Minister. But, as his later conduct proves, he was not moved by such considerations. Wellington, to quote Mr. Greville's words, "was utterly devoid of personal and selfish ambition, and there never was a man whose greatness was so thrust upon him." Nor can the fact that on the death of Canning, in the course of a few months, he became Prime Minister and carried Emancipation, affect any estimate of his conduct on the retirement of Lord Liverpool. It was his own famous maxim, that in "all circumstances the duty of a wise man is to choose the lesser of any two difficulties which beset him." When he came into office, the Clare Election had occurred, and it had not occurred when he refused to co-operate with Canning. Of the two difficulties which stared him in the face, Emancipation or civil war, he chose the lesser. He did not relieve the Catholics from any sympathy with them, or because he had changed his opinion on the justice and policy of relieving them, but to prevent the appalling alternative of rebellion in Ireland, of which there had not, in his view, been any immediate prospect when he acted with the anti-Catholic division of Lord Liverpool's late colleagues. In so doing, he virtually broke up his party and secured the speedy discomfiture of his Government. Resistance to parliamentary reform, the Corn Laws, and the extension of the currency was useless for the purpose of calming the fears or quelling the anger of the strict Tories who had been aroused by the cry of "The Church in Danger."

When, therefore, the quarrel with Huskisson ensued and the Canningites were also alienated, an end was put to Wellington's first and last premiership. But, to the time of his death, he always commanded an authority scarcely inferior to that of the responsible head of the Government. It is remarkable to observe from the entries in Mr. Greville's "Journal," that as early as 1839, Wellington's mental as well as his bodily condition appeared to be alarming to those who were in habitual association with him. The "last stage" of Marlborough and Swift seemed to them to be fast approaching, and the famous couplet is referred to·by Mr. Greville himself and by Lyndhurst, twice in the course of a few pages. In the next year, Mr. Greville describes the Duke as "a broken man," and mentions a seizure which he had in the House of Lords, whence he was carried home speechless to Apsley House. At the very time, however, that Mr. Greville was noting these melancholy symptoms, the Duke was in correspondence with the King of Prussia, by whom he had been asked to take the command of the forces of the German Confederation in the event of a war with France, and to whom he replied, that with the Queen's permission he was quite ready to do so, since he "felt as able as ever and as willing to command the King's army against France." It was, too, eight years after this that Wellington planned the masterly defence of London against the Chartists, a piece of strategy which was not by any means unworthy of his most vigorous days. On the whole, the world will concur in Mr. Greville's final estimate of the Duke of Wellington, that he was not merely a very great man, but that he was the only great man in the true sense of the terms who was living at the period of his death.

With Sir Robert Peel Mr. Greville describes his acquaintance as "slight and superficial." But on more than one occasion he appears to have been in confidential, if not direct, communication with him. In the negotiations of 1839 which preceded Peel's attempt to form an Administration and his discomfiture on the "Bed-chamber question," he acted as the informal intermediary between the Government and the Opposition. But he expresses his satisfaction that, on this occasion, he saw Graham instead of Peel himself, "by whom," he says, "I should have been met with a cold austerity of manner which would have disconcerted me, and I should have most certainly quitted him mortified and disappointed, without having effected any good." "Confound the fellow," he writes a little later, "what a cold feeler and cautious stepper he is!" But he seems to have considered Lord John Russell, on whose behalf he was more particularly acting, almost equally disagreeable. "Strange," he adds, "that two leaders should make themselves so personally obnoxious as they do by their manners and behaviour. Nevertheless, John Russell, though frigid and forbidding to strangers, is a more amiable man with his friends; but the other has no friends."

In after years he refers to Peel again as "so cold, so reserved, and his ways so little winning and attractive, that he cannot attach people to him personally." But in summing up his characteristics after his death, Mr. Greville says that "he was easy of access, courteous, and patient;" moreover, that "those who approached him generally left him gratified by his affability." The consensus of testimony from all quarters, however, is complete that there was in Peel's manner an absence of warmth and charm which was not only repellent, but in a certain sense humiliating to those who came into contact with him. Sir James Hudson, who was William IV.'s secretary, and who posted night and day to Rome to summon Peel to England in 1834, used to relate, as an example of this, that Peel did not even ask him to have lunch with him when he arrived, after the fatigues of his long and hurried journey.

How far the virulent animosity of Peel's former supporters may have been attributable to his want of politeness and what they stigmatised as his want of principle, is a problem which it would be difficult to solve. But it may be taken for granted that the ablest leader in the Protectionist revolt would have moderated the rancour of his attacks if he had not been treated with what appeared to be studied discourtesy by Peel, and if he could have hoped that Peel would have ever been induced to regard him as an eligible candidate for office. As it is, Lord Beaconsfield's Corn Law speeches have not done less in many quarters to create the current impression of Peel's character, than the cartoons of *Punch* to create the popular notion of Brougham's countenance. Both were extremely open to caricature, and both have been caricatured with great effect.

It was Peel's misfortune as a political chief, that he had too much common sense and too much information to be at any time a thorough-going partisan. It was by the accident of birth more than anything else that he was originally connected with the Tories. Mr. Greville tells a story of the manner in which the first Sir Robert Peel secured the Irish Secretaryship for his son, viz., by threatening Lord Liverpool with his secession to the Whigs if he was not provided with high office at once. The anecdote is probably not true, but there is nothing impossible about it. With his "cool head and temperament" Peel could never have been an extreme politician. He always perceived the difference between abstract principle and practical expediency. His political opinions were not articles of faith, but conclusions of reason. He saw that on all questions there was much to be said on both sides, and that it depended on surrounding circumstances whether one side or the other had the best of the argument. He knew, to use his own words, that "what at one time is consistent with sound policy, may be at another completely impolitic," and it was his fate on many memorable occasions to illustrate the proposition by his own example. While he enjoyed the full confidence of those who acted with him, he first opposed, and then supported, the Catholic Claims and the reform of the Currency Laws. It is, as we now know, a mere chance that he did not repeat the process in regard to parliamentary reform. As early as 1820 he asked, in a remarkable letter to Mr. Croker, "Can we resist—I mean not next session or the session after that—but can we resist for seven years reform in Parliament?" And answering in the negative, he continues, evidently with approval of the prospect he presents, to say that "if reform cannot be resisted, is it not more probable that Whigs and Tories will unite and carry through moderate reform than remain opposed to each other?"

But even if this had been added to his numerous tergiversations, his grand apostasy would still have been the repeal of the Corn Laws. Here he touched not only the sentiments, but the pockets of the country gentlemen, and even Mr. Greville, who was himself a Free-Trader, affirms that if he had belonged to Peel's party he should have felt "the same indignation and disgust" that they all did. It may well seem strange that the contemporaries of Peel, and Mr. Greville among them, should have forgotten that long before the crisis came he had declared his adherence to the principle of Free Trade, and had treated the Corn Laws as an exception to its application, of which the expediency depended on circumstances. In his memorable speech on the Tariff of 1842, he affirmed that "on the general principles of Free Trade there is now no great difference of opinion," and that "all agree in the broad rule that we should purchase in the cheapest market and sell in the dearest." The League had made the prolonged existence of the Corn Laws in their integrity impossible in the years between 1842 and 1845, and the question was between the sliding scale of the Government, the fixed duty of the Whigs, and the total abolition of the Repealers. The Irish Famine determined the course of Peel; or, according to the Duke of Wellington, as quoted by Mr. Greville, "rotten potatoes did it all: they put Peel in his damned fright." But in addition to "rotten potatoes," there came the "Edinburgh Letter" of Lord John Russell, with its denunciation of the Corn Laws as "the blight of commerce, the bane of agriculture, the source of bitter divisions among classes, the cause of penury, fever, mortality, and crime among the people."

After this manifesto, the maintenance of the sliding scale or the adoption of a fixed duty became equally impracticable. What could Peel do under the circumstances more or better than he did do? He summoned a Cabinet Council, the result of whose deliberations was that he resigned. Lord John Russell was sent for, and failed to form an Administration. Peel, therefore, had no alternative but to resume office. He came back again with all his colleagues except Lord Stanley, whose place as Colonial Secretary was taken by Mr. Gladstone, and the Corn Laws were repealed. After Peel's death, the Duke of Wellington declared in the House of Lords that one of his most marked characteristics was the love of truth, and that during his long connection with him he had never known him to deviate from the strictest veracity. Such praise from such a quarter leads Mr. Greville to suspect that "resentment and disappointment may have caused an unfair interpretation to be put upon his motives."

But with the great bulk of the people the motives of Peel were never in doubt. On the Catholic question the Tories made him the scapegoat of Wellington, because they were afraid openly to attack the Duke himself. But that did not interfere with the implicit reliance which they afterwards placed in him, more especially when, owing mainly to him, the Conservative reaction of 1841 secured for them a long tenure of power. On the question of Free Trade he was made, not the scapegoat, but the stepping-stone of Lord Beaconsfield. It was only by trampling Peel under foot that Mr. Disraeli could hope to ascend to the Treasury Bench. But with the middle class, both upper and lower, the most intelligent as well as the most wealthy section of the community, he never forfeited his popularity, and their opinion of him was raised by his independence and disinterestedness. He was emphatically one of themselves, and presented to their minds the embodiment of all their best and most distinctive qualities. He was a man of solid understanding, without a trace of extravagance in either his views or his actions. He was a financier to whose prudence and resource they could look with the most implicit confidence. He was, as Mr. Greville says he considered himself, " the Minister of the nation, whose mission it was to redress the balance which mistaken measures or partial legislation had deranged, and to combine the interests of all classes in one homogeneous system, by which the prosperity and happiness of the whole commonwealth would be promoted." His life was singularly decorous, and, in spite of his great wealth, his habits were simple and unostentatious. All this endeared him to the respectable classes, and gave him a unique place in their esteem.

It would be difficult to discover a more striking contrast to Sir Robert Peel in many of these particulars than Lord Melbourne. Both had strong common sense. But the common sense of Melbourne bore a close resemblance to the cynical shrewdness of the man of the world, and was backed by a fund of humour of which Peel was entirely destitute. Peel was a pattern of orthodox and domestic propriety. Melbourne, although his theological reading was wide, had no settled convictions, and was always getting into notoriety about his own wife or the wife of somebody else. Peel was by nature a politician, a master of details and precedents, and never more at home than in the House of Commons, on which, when he spoke, as Lord Beaconsfield has testified, "he played as if it were an old fiddle." Melbourne really detested politics, could bring himself only with difficulty to the examination of even great and important questions, and as. a speaker in the House of Commons was a complete failure. Peel's stiffness and want of cordiality seriously injured his prospects in public life. Melbourne's charm of manner, his urbanity and kindness, were the main things which prevented his public life from being a series of disasters. Peel was a *bourgeois* Tory, Melbourne was an aristocratic Whig, and while the one, under the guidance of his judgment, was always tending towards Liberalism, the other was in all his instincts, prejudices, and sympathies a Conservative throughout his career. It is true that he was included in the small band of politicians to whom the name of Liberal was first applied. He deserted Grey and Althorp as Palmerston deserted Wellington and Peel, and enrolled himself under the leadership of Canning. Mr. Greville says he hated parliamentary reform, although, as Home Secretary of the Grey Administration, he supported it; while of the repeal of the Corn Laws his view was expressed to the Queen, when he was sitting next to her at dinner at Windsor, with his usual vigour in the words, "Ma'am, it is a damned dishonest act."

It was his well-known divergence from the principles of Grey which led to his appointment as his successor in the premiership by William IV. in 1834. The King thought that so bad a Whig was the next best thing to a Tory, for which he exchanged him in six months, when Peel supplanted him—for even a shorter period. But it was then said of him that he understood William IV. more perfectly than anybody else, and it was in his ability to understand people and to adapt himself to them that his strength lay. The esteem and affection with which the Queen is known to have regarded him are frequently illustrated in the anecdotes which Mr. Greville has preserved. But Melbourne's thoughtfulness on Her Majesty's account, and his generosity towards an opponent whom he fervently disliked, are perhaps most pleasingly exemplified in the advice which he transmitted to Peel through Mr. Greville concerning the mode of transacting business with Her Majesty when he retired from office in 1841. He was, in fact, not a statesman, but a courtier. His Administration was one of the worst and most incompetent ever known. It nearly involved us in a war with France, and its Budgets disclosed an uninterrupted succession of deficits. Its Cabinet Councils were often the scene of disputes and recriminations between its members, and when matters proceeded more peacefully the Prime Minister went to sleep. Had it not been for Melbourne's tact and good-humour it would have broken up long before it was turned out. But he was not always equal to the occasion, and Mr. Greville gives a painful description of the "indecision, weakness, and pusillanimity" which marked some of his efforts to pacify his colleagues and prevent an open rupture between them.

In the Melbourne Administration which came to an end, to the satisfaction of everybody, in 1841, Lord John Russell and Lord Palmerston were Secretaries of State, one originally for the Home, and afterwards for the Colonial Department, and the other for Foreign Affairs. As politicians, both were immensely superior to the Prime Minister. Both possessed infinitely more force of character and knowledge of affairs. Moreover, both had deliberately chosen politics as the serious occupation of their lives, while he was always more or less of a statesman *malgré lui*. Russell was sedate, and without any trace of humour or imagination. His courage and his confidence in himself were almost without parallel, and throughout his public career he fully justified Sydney Smith's well-known jest, levelled at him in his youth. His political opinions came to him by inheritance. He had never had the slightest trouble in forming them. He accepted them, however, not with mere acquiescence, but with the strongest faith in their unassailable truth and wisdom. His principles were the principles of civil and religious liberty. He was above all things a Whig, and a representative of the Whig tradition. He believed implicitly in the infallibility of the whole series of Whig statesmen, from Somers to Fox, and he accepted it as a dispensation of Providence that the Great Revolution families should lead the people and govern the country from generation to generation. He entered public life with the same easy certainty of attaining to high office as that with which the son of the head of a commercial firm looks forward to a partnership when the term of his novitiate is over. He had not to make his own position; it was already made for him, and his success was merely a question of time and opportunity. He was in no sense brilliant, and it was not necessary that he should display brilliancy. Whatever abilities he possessed were sure to be readily and gladly acknowledged by his party. He had not to fight his way to the front rank, or push aside obstructive and pertinacious veterans who impeded his progress. In the course of nature he must arrive there, and no need existed for him to be impatient or obtrusive. Nothing was heard of him by the outside world for sixteen or seventeen years after he had become a member of the House of Commons. But he had established his footing there in a calm and unpretentious way.

As yet he was not a leader, or even a candidate for leadership. It was never suggested that he should enter into competition for it with Tierney, or

Brougham, or Althorp. But the chief of his party at last found an opening for him, and he was put forward to move the repeal of the Test and Corporation Act. That measure was practically already a dead letter in the Statute Book, and it was expunged from it with only a show of opposition from the Government of Wellington and Peel. But from that time forward the name of Russell became a household word among the large and influential congregations of Dissent. A year or two afterwards he was selected as one of the small committee by whom the Reform Bill was prepared, and, as Paymaster of the Forces, in the Grey Administration, he moved the first reading. But the conduct of the measure through its subsequent stages was undertaken by Althorp. Russell's gifts as a speaker were considerable. But he was not a great orator like Mr. Gladstone or Mr. Bright, or a first-rate debater like Mr. Canning or Sir James Graham. Occasionally, however, he rose to eloquence, and produced an immense effect on the audience he happened to be addressing.

> But see our statesmen when the steam is on,
> And languid Johnny glows to glorious John;
> When Hampden's thought, by Falkland's muses dress'd,
> Lights the pale cheek and swells the generous breast;
> When the pent heat expands the quickening soul,
> And foremost in the race the wheels of genius roll.

His vocabulary was not very copious, and this in some measure gave force to his diction. He did not use words which impart the nicer shades of distinction, and hence his speeches were commonly telling, because they were full of strong expressions.

The most instructive and, to all who take up the volume except for frivolous amusement, the most interesting portion of Mr. Greville's "Journals" is that which describes the triumph of Palmerston, and, indeed, were this work to be distributed into parts after the fashion of eighteenth-century epics, much of it might be entitled "The Triumph of Palmerston." So inexplicable, so miraculous does it seem to Greville, as it seemed to many of Palmerston's contemporaries, that one might almost expect to find the intervention of some god or goddess on his behalf. And, indeed, there is good reason why Mr. Greville and others should have felt this astonishment. Palmerston was generally hated by his colleagues in the Cabinet, was seldom in a majority of more than one, while on the Continent he was regarded by every European State as little less than the embodiment of the principle of evil. Yet he was uniformly victorious. How, and why? These questions are not answered by Mr. Greville. It may be said that Palmerston knew better than many of his friends and foes did his own mind, and that he devoted himself to realising it. It would, however, be more correct to say that he went his own way, he allowed nothing to interfere with him, he was never nonplussed, he never stopped to argue with those who desired to thwart or censure him, whether Prime Minister or Sovereign. He coolly pocketed all criticism and reprobation, and went on as if nothing had happened. But is this the only explanation of his extraordinary success? I think not.

Palmerston had, at the most critical period of his career, in 1840, the year in which he achieved his most dazzling victories over his colleagues, one instrument which, to a Minister, and especially a Foreign Minister, is of nearly overwhelming efficacy, and by his dexterous use of this instrument he contrived to carry all before him. What was it? It is no secret that he had in the late Lord Dalling—then Sir Henry Bulwer and Secretary of Legation at Paris—a fast friend. Lord Dalling was a diplomatist who believed in the value of knowledge acquired from every quarter and by every means. Wherever men, and especially women, congregated, he made it his business to gather information as to the doings and intentions of foreign Cabinets and statesmen. In this way he contrived to know much of what the French and other Cabinets determined before their sitting had been formally held. This knowledge he communicated to Palmerston, and the consequence was that Palmerston speedily became invincible in the Councils of Whitehall. He knew everything; he was never taken aback; he could not be imposed upon; and when any portion of his own policy was criticised, he brought to bear upon his critics such an entire armoury of facts and figures that they were compelled to admit that he had acted and spoken with good reason. To put it therefore in a sentence, the secret of Palmerston's invincibility was not merely the fact that he was a man who went his own way, but the further fact that he had the benefit of Sir Henry Bulwer's full, minute, and inspiring information.

It was immediately after the passage of the Reform Act that Russell was admitted to the Cabinet, and that the long and embittered rivalry between him and Palmerston commenced. The death of Canning had left Palmerston without a political chief, and he was on the look-out for a new political connection. He had been in office for nearly twenty years under successive Tory Administrations, from that of the Duke of Portland to that of Lord Liverpool. But he saw that the Whigs were in the ascendant, and having already separated himself from Wellington and Peel, he offered his services to Lord Grey. His wish was to lead in the Commons; a project which, if it had been realised, would have materially affected the prospects of Russell. It was arranged, therefore, that Althorp should take the lead of the House. But Palmerston was made Secretary for Foreign Affairs, and was in Lord Grey's Cabinet when Russell entered it. Palmerston resembled Russell in his courage and self-confidence. Nor was he inferior to him in his undeviating regard for his own interests.

But here the likeness between them ends. Palmerston's jaunty and *dégagé* air was proverbial from his youth to his extreme old age. He always appeared to be in excellent spirits, and did and said the most disagreeable things with an unruffled temper, and in all lightness of heart. He was not connected by the ties of at any rate near kindred with any of the great political houses among either the Tories or the Whigs. His Irish peerage gave him the great advantage of a recognised station which enabled him, though not without a struggle, to secure a hold upon "society," and in those days "society" meant, to those who were in it, politics, if they had any capacity and inclination for them. He was not rich, but he was extremely good-looking and pleasing in his manners. His long and intimate friendship—which ultimately resulted in marriage—with Lady Cowper, the sister of Lord Melbourne, and one of the three or four *grandes dames* of the period, was of the highest use in the furtherance of his political fortunes. He had much quickness, but little prudence or discretion. His industry was great, his information wide and varied, and his wit and humour abundant and ready in every emergency for either attack or defence. His head, rather than his heart, however, was the source of the many-sided sympathies with which he was credited.

Beneath the superficial *bonhomie* which fascinated everybody who approached him, there lurked a large reserve of craft and calculation. His joviality and apparent want of restraint covered and disguised an intelligence ever on the watch for his own advancement and the discomfiture of his adversaries. His sagacity was not deep and far-reaching. He acted far oftener from impulse than from deliberation. He was guided, to use M. Thiers' phrase, "par le caractère, non par la raison." Except in foreign affairs, where he was meddlesome to an unequalled degree, *laisser aller* was the maxim which he observed both in public and private. The bills of his tradesmen were not less unheeded by him than the growing requirements of the people. Although he would have had no difficulty in paying the former at once, their payment was invariably deferred until the sterner processes of the law were called into action. He was deeply interested in politics, but he was as free from political convictions as Melbourne. Although he concealed his treachery with greater art, he was as treacherous as Russell. His treachery and Russell's treachery indeed manifested themselves under different forms and in different ways. Until he had established his supremacy in his party, he was perpetually coquetting with his opponents. It was never quite certain whether he was going to "nobble" the Tories or "square" the Radicals.

Russell could never have pretended to be anything else than a Whig. It is true that in his later years he was compelled to concede much to the more advanced section of his followers. But he had no sympathy with either the Philosophical Radicals like Molesworth and Grote, or the Manchester Radicals like Milner-Gibson, Cobden, and Bright. Although he was forced by circumstances to renounce it, his famous declaration of "finality" expressed his permanent and unbiassed view of parliamentary reform. In quite another sense from that in which it was applied at first to the great measure of the Grey Administration he wanted the "Bill, the whole Bill, and nothing but the Bill." Still, if he never entertained the slightest notion of deserting his party, his practice of playing for his own hand was perpetually getting it into difficulties and embarrassments. At no time could his colleagues be sure that, as Bear Ellice expressed it, "Johnny was not at some of his dirty tricks." He was always springing mines under their feet, and making a bid for popularity without their knowledge and over their heads. They could never go to bed at night with the full assurance that they would not wake in the morning and find themselves confronted in the newspapers by a Stroud Letter, or an Edinburgh Letter, or a Durham Letter. They could never even rest in certainty that Russell would not denounce them in Parliament as he did denounce them on the conduct of the Crimean War.

Palmerston did not give them cause to apprehend anything of this kind. But they could not tell from one day to another to what he was going to commit them in the department under his charge. If he consulted them at all, they might just as well have kept their counsel to themselves as have given it to him. He did precisely what he pleased, whether they liked it or not. He had no notion of what subordination or community of responsibility means. But more than this: it was always on the cards that he might leave them in the lurch altogether. One day at Windsor, when a Council was held, Mr. Greville was present, when Lord Melbourne said to Lord

Clarendon of his own Administration and Foreign Secretary: "It is impossible this Government can go on; Palmerston in communication with the Tories—Palmerston and Ashley——" and then he stopped. Lord Clarendon replied: "What! you think Palmerston and the Tories will come together?" To which Lord Melbourne nodded assent. "And which," inquired Lord Clarendon, "will come to the other?" "Oh, I don't know," rejoined Lord Melbourne, and chuckled and grunted, laughed, and rubbed his hands.

It was a similar performance in the opposite direction which, according to Mr. Greville, led to the rupture between Palmerston and Russell ten years later. On that occasion he was flirting with the Radicals. They gave him a dinner at the Reform Club—"a sorry affair"—says Mr. Greville; "a rabble of men, not ten out of two hundred whom I knew by sight." They sent deputations to him from Finsbury and Islington about Kossuth, and he made them a speech—"a very Radical speech," it is called by Lord Malmesbury. It was not Palmerston's premature approval of the Emperor Napoleon's *coup d'état* in conversation with Count Walewski which really provoked his dismissal, however angry the Queen and the Prince Consort may have been about it. That Mr. Greville affirms was merely the pretext; "the *causa causans* was, without any doubt, the Islington speech and deputation, and his whole conduct in that affair." But Russell dare not have turned him out on grounds which would have drawn him and the Radicals even more closely together than before.

. In spite however of the dinner at the Reform Club and the Kossuth deputations, Palmerston was quite ready to open communications with Lord Derby when he was getting his Ministry together in 1852. According to Lord Malmesbury, Palmerston himself made the first advances ; and what a difference it would have made to Lord Derby if the alliance could have been formed ? Everybody will remember the account in " Endymion " of the band of gentlemen, only one of whom, and he in the House of Lords, had ever been in office before, who were called on to form an Administration, and how impossible, for this reason, the task appeared to them. But here in fact, although not in Lord Beaconsfield's fiction, was a gentleman ready to join them, who, despite the chops and changes of the political world, for more than forty years had hardly ever been out of office at all. A gentleman, whose attachment to the Treasury bench was so deep, sincere, and comprehensive, that it included every party in the State whose leaders happened for the time to sit on it, was at hand to instruct them in their duties, if they had only been wise enough to accept his assistance. But the arrangement failed because Palmerston would not, accommodating as he was, have anything to do with Protection, about which Lord Derby never proposed, and in all likelihood never seriously intended to propose, anything.

In less than a year Palmerston was in office once more, and he did not quit it again, except for one year and a hundred and thirteen days in 1858-59, until his ruling passion subsided in death. Once when he was Prime Minister, and Mr. Hayward was staying with him at Broadlands, Mr. Delane, who was there also, said, "Would you tell us, Lord Palmerston, the circumstances of your resignation in 1853?" "You need not trouble yourself about the circumstances," returned Lord Palmerston, "for I never resigned at all." The editor of *The Times*, primed with this piece of news, returned to his office, and incorporated it in a leader which appeared the next morning. At the Athenæum Club in the afternoon Mr. Hayward and Mr. Delane met. The former pointed out in the files of *The Times* how persistently that journal had asserted that Palmerston had resigned in 1853 on the question of the Black Sea fleet. Mr. Delane put his hands up to his head and exclaimed, "Good God! What it is to have to do with a daily newspaper." The story of the resignation, as *The Times* originally gave it, is repeated by Lord Malmesbury, with the addition that Palmerston was out of office for just ten days.

If Lord Palmerston had become a member of Lord Derby's Administration in 1852, he would have found himself associated in the person of its chief with one of the oldest of his Whig colleagues. Palmerston and Derby, with Melbourne and Russell, were in office together under Lord Grey in the memorable Reform

Government of 1830. The mere enumeration of these four names as those of men banded together for the furtherance of what the Tories of the day dreaded as revolutionary, serves to remind us of the enormous distance we have travelled since then. It is suggestive to observe in Mr. Greville's "Journals," although they refer to a period when all Lord Grey ever desired to do had been done for many years, how quietly he seems to assume that politics are and ought to be essentially an aristocratic business or diversion. In his view the work of government and legislation appears to be the appropriate, and should be the exclusive, occupation of people of rank or fortune, with a few assistants selected by them from among their adherents, whose humbler station or more limited means they are good enough to excuse on account of their superior capacity.

Perhaps Mr. Greville may have been a little old-fashioned in this as compared even with the majority of his associates. But the spirit which shut the door of the Cabinet in the face of Burke, which branded Canning as an upstart, and which pointed the finger of scorn at Disraeli as an adventurer, lasted much longer than the *régime* from which it took its origin. When Lord Derby decided to devote a portion of his leisure to political pursuits, this sentiment was far more general and active than when Mr. Greville wrote. Everybody would then have agreed that as a rule admitting of few exceptions men should be politicians because they were persons of importance, and not persons of importance because they were politicians. As the grandson and heir of a Whig peer of high rank, illustrious lineage, and vast estate, it would have been a reproach to Mr. Stanley if he had not taken his place in the House of Commons. It would have been equally censurable in the leaders of his party if they had not embraced the earliest opportunity of rewarding him with office and the assurance of promotion. He was Irish Secretary and Colonial Secretary with the Whigs, and then Colonial Secretary and thrice Prime Minister with the Tories. It was thus his singular privilege to be a member of each of the two Administrations by whom measures of parliamentary reform were passed in his lifetime.

Lord Derby's character appeals to the imagination more forcibly than that of any of the statesmen who were opposed to him. He has gathered around him almost as much of popular romance as Lord Beaconsfield himself. It is not of the same kind, and it does not arise from the same causes; but it is equally unfounded and nearly as absurd. He was so far from being a great statesman that he was not a statesman at all in any true and rational sense of the term. It is difficult to regard him even as a serious politician. He had plenty of political prejudices, but no political principles. As a leader he was not the chief so much as the figure-head of his party. In or out of office he reigned, but he did not govern. He was the sleeping partner, and gave the credit of his name to the firm of which Lord

Beaconsfield was the manager and business man. He represented no scheme of national policy, but only an exploded fallacy in political economy. He talked about "stemming the tide of democracy," which ended in his "dishing the Whigs" by outbidding them with the Radicals. He had neither large views nor wide sympathies. He had an imperious manner and a bad temper. He was an elegant, although not an erudite, scholar. Of knowledge beyond scholarship he had none. He belonged, as he himself said, to "the pre-scientific age," and he once undertook to swallow the boiler of the first steamer that should ever get across the Atlantic. All that Lord Malmesbury can claim for him as a politician is that as Lord Melbourne's Colonial Secretary he had care of the Bill for the Abolition of Slavery, and that as Prime Minister he was prompt in his recognition of Napoleon III., and passed the Reform Act of 1867.

It must be admitted, however, that he was an excellent landlord and a model country gentleman. He was also munificent in his charities, and did a great deal of good during the cotton famine in Lancashire. "But," Mr. Greville says, "the notion which is generally entertained of his being so high-minded and chivalrous is a mistake. He is not so in private life —that is, in his transactions on the Turf; and it is not likely that a man should be one thing in private and another in public life." Just before he became Prime Minister Mr. Greville saw him at Newmarket, amid a crowd of betting men and loose characters of every description, in uproarious spirits, chaffing, rowing, and shouting with laughter, and joking. "His amusement," Mr. Greville explains, "was to lay Lord Glasgow a wager that he did not sneeze in a given time, for which he took pinch after pinch of snuff." And yet it is certain that Lord Derby was a man of cultivated tastes, and of much keen wit as well as playful humour. He was, moreover, the most brilliant orator, and in all other respects the most considerable personage of his time, in the House of Lords. But, young or old, he always retained many of the leading characteristics of boyhood.

> The brilliant chief, irregularly great,
> Frank, haughty, rash, the Rupert of Debate;
> Nor gout, nor toil, his freshness can destroy,
> And Time still leaves all Eton in the boy.

X.

BERNAL OSBORNE.*

MORE than ten years have passed since the late Mr. Bernal Osborne retired from the House of Commons, and more than two since he died. Neither in the political nor social life of England has there, during this interval, appeared any one to fill the place which his departure left vacant; and there are those who believe that the want of some such censor as Osborne —so brilliant, so wise, above all so irresistibly dominant—is one of the causes of the decline of the House of Commons, carrying with it the decline and fall of statesmanship. Those who long sat with Osborne in the House of Commons may in some measure test for themselves the soundness of such a belief by questioning their imaginations a little, and asking whether certain things could have been hazarded, if on that favourite seat next below the gangway, which is the third from the floor, Bernal Osborne were sitting intent, with his hat inclined over his eyes, and ready to make his spring.

Be that as it may, he was a memorable, interest-

* Reprinted from *The Fortnightly Review*, October, 1884.

ing, and unique figure, while there is more of durability in the reputation he has left behind him than in the case of many whose distinction in their generation was of a higher degree. This is due to the striking aspects of an idiosyncrasy which, viewed in the aggregate of its qualities and its effects, was without a parallel in contemporary life. Other men in other ways were witty and wise, apt at phrase-making and quick at repartee, others shone after their manner in society; but none united to Osborne's social qualities those exuberant and unconquerable animal spirits which ruled his character, which may be even said to have decided his career, and which made their influence felt by all with whom he was brought into contact—with delight by some, with fear and trembling by others.

The peculiar power of Bernal Osborne cannot be better illustrated than by recalling some of the moments of sudden, delighted excitement once familiar to many who will read these lines. If the collective character of the House of Commons is to be studied as a drama, and its distinctive traits as a living organism, of which its individual members are parts, are to be observed to advantage, the ladies' gallery, or the benches under the clock, are the points from which any one (whether a member or not) can best look at the assembly objectively, and try to divine how it manages to be " wiser than any one in it." If, on the other hand, the real life of the House of Commons is to be studied analytically, one must not forget the side lobbies. Each of these is a chamber immediately contiguous to, and running parallel with, the whole length of the House itself. In these two rooms, strictly appropriated to members, one frequented by the habitual supporters of the Government, the other by the Opposition, there may be seen engaged in the writing of endless letters or talking with another, some languidly, some in deep earnest, many a score of the elective legislators of the realm. Here it is a follower of the Government in eager conversation with a Minister, or—more business-like still — with the indefatigable Patronage Secretary of the Treasury. Here, by twos and threes, are gentlemen whom the whips distinguish as "malcontents," conspiring with great animation and cheerfulness against political rivals who are not perhaps three yards distant from them.

The partitions which divide these rooms from the body of the House are of such a kind that occupants of it, whilst engaged in their correspondence, or conversing with their friends, always hear the murmurs of the House. One does not mostly distinguish the orator's words, but the interruptions are plainly audible—the cheers, the angry, the scornful interjections, the mighty, uproarious laugh, the "Order!" "Order!" "Order!" from the chair. At one moment the House is calm, and the member seated at the table determines he will finish his letters. Then he hears the sounds of a storm gathering, and resolves in sudden haste to postpone his epistles till to-morrow.

He knows when one speech is ended and another beginning, and the knowledge thus gained by the ear is reinforced by men coming out of the House and gliding in singly from moment to moment, or sometimes by an influx of members coming suddenly from out of the House because some well-known bore is on his legs.

But at last some speech ends, and one hears—or rather once did hear—"Dizzy's up," then another, and "Palmerston's up," then another, and "Gladstone is up." Thereupon men will quietly determine to shorten their literary labours, will composedly collect their papers, and before long go back into the House to hear what the chiefs have to say. But there used to be no such composure as this when the fibre of the well-known voice could be recognised through the partitions, and voices here, there, and everywhere, along both the side lobbies, were crying out: "Osborne is up." Then men of all sorts and conditions would bundle up incomplete documents with a haste that threatened confusion, and rush at once into the manufactory of statute law. The very doorkeepers used to cease from being solemnities, and be busy in carrying the infection, saying eagerly, "Mr. Osborne is up, sir."

Such was the common experience, and it at once constitutes a tribute to Osborne's powers, and suggests the question—Why? What was it that always guaranteed him a full House when he spoke? It is not enough to say that the people's representatives love a jester, and that they welcomed the relief afforded by Bernal Osborne's *persiflage* to the severer eloquence of other orators. It is certain that Osborne would not have received so eager and so gratified a hearing if he had not mingled much practical wisdom with his entertainment; if he had failed to confute, demonstrate, or instruct, as well as to divert; if his satire and pleasantry had not discharged the intellectual functions of dialectic as well as tickled the fancy. The truth is, that in many cases, and especially in debate, a joke is often a happy summary, a trenchant and bright compendium of a series of solemn argumentative processes. It flashes, in an instant, conviction on the hearer's mind; it causes the truth, which was previously obscured and is now suddenly enlightened, to penetrate into his being. It does briefly what volumes of vapid talk fail to effect. It is the concentration, because it is the enlivening and illumining, of argument.

When, for instance, in reply to demands that England should "put her foot down" at once in several quarters of the globe, Mr. John Morley tersely submitted that "England is not a centipede," could he have exposed more effectively the Chauvinistic fallacy of the patriots of the platform? Mr. Bagenal, in his interesting and, whether in respect of literary style, or of just appreciation of a biographer's duties, admirably executed memoir of Bernal Osborne, recently printed for private circulation, quotes a passage from one of the most brilliant of living writers, who has insisted that "the English, not being a logical people, and not having the clue of pure reason to guide them in their search after truth, would be passing their life in a political jury-box, for ever inquiring, were it not for the occasional service of the swift, trenchant argument of ridicule." Mr. Bagenal then proceeds to show with felicitous cogency that by his use of the weapon Bernal Osborne did good, wholesome service to the State, and became for that reason a power in Parliament.

Mr. Disraeli called him "the chartered libertine of debate," but the shrewd, sagacious assembly which gave him this licence knew well in its heart of hearts that whether by words of sterling sense, or by humorous allusions, or by political sarcasm, he was clearing the air of debate. So it was that when, for instance, he sprang to his feet after an intolerably dull speech from the Treasury bench, and entreated the House not to be carried away by the eloquence of the right hon. gentleman ; when he protested that the electors in one half of the small boroughs regard a vote neither as a right, nor a-trust nor a privilege, but a perquisite ; when he denounced the increase of military expenditure as a game of beggar-my-neighbour ; when he said of Lord Palmerston that "in a Cabinet the united ages of which would puzzle the oldest inhabitant, he was the youngest man—having a turn for extravagance, which is a folly of youth, and never being satisfied without squandering the public money ;" when he said each of these things he was giving pithy and pointed interpretation to what all knew to be a truth. What drew men crowding into the House when they heard the cry, "Osborne is up!" was not only a desire to hear Osborne speak, but to witness the effect—to see the House, as Pitt phrased it, "under the wand of the magician."

But great as was Osborne's faculty for wit of the intellectual kind, it attracted perhaps less notice than his over-brimming wealth of animal spirits. Whatever the extremes into which these led him, however disagreeable the names by which his freedom from all bashfulness and *mauvaise honte* might be called by his censors, it must be remembered that they were the accompaniments of unflagging courage, and, on the whole, of extraordinary public spirit and political independence. If Osborne had been made of different material, or if his gift of pleasantry had not been associated with such intrepidity, it is probable that he would never have entered political life. His father indeed had sat during thirty-four years in the House of Commons at a cost of nearly £70,000. But the son showed no early taste for public affairs, and at Cambridge, not mingling closely with the studious or even the intellectual men, he at once became a prince of society. "Superbly, aggressively handsome," writes one of his best friends, "with flashing dark eyes, with firm set defiant lips, with a strong ringing voice in speech, which became a fine tenor in song, with an utter absence of all guile, with not even a thought of self-repression, and in short with an absolutely unbounded audacity, he was something almost godlike in the midst of shy, sheepish young men of the common English types. It has been said that at Cambridge he played in private theatricals. Yes, he played Captain Absolute in 'The Rivals;' but there was no acting in it. He was simply himself—simply Bernal triumphant. It was perfect."

There is a story, not true to the letter, yet substantially founded on truth, which puts words into the mouth of a chaperon in those brilliant days: "Mr. Bernal danced twice with my Julia, and sang a duet with her, and he was so dreadfully handsome, and had such a bewitching tenor in singing, that I became alarmed lest he should trifle with her affections; and, determining to interpose, I asked him (in the phrase customary at that time) whether his intentions were honourable, and what do you think was his answer? He answered, 'Certainly not!' and in so ringing a voice that you might have heard him in the next room. My first impulse was to be angry, and to think he might have had the grace to say something more 'roundabout;' but I was wrong. Would that all men were so honest, so bold, so determined, and so free from guile." He went into the army, and afterwards was attached as an aide-de-camp to Lord Normanby's viceregal court in Ireland. His father had not helped him at all to obtain that appointment; and with a humour delightful to think of at even this distance of time, he used to say: "I got that entirely by my own merit." He acquired distinction and vogue as a brilliant young man of fashion, first in Dublin and afterwards in London. In 1841 he became, more by accident than design, candidate in the Whig interest for High Wycombe. He carried the seat entirely by the spirit and pluck, by the inexhaustible fun and go which he brought to the contest.

These, indeed, were the qualities which never deserted him throughout a public career of nearly half a century, and which stood him in such extraordinary good stead at the nine opposed elections which he fought. No man ever less nursed a constituency or had such a contempt and incapacity for the process as Osborne. Middlesex, Dover, Liskeard, Nottingham, and Waterford, each in turn accepted him, not because he paid them any careful suit or flattered their local vanity, or subscribed to their local institutions, but because he took them by storm and carried them with a rush. The greater the resistance offered to him the more uncontrollable, the more audacious, and often the more successful he was. It was a radiant, boisterous life, and the ardour, no less than the literary power with which Mr. Bagenal has loyally followed his hero from contest to contest, is delightful to those friends of Osborne's who have been allowed to read pages withheld from the eye of the public. He declined to pledge himself to a party or a Minister; he set himself against Lord Palmerston when his power and popularity were at their zenith; he required that his election expenses should be kept down to a figure which, in those days, seemed not so much modest as mean; he trampled on the Protestant susceptibilities of the English public at a time when the "No Popery" cry woke a real echo in the country; and yet, though he did all these things by turns, and not infrequently many of them together, he was one of the most popular parliamentary candidates of his time.

A bearing so fearless as Osborne's, a contempt so robust for all conventionalities and prejudices, a diction so clear, so incisive, so ready a wit, so powerful, so thrilling a voice, with a delivery always animated and firm, always even triumphant and masterful, compelled the admiration of the multitude. Only a man who had immense physical strength, as well as personal fearlessness and hardihood, could have fought the battle of his second Middlesex election, or could have passed the ordeal described so amusingly by himself at Waterford. "I am," he said to a friend shortly after he had been victorious at the latter of these places, "slowly recovering from the success of an Irish election." Most men with half of Osborne's experience would, long before this, have registered a resolve to retire into private life.

What would have discouraged and deterred others only served to stimulate Osborne. Angry crowds, surging before platforms and accentuating their anger with missiles hurled at the speaker's head, the waving of bludgeons, the smashing of windows, the howls of infuriated electors, accusations, calumnies, abuse of every kind were to Osborne part of the fun of the business, into which he entered with a laugh and a jest. Upon one occasion, at Waterford, one of his enemies in the mob below fired a pistol. Osborne was not daunted for an instant. "If," he exclaimed, "my good friend, you would only have the goodness to go off, like your pistol, I should be for ever indebted to you." Upon the same occasion he would certainly have been lynched if he had not succeeded in getting out of a second-floor window, and so effecting an entrance to a draper's shop, where he passed the night stowed away in a bundle of blankets. The town itself was wrecked. Osborne had shown no sign of flinching throughout. He was equally impervious to alarm when plunged in the midst of contests which, less tempestuous and perilous, were sufficiently trying to the nerves at Liskeard and Nottingham.

His extraordinary animal spirits, therefore, rested upon a strong basis of rare personal courage, and in the audacity of his manner there was nothing which went beyond, or had not its exact counterpart in, the defiant daring of his nature. A temperament and attributes of this sort are sure to command ascendance, and to secure recognition. He always used to be neatly, appropriately, and faultlessly dressed, and was not tolerant of those who fell into less careful habits. He had not been in Parliament an hour before he disclosed his characteristic audacity and a disregard so disdainful of all self-repression, that he needs must begin undertaking to enforce the rules of the House! Descrying a college friend, not then a member, who was occupying, by the Speaker's leave, a seat under the gallery, he came and sat next him, and joyously used his new privilege by putting on his hat, as a member is entitled to do. Presently a gentleman, less trim and spruce, came and took his place close to Osborne, putting on, as the newly-elected member for Wycombe had done, his hat—a hat as remarkable for its shabbiness, as Osborne's was for its brilliancy and military smartness. Osborne was so new to Parliament as to be shocked at the sight of this ill-brushed and ill-conditioned article of head-gear, and imagining that so lamentable an offender in the matter of apparel could not be really a Member of Parliament, he actually put him to the test. "Pray, sir," he said, severely looking at him, "are you a member?"

Instances of this kind might be indefinitely multiplied from Mr. Bagenal's delightful volume. When Osborne was not attracting the attention of the House of Commons by formally taking part in its debates, he was, as often as not, making his presence felt by his audible asides, and his satirical comments on those who sat near him. He took a particular pleasure in teasing sedate Liberals, and taking a rise out of severely respectable Radicals. The fun he threw into these sallies cannot be conveyed by language, and depended for its original effect upon the time, the place, and the manner of the man, but one may speak of the way in which it told. Those good Radicals contracted such an awe of Osborne, that in the vain hope of keeping him at a distance, to Osborne's immense delight, they used meekly to call him " Sir." It was the same in social life. Only one who was indeed "a chartered libertine" of the drawing-room and dinner-table could have indulged so systematically, and with such impunity, his peculiar method of raising a laugh by selecting a butt who was frequently a person of high position and decorous gravity, and directing at him, for the entertainment of the company, his shafts of satire and chaff.

How, it may be asked, is the circumstance to be explained—first, that his wildest extravagances were universally tolerated in society ; secondly, that independently of his wit and its intellectual value, he was a distinct power in the House of Commons ? As regards the former, it is enough to say that his perfectly natural and absolutely spontaneous freedom came of his southern blood, and was endured, and appreciated, because it presented so marked a contrast to the pervading tone of English life. In England, where the national virtue is a dignified self-restraint, there is always room for one man of the most opposite sort. Count d'Orsay, who with all his high-breeding and genuine kindliness was, to say the least, bold in society, affords another instance of this truth. With reference to the second question, it should not be forgotten that Osborne possessed an immense store of masculine common sense, of sound judgment, and even of accurate prevision. On the ballot, on Ireland—especially on the Irish Church, and the position and dangers of landowners—he held opinions that were distinctly in advance of his day. He saw the turn which, on the day after to-morrow, matters were likely to take, the crises which must inevitably arise, and he anticipated many of the troubles which legislation has since attempted to remove.

This shrewdness and solidity of thought, added to his undoubted sincerity and his tenacious adherence to the opinions he had once espoused, even when they were involved in a storm of unpopularity, were quite enough, without his endowments and achievements as an orator and a debater, to secure him a position at St. Stephen's. As an orator his voice was, as has been said above, fine, rich, and musical, but, above all, penetrating; his sentences were not only bright, but were well turned; the literary form in which he spoke was capital, and he was always light in hand. Towards the close of his life he was in the habit of saying that his high animal spirits and loud voice had been his bane. That the voice reacts on the character, and consequently on the reputation, is true, but a low voice, as well as a strong one, may tempt its owner to indulge in satirical speech. Rogers used to excuse himself for the ill-natured remarks he was reproached with making, by murmuring, "I have so low a voice that, if I didn't say bitter things, no one would ever hear me at all." But for Osborne to reproach himself either with his voice or his spirits, was much as if he had reproached himself with being Bernal Osborne; certainly none who knew him can be favoured with imagination enough to conceive Bernal Osborne with a voice meek and low, and a temperament submissive and chastened.

By his power as a speaker he climbed the first and most difficult part of the steep which leads to high political eminence, with a success so decisive as to be recognised in the most complete of all ways—by the offer of office under the Crown. The office he consented to take was (amongst the non-Cabinet offices), a high and important one, the Secretaryship of the Admiralty; but, the First Lord being also a member of the House of Commons, it followed that Osborne was not in general called upon to answer questions touching the conduct of his department. As a consequence his new official position, notwithstanding its dignity, was disadvantageous to Osborne in its influence on his subsequent career. The change necessarily withdrew him in great measure from the debates, while it did not give him that invaluable practice and discipline which would have completed his political training, and which he would have received if he had been charged with the task of representing a department in the House of Commons.

We may conjecture—no one can do more—that if that duty had been cast upon him, he would have executed it with success; because his vigour and ability would have easily enabled him to master the business, and the duty of giving authoritative explanations in the House to ill-informed and sometimes foolish questioners would have afforded him the best possible opportunities of using with due moderation his powers of banter and sarcasm. As it was, his official position condemned him in general to silence; and when at last, after an interval of five or six years, he found himself unleashed by the change of Government, and hastened to use his recovered freedom, he uttered the speech which Disraeli amusingly called the "shriek of liberty." The gibe was the more successful since the time was one when, the Liberal party being in a shattered state, Osborne's piece of invective was a sheer waste of power.

Osborne never seemed to fail in a speech. He

was a real, honest sharer of those simple old Radical opinions pleasantly styled "shoemakers' politics," but he never allowed himself to "preach" on such subjects, nor even, indeed, to touch them without taking care to be witty. He once, indeed, thought that he had failed. The great speech that he made in 1864 against going to war with Germany was in every point of view admirable, and tended to govern events, but it was—rightly, of course—a grave speech, and Osborne missed—missed even with pain—those signs of enjoyment on the part of the House which before had always greeted his efforts.

But whatever his sterner potentialities, the line that he adopted and the triumphs that he won were those that best suited his taste. He delighted to dwell in a blaze of celebrity and in a very tempest of social and political action. These were his natural elements. He did not lack dignity, but his nature was wholly foreign to calm and repose. At his Irish home at New Town Anner, he is supposed to have studied and meditated much, and he was unquestionably a well-read man; but the incurable fault he must ever have found in all books was that of their being behindhand, and not close up, alongside with him, in the very front and van of life. Certain it is that at New Town Anner he appeared to those who knew him, and whom he entertained with the kindest and most thoughtful hospitality beneath his roof, to pay much more heed to life, actual life, than to books.

But one of the many attractions which made him so delightful a host was of an intellectual kind. Speaking always in the most generous spirit, and with an admirable breadth of view, he would touch the questions of Ireland—the Ireland close outside his park gates ; and if he had been the dullest instead of the brightest of men, he could not have spoken more wisely. Certain, too, it is that whatever his literary studies during the parliamentary recess on the other side of St. George's Channel, he had no time for anything of the sort in London. In Pall Mall it would have been as accurate to speak of him as a recluse as a student. No one there ever saw him "in his library," "in his study," in any sort of masculine den. He was always astir. His way of living was to be alive. He was too highly gifted intellectually to be averse from contemplative moods ; but he liked to think aloud, and his thinking was rendered all the more sound by the clear, vigorous diction which expressed it, and the accompaniment might, as musicians would say, of his glorious, soul-stirring voice.

Bernal Osborne was ever true and steadfast in friendship ; and one of the ways in which he proved his loyalty may be mentioned here. When the shafts of his ridicule and his banter came flying around, there were always a few—some were women and some were men—who seemed each of them to have a charmed life. The truth is that to him they were sacred. Distinguished from mere acquaintances, they were really his friends. He never struck at a friend.

THE END.

CHARLES DICKENS AND EVANS, CRYSTAL PALACE PRESS.

11, HENRIETTA STREET, COVENT GARDEN, W.C.

APRIL, 1886.

A

Catalogue of Books

PUBLISHED BY

CHAPMAN & HALL, LIMITED,

INCLUDING

Drawing Examples, Diagrams, Models, Instruments, etc.,

ISSUED UNDER THE AUTHORITY OF

THE SCIENCE AND ART DEPARTMENT, SOUTH KENSINGTON,

FOR THE USE OF SCHOOLS AND ART AND SCIENCE CLASSES.

THOMAS CARLYLE'S WORKS.

MESSRS. CHAPMAN & HALL beg to announce that an entirely New Edition of the Writings of MR. CARLYLE, to be completed in Seventeen Volumes, demy 8vo, is now publishing, called

THE ASHBURTON EDITION.

This Edition is handsomely printed and contains the Portraits and Illustrations, and is issued in Monthly Volumes, at Eight Shillings a Volume, viz. :

VOL. 1. THE FRENCH REVOLUTION. Vol. I. [Ready.
,, 2. THE FRENCH REVOLUTION AND PAST AND PRESENT.
  [Ready.
,, 3. SARTOR RESARTUS; HEROES AND HERO WORSHIP.
  [Ready.
,, 4. LIFE OF JOHN STERLING—LIFE OF SCHILLER.
  [Ready.
,, 5. LATTER-DAY PAMPHLETS—EARLY KINGS OF NORWAY—ESSAY ON THE PORTRAIT OF JOHN KNOX.
  [Ready.
,, 6. LETTERS AND SPEECHES OF OLIVER CROMWELL.
  Vol. 1. [Ready.
,, 7.   Ditto   ditto   ,, 2.   [Ready.
,, 8.   Ditto   ditto   ,, 3.   [Ready.
,, 9. HISTORY OF FREDERICK THE GREAT. Vol. I. [Ready.
,, 10. Ditto   ditto   ,, 2.   [Ready.
,, 11. Ditto   ditto   ,, 3.
,, 12. Ditto   ditto   ,, 4.
,, 13. Ditto   ditto   ,, 5.
,, 14. Ditto   ditto   ,, 6.
,, 15. CRITICAL AND MISCELLANEOUS ESSAYS. Vol. I.
,, 16. Ditto   ditto   ,, 2.
,, 17. Ditto   ditto   ,, 3.

Ten Volumes are now ready.

BOOKS

PUBLISHED BY

CHAPMAN & HALL, LIMITED.

ABLETT (T. R.)—
WRITTEN DESIGN. Oblong, sewed, 6d.

ABOUT (EDMOND)—
HANDBOOK OF SOCIAL ECONOMY; OR, THE
WORKER'S A B C. From the French. With a Biographical and Critical Introduction by W. FRASER RAE. Second Edition, revised. Crown 8vo, 4s.

THE ARMIES OF THE NATIVE STATES OF INDIA.
Reprinted from the *Times* by permission. Crown 8vo, 4s.

BADEN-POWELL (GEORGE)—
STATE AID AND STATE INTERFERENCE. Illustrated by Results in Commerce and Industry. Crown 8vo, 9s.

BARTLEY (G. C. T.)—
A HANDY BOOK FOR GUARDIANS OF THE POOR.
Crown 8vo, cloth, 3s.

BAYARD: HISTORY OF THE GOOD CHEVALIER,
SANS PEUR ET SANS REPROCHE. Compiled by the LOYAL SERVITEUR; translated into English from the French of Loredan Larchey. With over 200 Illustrations. Royal 8vo, 21s.

BELL (DR. JAMES), Principal of the Somerset House Laboratory—
THE CHEMISTRY OF FOODS. With Microscopic Illustrations.
PART I. TEA, COFFEE, SUGAR, ETC. Large crown 8vo, 2s. 6d.
PART II. MILK BUTTER, CEREALS, PREPARED STARCHES, ETC. Large crown 8vo, 3s.

A 2

BENNET (WILLIAM)—
   KING OF THE PEAK: a Romance. With Portrait.
   Crown 8vo, 6s.

BENSON (W.)—
   MANUAL OF THE SCIENCE OF COLOUR. Coloured
   Frontispiece and Illustrations. 12mo, cloth, 2s. 6d.
   PRINCIPLES OF THE SCIENCE OF COLOUR. Small
   4to, cloth, 15s.

BINGHAM (CAPT. THE HON. D.)—
   A SELECTION FROM THE LETTERS AND
   DESPATCHES OF THE FIRST NAPOLEON. With Explanatory Notes.
   3 vols. demy 8vo, £2 2s.
   THE BASTILLE: Its History and Chronicles. [*In the Press.*

BIRDWOOD (SIR GEORGE C. M.), C.S.I.—
   THE INDUSTRIAL ARTS OF INDIA. With Map and
   174 Illustrations. New Edition. Demy 8vo, 14s.

BLACKIE (JOHN STUART), F.R.S.E.—
   THE SCOTTISH HIGHLANDERS AND THE LAND
   LAWS. Demy 8vo, 9s.
   ALTAVONA: FACT AND FICTION FROM MY LIFE
   IN THE HIGHLANDS. Third Edition. Crown 8vo, 6s.

BLATHERWICK (DR.)—
   PERSONAL RECOLLECTIONS OF PETER STONNOR,
   Esq. With Illustrations by JAMES GUTHRIE and A. S. BOYD. Large crown 8vo, 6s.

BLOOMFIELD'S (BENJAMIN LORD), MEMOIR OF—
   MISSION TO THE COURT OF BERNADOTTE. Edited by GEORGIANA,
   BARONESS BLOOMFIELD, Author of "Reminiscences of Court and Diplomatic Life."
   With Portraits. 2 Vols. demy 8vo, 28s.

BOYLE (FREDERICK)—
   ON THE BORDERLAND—BETWIXT THE REALMS
   OF FACT AND FANCY. Crown 8vo, 10s. 6d.

BOULGER (DEMETRIUS C.)—
   GENERAL GORDON'S LETTERS FROM THE
   CRIMEA, THE DANUBE, AND ARMENIA. 2nd Edition. Crown 8vo, 5s.

BRADLEY (THOMAS), of the Royal Military Academy, Woolwich—

ELEMENTS OF GEOMETRICAL DRAWING. In Two Parts, with Sixty Plates. Oblong folio, half bound, each Part 16s.

BRAY (MRS.)—

AUTOBIOGRAPHY OF (born 1789, died 1883). Author of the "Life of Thomas Stothard, R.A.," "The White Hoods," &c. Edited by JOHN A. KEMPE. With Portraits. Crown 8vo, 10s. 6d.

MRS. BRAY'S NOVELS AND ROMANCES.

New and Revised Editions, with Frontispieces. 3s. 6d. each.

THE WHITE HOODS; a Romance of Flanders.
DE FOIX; a Romance of Bearn.

THE TALBA; or, The Moor of Portugal.
THE PROTESTANT; a Tale of the Times of Queen Mary.

NOVELS FOUNDED ON TRADITIONS OF DEVON AND CORNWALL.

FITZ OF FITZFORD; a Tale of Destiny.
HENRY DE POMEROY; or, the Eve of St. John.
TRELAWNY OF TRELAWNE; or, a Romance of the West.

WARLEIGH; or, The Fatal Oak.
COURTENAY OF WALREDDON; a Romance of the West.
HARTLAND FOREST AND ROSETEAGUE.

MISCELLANEOUS TALES.
A FATHER'S CURSE AND A DAUGHTER'S SACRIFICE.
TRIALS OF THE HEART.

BROADLEY (A. M.)—

HOW WE DEFENDED ARABI AND HIS FRIENDS.
A Story of Egypt and the Egyptians. Illustrated by FREDERICK VILLIERS. Demy 8vo, 12s.

BROMLEY-DAVENPORT (the late W.), M.P.—

SPORT: Fox Hunting, Salmon Fishing, Covert Shooting, Deer Stalking. With numerous Illustrations by General CREALOCK, C.B. Small 4to, 21s.
A New and Cheaper Edition. Crown 8vo, 6s.

BUCKLAND (FRANK)—

LOG-BOOK OF A FISHERMAN AND ZOOLOGIST.
With numerous Illustrations. Fourth Thousand. Crown 8vo, 5s.

BURCHETT (R.)—

DEFINITIONS OF GEOMETRY. New Edition. 24mo, cloth, 5d.

LINEAR PERSPECTIVE, for the Use of Schools of Art. New Edition. With Illustrations. Post 8vo, cloth, 7s.

PRACTICAL GEOMETRY: The Course of Construction of Plane Geometrical Figures. With 137 Diagrams. Eighteenth Edition. Post 8vo, cloth, 5s.

BURLEIGH (BENNET G.)—

DESERT WARFARE: Being the Chronicle of the Eastern Soudan Campaign. With Maps. Demy 8vo, 12s.

CAMPION (J. S.).—

ON THE FRONTIER. Reminiscences of Wild Sports, Personal Adventures, and Strange Scenes. With Illustrations. Second Edition. Demy 8vo, 16s.

ON FOOT IN SPAIN. With Illustrations. Second Edition. Demy 8vo, 16s.

CARLYLE BIRTHDAY BOOK. Second Edition. Small fcap. 8vo, 3s.

CHAMPEAUX (ALFRED)—

TAPESTRY. With Woodcuts. Cloth, 2s. 6d.

CHURCH (A. H.), M.A., Oxon.—

ENGLISH PORCELAIN. A Handbook to the China made in England during the Eighteenth Century, as illustrated by Specimens chiefly in the National Collection. With numerous Illustrations. Large crown 8vo, 3s.

ENGLISH EARTHENWARE. A Handbook to the Wares made in England during the 17th and 18th Centuries, as illustrated by Specimens in the National Collections. With 49 Illustrations. Crown 8vo, 3s.

PLAIN WORDS ABOUT WATER. Illustrated. Crown 8vo, sewed, 6d.

FOOD: A Short Account of the Sources, Constituents, and Uses of Food. Crown 8vo, cloth, 3s.

PRECIOUS STONES: considered in their Scientific and Artistic Relations. With Illustrations. Crown 8vo, 2s. 6d.

CLINTON (R. H.)—
A COMPENDIUM OF ENGLISH HISTORY, from the Earliest Times to A.D. 1872. With Copious Quotations on the Leading Events and the Constitutional History, together with Appendices. Post 8vo, 7s. 6d.

COBDEN, RICHARD, LIFE OF. By JOHN MORLEY. With Portrait. 2 vols. Demy 8vo, 32s.

New Edition. Portrait. Crown 8vo, 7s. 6d.

Popular Edition, with Portrait, sewed, 1s.; cloth, 2s.

CHAPMAN & HALL'S ONE SHILLING SERIES OF BOOKS.—*Crown 8vo, sewed.*

MEMOIRS OF A STOMACH. Written by Himself, that all who eat may read. Edited by a Minister of the Interior. 1s.

FAST AND LOOSE. A Novel. By ARTHUR GRIFFITHS, Author of "The Chronicles of Newgate." 1s.

A SINGER'S STORY, as related by the Author of "Flitters, Tatters, and the Counsellor." 1s.

NUMBER NINETY-NINE. A Novel. By ARTHUR GRIFFITHS. 1s.

THE CASE OF REUBEN MALACHI. By H. SUTHERLAND EDWARDS. 1s.

SARTOR RESARTUS. By THOMAS CARLYLE. Crown 8vo, sewed, 1s.

CHAPMAN & HALL'S SERIES OF POPULAR NOVELS.

New and Cheaper Editions of Popular Novels. Crown 8vo.

KARMA. By A. P. SINNETT. 3s. 6d.
MOLOCH. A Story of Sacrifice. By MRS. CAMPBELL PRAED, Author of "Nadine.' 6s.
FAUCIT OF BALLIOL. By HERMAN MERIVALE. 6s.
AN AUSTRALIAN HEROINE. By MRS. CAMPBELL PRAED. 6s.
STORY OF AN AFRICAN FARM. By RALPH IRON. 5s.
TO LEEWARD. By F. MARION CRAWFORD. New Edition. 5s.
AN AMERICAN POLITICIAN. By F. MARION CRAWFORD. 5s.
TIE AND TRICK. By HAWLEY SMART. 6s.

COOKERY—
THE PYTCHLEY BOOK OF REFINED COOKERY AND BILLS OF FARE. By MAJOR L——. Second Edition. Large crown 8vo, 8s.

OFFICIAL HANDBOOK FOR THE NATIONAL TRAINING SCHOOL FOR COOKERY. Containing Lessons on Cookery; forming the Course of Instruction in the School. Compiled by "R. O. C." Fourteenth Thousand. Large crown 8vo, 8s.

BREAKFAST AND SAVOURY DISHES. By "R. O. C." Seventh Thousand. Crown 8vo, 1s

COOKERY—Continued—

HOW TO COOK FISH. A Series of Lessons in Cookery, from the Official Handbook to the National Training School for Cookery, South Kensington. Compiled by " R. O. C." Crown 8vo, sewed, 3d.

SICK-ROOM COOKERY. From the Official Handbook to the National School for Cookery, South Kensington. Compiled by "R. O. C." Crown 8vo, sewed, 6d.

THE KINGSWOOD COOKERY BOOK. By H. F. WICKEN. Crown 8vo, 2s.

COURTNEY (W. L.)—

CONSTRUCTIVE ETHICS: A Review of Modern Philosophy and its Three Stages of Interpretation, Criticism, and Reconstruction. Demy 8vo. [*In April*.

CRAIK (GEORGE LILLIE)—

ENGLISH OF SHAKESPEARE. Illustrated in a Philological Commentary on his "Julius Cæsar." Seventh Edition. Post 8vo, cloth, 5s.

OUTLINES OF THE HISTORY OF THE ENGLISH LANGUAGE. Tenth Edition. Post 8vo, cloth, 2s. 6d.

CRAWFORD (F. MARION)—

TO LEEWARD. Crown 8vo, 5s.

AN AMERICAN POLITICIAN. Crown 8vo, 5s.

CRIPPS (WILFRED)—

COLLEGE AND CORPORATION PLATE. A Handbook for the Reproduction of Silver Plate. With numerous Illustrations. Large crown 8vo, cloth, 2s. 6d.

DAVITT (MICHAEL)—

LEAVES FROM A PRISON DIARY; or, Lectures to a Solitary Audience. 2 vols. Crown 8vo, 21s.
In one vol. Crown 8vo, cloth, 6s.
Cheap Edition. Crown 8vo, sewed, Ninth Thousand, 1s. 6d.

DAUBOURG (E.)—

INTERIOR ARCHITECTURE. Doors, Vestibules, Staircases, Anterooms, Drawing, Dining, and Bed Rooms, Libraries, Bank and Newspaper Offices, Shop Fronts and Interiors. Half-imperial, cloth, £2 12s. 6d.

DAVIDSON (ELLIS A.)—

PRETTY ARTS FOR THE EMPLOYMENT OF LEISURE HOURS. A Book for Ladies. With Illustrations. Demy 8vo, 6s.

DAY (WILLIAM)—

THE RACEHORSE IN TRAINING, with Hints on Racing and Racing Reform, to which is added a Chapter on Shoeing. Fifth Edition. 8vo, 9s.

D'HAUSSONVILLE (VICOMTE)—
SALON OF MADAME NECKER. Translated by H. M.
TROLLOPE. 2 vols. Crown 8vo, 18s.

DE KONINCK (L. L.) and DIETZ (E.)—
PRACTICAL MANUAL OF CHEMICAL ASSAYING,
as applied to the Manufacture of Iron. Edited, with notes, by ROBERT MALLET.
Post 8vo, cloth, 6s.

DICKENS (CHARLES)—See pages 32—38.
THE LETTERS OF CHARLES DICKENS. Edited
by his Sister-in-Law and his Eldest Daughter. Two vols. uniform with " The
Charles Dickens Edition " of his Works. Crown 8vo, 8s.
THE CHARLES DICKENS BIRTHDAY BOOK.
Compiled and Edited by his Eldest Daughter. With Five Illustrations by his
Youngest Daughter. In a handsome fcap. 4to volume, 12s.

DRAGE (GEOFFREY)—
CRIMINAL CODE OF THE GERMAN EMPIRE.
Translated with Prolegomena, and a Commentary, by G. DRAGE. Crown 8vo, 8s.

DRAYSON (LIEUT.-COL. A. W.)—
THE CAUSE OF THE SUPPOSED PROPER MOTION
OF THE FIXED STARS. Demy 8vo, cloth, 10s.
PRACTICAL MILITARY SURVEYING AND
SKETCHING. Fifth Edition. Post 8vo, cloth, 4s. 6d.

DREAMS BY A FRENCH FIRESIDE. Translated from the
German by MARY O'CALLAGHAN. Illustrated by Fred Roe. Crown 8vo, 7s. 6d.

DUPANLOUP, MONSEIGNEUR (BISHOP OF ORLEANS),
LIFE OF. By ABBÉ F. LAGRANGE. Translated from the French by LADY
HERBERT. With Two Portraits. 2 vols. 8vo, 32s.

DYCE'S COLLECTION. A Catalogue of Printed Books and
Manuscripts bequeathed by the REV. ALEXANDER DYCE to the South Kensington Museum. 2 vols. Royal 8vo, half-morocco, 14s.
A Collection of Paintings, Miniatures, Drawings, Engravings,
Rings, and Miscellaneous Objects, bequeathed by the REV. ALEXANDER DYCE
to the South Kensington Museum. Royal 8vo, half-morocco, 6s. 6d.

DYCE (WILLIAM), R.A.—
DRAWING-BOOK OF THE GOVERNMENT SCHOOL
OF DESIGN; OR, ELEMENTARY OUTLINES OF ORNAMENT. Fifty
selected Plates. Folio, sewed, 5s.; 18s.
Text to Ditto. Sewed, 6d.

EDWARDS, H. SUTHERLAND—
FAMOUS FIRST-NIGHT REPRESENTATIONS.
[*In the Press.*]

EGYPTIAN ART—
A HISTORY OF ART IN ANCIENT EGYPT. By
G. PERROT and C. CHIPIEZ. Translated by WALTER ARMSTRONG. With over 600 Illustrations. 2 vols. Imperial 8vo, £2 2s.

ELLIS (A. B., Major 1st West India Regiment)—
WEST AFRICAN ISLANDS. Demy 8vo. 14s.
THE HISTORY OF THE WEST INDIA REGI-
MENT. With Maps and Coloured Frontispiece and Title-page. Demy 8vo. 18s.
THE LAND OF FETISH. Demy 8vo. 12s.

ENGEL (CARL)—
A DESCRIPTIVE AND ILLUSTRATED CATALOGUE
OF THE MUSICAL INSTRUMENTS in the SOUTH KENSINGTON MUSEUM, preceded by an Essay on the History of Musical Instruments. Second Edition. Royal 8vo, half-morocco, 12s.
MUSICAL INSTRUMENTS. With numerous Woodcuts.
Large crown 8vo, cloth, 2s. 6d.

ESCOTT (T. H. S.)—
ENGLAND. ITS PEOPLE, POLITY, AND PURSUITS.
New and Revised Edition. Fifth Thousand. 8vo, 8s.
PILLARS OF THE EMPIRE : Short Biographical
Sketches. 8vo, 10s. 6d.

EWALD (ALEXANDER CHARLES), F.S.A.—
REPRESENTATIVE STATESMEN : Political Studies.
2 vols. Large crown 8vo, £1 4s.
SIR ROBERT WALPOLE. A Political Biography,
1676-1745. Demy 8vo, 18s.

FANE (VIOLET)—
QUEEN OF THE FAIRIES (A Village Story), and other
Poems. Crown 8vo, 6s.
ANTHONY BABINGTON: a Drama. Crown 8vo, 6s.

FEARNLEY (W.)—
LESSONS IN HORSE JUDGING, AND THE SUM-
MERING OF HUNTERS. With Illustrations. Crown 8vo, 4s.

FLEMING (GEORGE), F.R.C.S.—

ANIMAL PLAGUES: THEIR HISTORY, NATURE, AND PREVENTION. 8vo, cloth, 15s.

PRACTICAL HORSE-SHOEING. With 37 Illustrations. Fifth Edition, enlarged. 8vo, sewed, 2s.

RABIES AND HYDROPHOBIA: THEIR HISTORY, NATURE, CAUSES, SYMPTOMS, AND PREVENTION. With 8 Illustrations. 8vo, cloth, 15s.

FORSTER (JOHN), M.P. for Berwick—

THE CHRONICLE OF JAMES I., KING OF ARAGON, SURNAMED THE CONQUEROR. Written by Himself. Translated from the Catalan by the late JOHN FORSTER, M.P. for Berwick. With an Historical Introduction by DON PASCUAL DE GAYANGOS. 2 vols. Royal 8vo, 28s.

FORSTER (JOHN)—

THE LIFE OF CHARLES DICKENS. With Portraits and other Illustrations. 3 vols. 8vo, cloth, £2 2s.

THE LIFE OF CHARLES DICKENS. Uniform with the Illustrated Library Edition of Dickens's Works. 2 vols. Demy 8vo, £1 8s.

THE LIFE OF CHARLES DICKENS. Uniform with the Library Edition. Post 8vo, 10s. 6d.

THE LIFE OF CHARLES DICKENS. Uniform with the "C. D." Edition. With Numerous Illustrations. 2 vols. 7s.

THE LIFE OF CHARLES DICKENS. Uniform with the Household Edition. With Illustrations by F. BARNARD. Crown 4to, cloth, 5s.

WALTER SAVAGE LANDOR: a Biography, 1775–1864. With Portrait. A New and Revised Edition. Demy 8vo, 12s.

FORTNIGHTLY REVIEW—

FORTNIGHTLY REVIEW.—First Series, May, 1865, to Dec. 1866. 6 vols. Cloth, 13s. each.

New Series, 1867 to 1872. In Half-yearly Volumes. Cloth, 13s. each.

From January, 1873, to the present time, in Half-yearly Volumes. Cloth, 16s. each.

CONTENTS OF FORTNIGHTLY REVIEW. From the commencement to end of 1878. Sewed, 2s.

FORTNUM (C. D. E.)—

A DESCRIPTIVE AND ILLUSTRATED CATALOGUE OF THE BRONZES OF EUROPEAN ORIGIN in the SOUTH KENSINGTON MUSEUM, with an Introductory Notice. Royal 8vo, half-morocco, £1 10s.

A DESCRIPTIVE AND ILLUSTRATED CATALOGUE OF MAIOLICA, HISPANO-MORESCO, PERSIAN, DAMASCUS, AND RHODIAN WARES in the SOUTH KENSINGTON MUSEUM. Royal 8vo, half-morocco, £2.

MAIOLICA. With numerous Woodcuts. Large crown 8vo, cloth, 2s. 6d.

BRONZES. With numerous Woodcuts. Large crown 8vo, cloth, 2s. 6d.

FRANCATELLI (C. E.)—

ROYAL CONFECTIONER: English and Foreign. A Practical Treatise. Fourth Edition. With Illustrations. Crown 8vo, 5s.

FRANKS (A. W.)—

JAPANESE POTTERY. Being a Native Report. Numerous Illustrations and Marks. Large crown 8vo, cloth, 2s. 6d.

GALLENGA (ANTONIO)—

EPISODES OF MY SECOND LIFE. 2 vols. Demy 8vo, 28s.

IBERIAN REMINISCENCES. Fifteen Years' Travelling Impressions of Spain and Portugal. With a Map. 2 vols. Demy 8vo, 32s.

GASNAULT (PAUL) and GARNIER (ED.)—

FRENCH POTTERY. With Illustrations. Crown 8vo, 3s.

GORDON (GENERAL)—

LETTERS FROM THE CRIMEA, THE DANUBE, AND ARMENIA. Edited by DEMETRIUS C. BOULGER. Second Edition. Crown 8vo, 5s.

GORST (J. E.), Q.C., M.P.—

An ELECTION MANUAL. Containing the Parliamentary Elections (Corrupt and Illegal Practices) Act, 1883, with Notes. Third Edition. Crown 8vo, 1s. 6d.

GRESWELL (WILLIAM), M.A., F.R.C.I.—

OUR SOUTH AFRICAN EMPIRE. With Map. 2 vols.
Crown 8vo, 21s.

GRIFFIN (SIR LEPEL HENRY), K.C.S.I.—

THE GREAT REPUBLIC. Second Edition. Crown 8vo,
4s. 6d.

GRIFFITHS (MAJOR ARTHUR), H.M. Inspector of Prisons—

CHRONICLES OF NEWGATE. Illustrated. New
Edition. Demy 8vo, 16s.

MEMORIALS OF MILLBANK: or, Chapters in Prison
History. With Illustrations by R. Goff and Author. New Edition. Demy 8vo,
12s.

HALL (SIDNEY)—

A TRAVELLING ATLAS OF THE ENGLISH COUN-
TIES. Fifty Maps, coloured. New Edition, including the Railways, corrected
up to the present date. Demy 8vo, in roan tuck, 10s. 6d.

HARDY (LADY DUFFUS)—

DOWN SOUTH. Demy 8vo. 14s.

THROUGH CITIES AND PRAIRIE LANDS. Sketches
of an American Tour. Demy 8vo, 14s.

HATTON (JOSEPH) and HARVEY (REV. M.)—

NEWFOUNDLAND. The Oldest British Colony. Its
History, Past and Present, and its Prospects in the Future. Illustrated from
Photographs and Sketches specially made for this work. Demy 8vo, 18s.

TO-DAY IN AMERICA. Studies for the Old World and
the New. 2 vols. Crown 8vo, 18s.

HAWKINS (FREDERICK)—

ANNALS OF THE FRENCH STAGE: FROM ITS
ORIGIN TO THE DEATH OF RACINE. 4 Portraits. 2 vols. Demy 8vo,
28s.

HILDEBRAND (HANS)—

INDUSTRIAL ARTS OF SCANDINAVIA IN THE
PAGAN TIME. Illustrated. Crown 8vo, 2s 6d.

HILL (MISS G.)—

THE PLEASURES AND PROFITS OF OUR LITTLE POULTRY FARM. Small 8vo, 3s.

HOLBEIN—

TWELVE HEADS AFTER HOLBEIN. Selected from Drawings in Her Majesty's Collection at Windsor. Reproduced in Autotype, in portfolio. £1 16s.

HOLLINGSHEAD (JOHN)—

FOOTLIGHTS. Crown 8vo. 7s. 6d.

HOVELACQUE (ABEL)—

THE SCIENCE OF LANGUAGE: LINGUISTICS, PHILOLOGY, AND ETYMOLOGY. With Maps. Large crown 8vo, cloth, 5s.

HUMPHRIS (H. D.)—

PRINCIPLES OF PERSPECTIVE. Illustrated in a Series of Examples. Oblong folio, half-bound, and Text 8vo, cloth, £1 1s.

INTERNATIONAL POLICY: Essay on the Foreign Relations of England. By FREDERIC HARRISON, PROF. BEESLEY, RICHARD CONGREVE, and others. New Edition. Crown 8vo, 2s. 6d.

IRON (RALPH)—

THE STORY OF AN AFRICAN FARM. New Edition. Crown 8vo, 5s.

JARRY (GENERAL)—

OUTPOST DUTY. Translated, with TREATISES ON MILITARY RECONNAISSANCE AND ON ROAD-MAKING. By Major-Gen. W. C. E. NAPIER. Third Edition. Crown 8vo, 5s.

JEANS (W. T.)—

CREATORS OF THE AGE OF STEEL. Memoirs of Sir W. Siemens, Sir H. Bessemer, Sir J. Whitworth, Sir J. Brown, and other Inventors. Second Edition. Crown 8vo, 7s. 6d.

JOHNSON (DR. SAMUEL)—

LIFE AND CONVERSATIONS OF DR. SAMUEL JOHNSON. By A. MAIN. Crown 8vo, 10s. 6d.

JONES (CAPTAIN DOUGLAS), R.A.—
NOTES ON MILITARY LAW. Crown 8vo, 4s.

JONES COLLECTION (HANDBOOK OF THE) IN THE SOUTH
KENSINGTON MUSEUM. Illustrated. Large crown 8vo, 2s. 6d.

KEMPIS (THOMAS Ã)—
OF THE IMITATION OF CHRIST. Four Books.
Beautifully Illustrated Edition. Demy 8vo, 16s.

KENNARD (MRS. EDWARD)—
TWILIGHT TALES. Illustrated by EDITH ELLISON.
Crown 8vo, 7s. 6d.

KENT (CHARLES)—
HUMOUR AND PATHOS OF CHARLES DICKENS,
WITH ILLUSTRATIONS OF HIS MASTERY OF THE TERRIBLE
AND PICTURESQUE. Portrait. Crown 8vo, 6s.

KLACZKO (M. JULIAN)—
TWO CHANCELLORS: PRINCE GORTCHAKOF AND
PRINCE BISMARCK. Translated by MRS. TAIT. New and cheaper Edition, 6s.

LACORDAIRE'S JESUS CHRIST; GOD; AND GOD AND
MAN. Conferences delivered at Notre Dame in Paris. New Edition in 1 vol.
Crown 8vo, 6s.

LAING (S.)—
MODERN SCIENCE AND MODERN THOUGHT.
Third Edition. With a Supplementary Chapter on Gladstone's "Dawn of Creation
and Drummond's "Natural Law of the Spiritual World." Demy 8vo, 7s. 6d.

LAVELEYE (ÉMILE DE)—
THE ELEMENTS OF POLITICAL ECONOMY.
Translated by W. POLLARD, B.A., St. John's College, Oxford. Crown 8vo, 6s.

LANDOR'S WORKS. 8 vols. Demy 8vo, 14s. each volume.
All the Volumes can be supplied excepting Vol. II., *which is out of print.*

LECTURES ON AGRICULTURAL SCIENCE, AND OTHER
PROCEEDINGS OF THE INSTITUTE OF AGRICULTURE, SOUTH
KENSINGTON, 1883-4. Crown 8vo, sewed, 2s.

LEFEVRE (ANDRÉ)—

PHILOSOPHY, Historical and Critical. Translated, with an Introduction, by A. W. KEANE, B.A. Large crown 8vo, 7s. 6d.

LESLIE (R. C.)—

A SEA PAINTER'S LOG. With Illustrations by the Author. Crown 8vo. [*In the Press.*

LETOURNEAU (DR. CHARLES)—

SOCIOLOGY. Based upon Ethnology. Translated by HENRY M. TROLLOPE. Large crown 8vo, 10s.

BIOLOGY. Translated by WILLIAM MACCALL. With Illustrations. Large crown 8vo, 6s.

LILLY (W. S.)—

SOME CHAPTERS ON EUROPEAN HISTORY. With an Introductory Dialogue on the Philosophy of History. 2 vols. Demy 8vo, 21s.

ANCIENT RELIGION AND MODERN THOUGHT. A New and Revised Edition. Demy 8vo, 12s.

LONG (JAMES)—

DAIRY FARMING. To which is added a Description of the Chief Continental Systems. With numerous Illustrations. Crown 8vo, 9s.

LOW (C. R.)—

SOLDIERS OF THE VICTORIAN AGE. 2 vols. Demy 8vo, £1 10s.

LYTTON (ROBERT, EARL)—

POETICAL WORKS—
    FABLES IN SONG. 2 vols. Fcap 8vo, 12s.
    THE WANDERER. Fcap. 8vo, 6s.
    POEMS, HISTORICAL AND CHARACTERISTIC. Fcap. 6s.

MALLET (ROBERT)—

PRACTICAL MANUAL OF CHEMICAL ASSAYING, as applied to the Manufacture of Iron. By L. L. DE KONINCK and E. DIETZ. Edited, with notes, by ROBERT MALLET. Post 8vo, cloth, 6s.

MASKELL (ALFRED)—
 RUSSIAN ART AND ART OBJECTS IN RUSSIA.
 A Handbook to the Reproduction of Goldsmiths' Work, &c., from that Country. Crown 8vo, 4s. 6d.

MASKELL (WILLIAM)—
 A DESCRIPTION OF THE IVORIES, ANCIENT AND MEDIÆVAL, in the SOUTH KENSINGTON MUSEUM, with a Preface With numerous Photographs and Woodcuts. Royal 8vo, half-morocco, £1 1s.
 IVORIES: ANCIENT AND MEDIÆVAL. With numerous Woodcuts. Large crown 8vo, cloth, 2s. 6d.
 HANDBOOK TO THE DYCE AND FORSTER COLLECTIONS. With Illustrations. Large crown 8vo, cloth, 2s. 6d.

MEREDITH (GEORGE)—
 MODERN LOVE AND POEMS OF THE ENGLISH ROADSIDE, WITH POEMS AND BALLADS. Fcap. cloth, 6s.

GEORGE MEREDITH'S WORKS.

A New and Uniform Edition. In Six-Shilling Volumes. Crown 8vo:

DIANA OF THE CROSSWAYS. [Ready.
EVAN HARRINGTON. [Ready.
THE ORDEAL OF RICHARD FEVEREL. A History of a Father and Son. [Ready.
THE ADVENTURES OF HARRY RICHMOND. [Ready.
SANDRA BELLONI. Originally EMILIA IN ENGLAND.
[Ready.
VITTORIA. [Ready.
RHODA FLEMING.
BEAUCHAMP'S CAREER.
THE EGOIST.

MERIVALE (HERMAN CHARLES)—
 BINKO'S BLUES. A Tale for Children of all Growths. Illustrated by EDGAR GIBERNE. Small crown 8vo, 5s.
 THE WHITE PILGRIM, and other Poems. Crown 8vo, 9s.
 FAUCIT OF BALLIOL. Crown 8vo, 6s.

B

MILITARY BIOGRAPHIES—
 FREDERICK THE GREAT. By COL. C. B. BRACKENBURY;
 with Maps and Portrait. Large crown 8vo, 4s.
 LOUDON. A Sketch of the Military Life of Gideon
 Ernest, Freicherr von Loudon, sometime Generalissimo of the Austrian Forces.
 By COL. G. B. MALLESON, C.S.I. With Portrait and Maps. Large crown
 8vo, 4s.
 TURENNE. By H. M. HOZIER. With Portrait and Two
 Maps. Large crown 8vo, 4s.
 PARLIAMENTARY GENERALS OF THE GREAT
 CIVIL WAR. By MAJOR WALFORD, R.A. With Maps. Crown 8vo, 4s.

MOLESWORTH (W. NASSAU)—
 HISTORY OF ENGLAND FROM THE YEAR 1830
 TO THE RESIGNATION OF THE GLADSTONE MINISTRY, 1874.
 Twelfth Thousand. 3 vols. Crown 8vo, 18s.
 ABRIDGED EDITION. Large crown, 7s. 6d.

MOLTKE (FIELD-MARSHAL COUNT VON)—
 POLAND : AN HISTORICAL SKETCH. An Authorised
 Translation, with Biographical Notice by E. S. BUCHHEIM. Crown 8vo, 4s. 6d.

MORLEY (HENRY)—
 TABLES OF ENGLISH LITERATURE. Containing
 20 Charts. Second Edition, with Index. Royal 4to, cloth, 12s.
 In Three Parts. Parts I. and II., containing Three Charts, each 1s. 6d.
 Part III. in Sections, 1, 2, and 5, 1s. 6d. each; 3 and 4 together, 3s.
 ⁎ The Charts sold separately.

MORLEY (JOHN)—
 LIFE AND CORRESPONDENCE OF RICHARD
 COBDEN. Fourth Thousand. 2 vols. Demy 8vo £1 12s.
 Popular Edition. With Portrait. 4to, sewed, 1s. Bound
 in cloth, 2s.

MUNTZ (EUGÈNE), From the French of—
 RAPHAEL : HIS LIFE, WORKS, AND TIMES.
 Edited by W. ARMSTRONG. With 155 Wood Engravings and 41 Full-page Plates
 Imperial 8vo, 36s.

MURPHY (J. M.)—
 RAMBLES IN NORTH - WEST AMERICA. With
 Frontispiece and Map. 8vo, 16s.

URRAY (ANDREW), F.L.S.—
 ECONOMIC ENTOMOLOGY. APTERA. With numerous Illustrations. Large crown 8vo, 7s. 6d.

NAPIER (MAJ.-GEN. W. C. E.)—
TRANSLATION OF GEN. JARRY'S OUTPOST DUTY.
With TREATISES ON MILITARY RECONNAISSANCE AND ON ROAD-MAKING. Third Edition. Crown 8vo, 5s.

NAPOLEON. A Selection from the Letters and Despatches of the First Napoleon. With Explanatory Notes by Captain the Hon. D. BINGHAM. 3 vols. Demy 8vo, £2 2s.

NECKER (MADAME)—
THE SALON OF MADAME NECKER. By VICOMTE D'HAUSSONVILLE. Translated by H. M. TROLLOPE. 2 vols. Crown 8vo 18s.

NESBITT (ALEXANDER)—
GLASS. Illustrated. Crown 8vo, cloth, 2s. 6d.

NEVINSON (HENRY)—
A SKETCH OF HERDER AND HIS TIMES. With a Portrait. Demy 8vo, 14s.

NEWTON (E. TULLEY), F.G.S.—
THE TYPICAL PARTS IN THE SKELETONS OF A CAT, DUCK, AND CODFISH, being a Catalogue with Comparative Description arranged in a Tabular form. Demy 8vo, cloth, 3s.

NORMAN (C. B.), late of the 90th Light Infantry and Bengal Staff Corps—
TONKIN; OR, FRANCE IN THE FAR EAST. With Maps. Demy 8vo, 14s.

O'GRADY (STANDISH)—
TORYISM AND THE TORY DEMOCRACY. Crown 8vo, 5s.

OLIVER (PROFESSOR), F.R.S., &c.,—
ILLUSTRATIONS OF THE PRINCIPAL NATURAL ORDERS OF THE VEGETABLE KINGDOM, PREPARED FOR THE SCIENCE AND ART DEPARTMENT, SOUTH KENSINGTON. With 109 Plates. Oblong 8vo, plain, 16s.; coloured, £1 6s.

OXENHAM (REV. H. N.)—
MEMOIR OF LIEUTENANT RUDOLPH DE LISLE, R.N., OF THE NAVAL BRIGADE. [*In the Press.*
SHORT STUDIES, ETHICAL AND RELIGIOUS. Demy 8vo. 12s.
SHORT STUDIES IN ECCLESIASTICAL HISTORY AND BIOGRAPHY. Demy 8vo, 12s.

PERROT (GEORGES) and CHIPIEZ (CHARLES)—

A HISTORY OF ANCIENT ART IN PHŒNICIA AND ITS DEPENDENCIES. Translated from the French by WALTER ARMSTRONG, B.A. Oxon. Containing 644 Illustrations in the text, and 10 Steel and Coloured Plates. 2 vols. Imperial 8vo, 42s.

A HISTORY OF ART IN CHALDÆA AND ASSYRIA. Translated by WALTER ARMSTRONG, B.A. Oxon. With 452 Illustrations. 2 vols. Imperial 8vo, 42s.

A HISTORY OF ART IN ANCIENT EGYPT. Translated from the French by W. ARMSTRONG, B A. Oxon. With over 600 Illustrations. 2 vols. Imperial 8vo, 42s.

PIASSETSKY (P.)—

RUSSIAN TRAVELLERS IN MONGOLIA AND CHINA. Translated by GORDON-CUMMING. With 75 Illustrations. 2 vols. Crown 8vo, 24s.

PITT TAYLOR (FRANK)—

THE CANTERBURY TALES. Selections from the Tales of GEOFFREY CHAUCER rendered into Modern English, with close adherence to the language of the Poet. With Frontispiece. Crown 8vo, 6s.

POLLEN (J. H.)—

ANCIENT AND MODERN FURNITURE AND WOODWORK IN THE SOUTH KENSINGTON MUSEUM. With an Introduction, and Illustrated with numerous Coloured Photographs and Woodcuts. Royal 8vo, half-morocco, £1 1s.

GOLD AND SILVER SMITH'S WORK. With numerous Woodcuts. Large crown 8vo, cloth, 2s. 6d.

ANCIENT AND MODERN FURNITURE AND WOODWORK. With numerous Woodcuts. Large crown 8vo, cloth, 2s. 6d.

POYNTER (E. J.), R.A.—

TEN LECTURES ON ART. Third Edition. [*In the Press.*

PRAED (MRS. CAMPBELL)—
AUSTRALIAN LIFE: Black and White. With Illustration. Crown 8vo, 8s.
AN AUSTRALIAN HEROINE. Crown 8vo, 6s.
MOLOCH. A Story of Sacrifice. Crown 8vo, 6s.

PRINSEP (VAL), A.R.A.—
IMPERIAL INDIA. Containing numerous Illustrations and Maps. Second Edition. Demy 8vo, £1 1s.

PYTCHLEY COOKERY BOOK—
THE PYTCHLEY BOOK OF REFINED COOKERY AND BILLS OF FARE. By Major L——. Second Edition. Large crown 8vo, 8s.

RADICAL PROGRAMME, THE. From the *Fortnightly Review*, with additions. With a Preface by the RIGHT HON. J. CHAMBERLAIN, M.P. Thirteenth Thousand. Crown 8vo, 2s. 6d.

RAMSDEN (LADY GWENDOLEN)—
A BIRTHDAY BOOK. Illustrated. Containing 46 Illustrations from Original Drawings, and numerous other Illustrations. Royal 8vo, 21s.

REDGRAVE (GILBERT)—
OUTLINES OF HISTORIC ORNAMENT. Translated from the German. Edited by GILBERT REDGRAVE. With numerous Illustrations. Crown 8vo, 4s.

REDGRAVE (GILBERT R.)—
MANUAL OF DESIGN, compiled from the Writings and Addresses of RICHARD REDGRAVE, R.A. With Woodcuts. Large crown 8vo, cloth, 2s. 6d.

REDGRAVE (RICHARD)—
ELEMENTARY MANUAL OF COLOUR, with a Catechism on Colour. 24mo, cloth, 9d.

REDGRAVE (SAMUEL)—
A DESCRIPTIVE CATALOGUE OF THE HISTORICAL COLLECTION OF WATER-COLOUR PAINTINGS IN THE SOUTH KENSINGTON MUSEUM. With numerous Chromo-lithographs and other Illustrations. Royal 8vo, £1 1s.

RENAN (ERNEST)—

> RECOLLECTIONS OF MY YOUTH. Translated from the original French, and revised by MADAME RENAN. Crown 8vo, 8s.

RIANO (JUAN F.)—

> THE INDUSTRIAL ARTS IN SPAIN. Illustrated. Large crown 8vo, cloth, 4s.

ROBINSON (JAMES F.)—

> BRITISH BEE FARMING. Its Profits and Pleasures. Large crown 8vo, 5s.

ROBINSON (J. C.)—

> ITALIAN SCULPTURE OF THE MIDDLE AGES AND PERIOD OF THE REVIVAL OF ART. With 20 Engravings. Royal 8vo, cloth, 7s. 6d.

ROBSON (GEORGE)—

> ELEMENTARY BUILDING CONSTRUCTION. Illustrated by a Design for an Entrance Lodge and Gate. 15 Plates. Oblong folio, sewed, 8s.

ROBSON (REV. J. H.), M.A., LL.M.—

> AN ELEMENTARY TREATISE ON ALGEBRA. Post 8vo, 6s.

ROCK (THE VERY REV. CANON), D.D.—

> ON TEXTILE FABRICS. A Descriptive and Illustrated Catalogue of the Collection of Church Vestments, Dresses, Silk Stuffs, Needlework, and Tapestries in the South Kensington Museum. Royal 8vo, half-morocco, £1 11s. 6d.
>
> TEXTILE FABRICS. With numerous Woodcuts. Crown 8vo, cloth, 2s. 6d.

ROLAND (ARTHUR)—
FARMING FOR PLEASURE AND PROFIT. Edited
by WILLIAM ABLETT. 8 vols. Crown 8vo, 5s. each.
> DAIRY-FARMING, MANAGEMENT OF COWS, &c.
> POULTRY-KEEPING.
> TREE-PLANTING, FOR ORNAMENTATION OR PROFIT.
> STOCK-KEEPING AND CATTLE-REARING.
> DRAINAGE OF LAND, IRRIGATION, MANURES, &c.
> ROOT-GROWING, HOPS, &c.
> MANAGEMENT OF GRASS LANDS, LAYING DOWN GRASS, ARTIFICIAL GRASSES, &c.
> MARKET GARDENING, HUSBANDRY FOR FARMERS AND GENERAL CULTIVATORS.

RUSDEN (G. W.), for many years Clerk of the Parliament in Victoria—
A HISTORY OF AUSTRALIA. With a Coloured Map.
3 vols. Demy 8vo, 50s.

A HISTORY OF NEW ZEALAND. With Maps. 3 vols.
Demy 8vo, 50s.

SCOTT (A. DE C., MAJOR-GENERAL, late Royal Engineers)—
LONDON WATER: a Review of the Present Condition and
Suggested Improvements of the Metropolitan Water Supply. Crown 8vo, sewed, 2s

SCOTT-STEVENSON (MRS.)—
ON SUMMER SEAS. Including the Mediterranean, the
Ægean, the Ionian, and the Euxine, and a voyage down the Danube. With a Map. Demy 8vo, 16s.

OUR HOME IN CYPRUS. With a Map and Illustra-
tions. Third Edition. Demy 8vo, 14s.

OUR RIDE THROUGH ASIA MINOR. With Map.
Demy 8vo, 18s.

SHEPHERD (MAJOR), R.E.—
PRAIRIE EXPERIENCES IN HANDLING CATTLE
AND SHEEP. With Illustrations and Map. Demy 8vo, 10s. 6d.

SHIRREFF (MISS)—
HOME EDUCATION IN RELATION TO THE
KINDERGARTEN. Two Lectures. Crown 8vo, 1s. 6d.

SIMMONDS (T. L.)—
ANIMAL PRODUCTS: their Preparation, Commercial
Uses, and Value. With numerous Illustrations. Large crown 8vo, 7s. 6d.

SINNETT (A. P.)—
ESOTERIC BUDDHISM. Annotated and enlarged by
the Author. Fifth Edition. Crown 8vo, 6s.
KARMA. A Novel. New Edition. Crown 8vo, 3s. 6d.

SINNETT (MRS.)—
THE PURPOSE OF THEOSOPHY. Crown 8vo, 3s.

SMART (HAWLEY)—
TIE AND TRICK. Crown 8vo, 6s.

SMITH (MAJOR R. MURDOCK), R.E.—
PERSIAN ART. Second Edition, with additional Illustrations. Large crown 8vo, 2s.

STORY (W. W.)—
ROBA DI ROMA. Seventh Edition, with Additions and Portrait. Crown 8vo, cloth, 10s. 6d.
CASTLE ST. ANGELO. With Illustrations. Crown 8vo, 10s. 6d.

SUTCLIFFE (JOHN)—
THE SCULPTOR AND ART STUDENT'S GUIDE
to the Proportions of the Human Form, with Measurements in feet and inches of Full-Grown Figures of Both Sexes and of Various Ages. By Dr. G. SCHADOW, Member of the Academies, Stockholm, Dresden, Rome, &c. &c. Translated by J. J. WRIGHT. Plates reproduced by J. SUTCLIFFE. Oblong folio, 31s. 6d.

TAINE (H. A.)—
NOTES ON ENGLAND. Translated, with Introduction, by W. FRASER RAE. Eighth Edition. With Portrait. Crown 8vo, 5s.

TANNER (PROFESSOR), F.C.S.—
HOLT CASTLE; or, Threefold Interest in Land. Crown 8vo, 4s. 6d.
JACK'S EDUCATION; OR, HOW HE LEARNT FARMING. Second Edition. Crown 8vo, 3s. 6d.

TEMPLE (SIR RICHARD), BART., M.P., G.C.S.I.—
COSMOPOLITAN ESSAYS. With Maps. Demy 8vo.
[*In the Press.*

TOPINARD (DR. PAUL)—
ANTHROPOLOGY. With a Preface by Professor PAUL BROCA. With numerous Illustrations. Large crown 8vo, 7s. 6d.

TOVEY (LIEUT.-COL., R.E.)—
MARTIAL LAW AND CUSTOM OF WAR; or, Military Law and Jurisdiction in Troublous Times. Crown 8vo, 6s.

TRAILL (H. D.)—
THE NEW LUCIAN. Being a Series of Dialogues of the Dead. Demy 8vo, 12s.

TROLLOPE (ANTHONY)—
AYALA'S ANGEL. Crown 8vo. 6s.
LIFE OF CICERO. 2 vols. 8vo. £1 4s.
THE CHRONICLES OF BARSETSHIRE. A Uniform Edition, in 8 vols., large crown 8vo, handsomely printed, each vol. containing Frontispiece. 6s. each.

THE WARDEN and BARCHESTER TOWERS. 2 vols.
DR. THORNE.
FRAMLEY PARSONAGE.

THE SMALL HOUSE AT ALLINGTON. 2 vols.
LAST CHRONICLE OF BARSET. 2 vols.

UNIVERSAL—
UNIVERSAL CATALOGUE OF BOOKS ON ART. Compiled for the use of the National Art Library, and the Schools of Art in the United Kingdom. In 2 vols. Crown 4to, half-morocco, £2 2s.
Supplemental Volume to Ditto. Crown 8vo, 8s. nett.

VERON (EUGENE)—
ÆSTHETICS. Translated by W. H. ARMSTRONG. Large crown 8vo, 7s. 6d.

WALE (REV. HENRY JOHN), M.A.—
MY GRANDFATHER'S POCKET BOOK, from 1701 to 1796. Author of "Sword and Surplice." Demy 8vo, 12s.

WALKER (MRS.)—
EASTERN LIFE AND SCENERY, with Excursions to Asia Minor, Mitylene, Crete, and Roumania. 2 vols., crown 8vo.
[*In the Press.*

WESTWOOD (J. O.), M.A., F.L.S., &c.—
CATALOGUE OF THE FICTILE IVORIES IN THE SOUTH KENSINGTON MUSEUM. With an Account of the Continental Collections of Classical and Mediæval Ivories. Royal 8vo, half-morocco, £1 4s.

WHIST HANDBOOKS. By AQUARIUS—
THE HANDS AT WHIST. 32mo, cloth gilt, 1s.
EASY WHIST. 32mo, cloth gilt, 1s.
ADVANCED WHIST. 32mo, cloth gilt, 1s.

WHITE (WALTER)—

A MONTH IN YORKSHIRE. With a Map. Fifth Edition. Post 8vo, 4s.

A LONDONER'S WALK TO THE LAND'S END, AND A TRIP TO THE SCILLY ISLES. With 4 Maps. Third Edition. Post 8vo, 4s.

WICKEN (H. F.)—

THE KINGSWOOD COOKERY BOOK. Crown 8vo, 2s.

WILL-O'-THE-WISPS, THE. Translated from the German of Marie Petersen by CHARLOTTE J. HART. With Illustrations. Crown 8vo, 7s. 6d.

WORNUM (R. N.)—

ANALYSIS OF ORNAMENT: THE CHARACTERISTICS OF STYLES. An Introduction to the History of Ornamental Art. With many Illustrations. Ninth Edition. Royal 8vo, cloth, 8s.

WORSAAE (J. J. A.)—

INDUSTRIAL ARTS OF DENMARK, FROM THE EARLIEST TIMES TO THE DANISH CONQUEST OF ENGLAND. With Maps and Illustrations. Crown 8vo, 3s. 6d.

YEO (DR. J. BURNEY)—

CLIMATE AND HEALTH RESORTS. New Edition. Crown 8vo, 10s. 6d.

YOUNGE (C. D.)—

PARALLEL LIVES OF ANCIENT AND MODERN HEROES. New Edition. 12mo, cloth, 4s. 6d.

SOUTH KENSINGTON MUSEUM
DESCRIPTIVE AND ILLUSTRATED CATALOGUES.
Royal 8vo, half-bound.

BRONZES OF EUROPEAN ORIGIN. By C. D. E. FORTNUM.
£1 10s.

DYCE'S COLLECTION OF PRINTED BOOKS AND MANUSCRIPTS. 2 vols. 14s.

DYCE'S COLLECTION OF PAINTINGS, ENGRAVINGS, &c. 6s. 6d.

FURNITURE AND WOODWORK, ANCIENT AND MODERN. By J. H. POLLEN. £1 1s.

GLASS VESSELS. By A. NESBITT. 18s.

GOLD AND SILVER SMITH'S WORK. By J. G. POLLEN.
£1 6s.

IVORIES, ANCIENT AND MEDIÆVAL. By W. MASKELL.
21s.

IVORIES, FICTILE. By J. O. WESTWOOD. £1 4s.

MAIOLICA, HISPANO-MORESCO, PERSIAN, DAMASCUS AND RHODIAN WARES. By C. D. E. FORTNUM. £2.

MUSICAL INSTRUMENTS. By C. ENGEL. 12s.

SCULPTURE, ITALIAN SCULPTURE OF THE MIDDLE AGES. By J. C. ROBINSON. Cloth, 7s. 6d.

SWISS COINS. By R. S. POOLE. £2 10s.

TEXTILE FABRICS. By Rev. D. ROCK. £1 11s. 6d.

WATER-COLOUR PAINTING. By S. REDGRAVE. £1 1s.

UNIVERSAL CATALOGUE OF BOOKS ON ART. 2 vols.
Small 4to, £1 1s. each.

UNIVERSAL CATALOGUE OF BOOKS ON ART. Supplementary vol. 8s. nett.

SOUTH KENSINGTON MUSEUM SCIENCE AND ART HANDBOOKS.

Handsomely printed in large crown 8vo.

Published for the Committee of the Council on Education.

THE ART OF THE SARACENS IN EGYPT. By STANLEY LANE POOLE. With Illustrations. [*In the Press.*

ENGLISH PORCELAIN. By A. H. CHURCH, M.A. With numerous Illustrations. 3s.

RUSSIAN ART AND ART OBJECTS IN RUSSIA. By ALFRED MASKELL. With Illustrations. 4s. 6d.

FRENCH POTTERY. By PAUL GASNAULT and EDOUARD GARNIER. With Illustrations and marks. 3s.

ENGLISH EARTHENWARE: A Handbook to the Wares made in England during the 17th and 18th Centuries. By PROF. CHURCH. With Illustrations. 3s.

INDUSTRIAL ARTS OF DENMARK. From the Earliest Times to the Danish Conquest of England. By J. J. A. WORSAAE, Hon. F.S.A., &c. &c. With Illustrations. 3s. 6d.

INDUSTRIAL ARTS OF SCANDINAVIA IN THE PAGAN TIME. By HANS HILDEBRAND, Royal Antiquary of Sweden. With Illustrations. 2s. 6d.

PRECIOUS STONES. By PROFESSOR CHURCH. With Illustrations. 2s. 6d.

INDUSTRIAL ARTS OF INDIA. By Sir GEORGE C. M. BIRDWOOD, C.S.I. With Map and Illustrations. Demy 8vo, 14s.

HANDBOOK TO THE DYCE AND FORSTER COLLECTIONS. By W. MASKELL. With Illustrations. 2s. 6d.

INDUSTRIAL ARTS IN SPAIN. By JUAN F. RIANO. With Illustrations. 4s.

GLASS. By ALEXANDER NESBITT. With Illustrations. 2s. 6d.

GOLD AND SILVER SMITH'S WORK. By JOHN HUNGERFORD POLLEN. With Illustrations. 2s. 6d.

TAPESTRY. By ALFRED CHAMPEAUX. With Illustrations. 2s. 6d.

BRONZES. By C. DRURY E. FORTNUM, F.S.A. With Illustrations. 2s. 6d.

PLAIN WORDS ABOUT WATER. By A. H. CHURCH, M.A. Oxon. With Illustrations. Sewed, 6d.

SOUTH KENSINGTON MUSEUM SCIENCE & ART HANDBOOKS—*Continued.*

ANIMAL PRODUCTS: their Preparation, Commercial Uses, and Value. By T. L. SIMMONDS. With Illustrations. 7s. 6d.

FOOD: A Short Account of the Sources, Constituents, and Uses of Food. By A. H. CHURCH, M.A. Oxon. 3s.

ECONOMIC ENTOMOLOGY. By ANDREW MURRAY, F.L.S. APTERA. With Illustrations. 7s. 6d.

JAPANESE POTTERY. Being a Native Report. Edited by A. W. FRANKS. With Illustrations and Marks. 2s. 6d.

HANDBOOK TO THE SPECIAL LOAN COLLECTION of Scientific Apparatus. 3s.

INDUSTRIAL ARTS: Historical Sketches. With Illustrations. 3s.

TEXTILE FABRICS. By the Very Rev. DANIEL ROCK, D.D. With Illustrations. 2s. 6d.

JONES COLLECTION IN THE SOUTH KENSINGTON MUSEUM. With Portrait and Illustrations. 2s. 6d.

COLLEGE AND CORPORATION PLATE. By WILFRED CRIPPS. With Illustrations. Cloth, 2s. 6d.

IVORIES: ANCIENT AND MEDIÆVAL. By WILLIAM MASKELL. With Illustrations. 2s. 6d.

ANCIENT AND MODERN FURNITURE AND WOOD-WORK. By JOHN HUNGERFORD POLLEN. With Illustrations. 2s. 6d.

MAIOLICA. By C. DRURY E. FORTNUM, F.S.A. With Illustrations. 2s. 6d.

THE CHEMISTRY OF FOODS. With Microscopic Illustrations. By JAMES BELL, Principal of the Somerset House Laboratory.
Part I.—Tea, Coffee, Cocoa, Sugar, &c. 2s. 6d.
Part II.—Milk, Butter, Cereals, Prepared Starches, &c. 3s.

MUSICAL INSTRUMENTS. By CARL ENGEL. With Illustrations. 2s. 6d.

MANUAL OF DESIGN, compiled from the Writings and Addresses of RICHARD REDGRAVE, R.A. By GILBERT R. REDGRAVE. With Illustrations. 2s. 6d.

PERSIAN ART. By MAJOR R. MURDOCK SMITH, R.E. Second Edition, with additional Illustrations. 2s.

CARLYLE'S (THOMAS) WORKS.

THE ASHBURTON EDITION.

An entirely New Edition of the Writings of Mr. CARLYLE, to be completed in Seventeen Volumes, demy 8vo, is now publishing. For Particulars see page 2.

CHEAP AND UNIFORM EDITION.

23 vols., Crown 8vo, cloth, £7 5s.

THE FRENCH REVOLUTION: A History. 2 vols., 12s.

OLIVER CROMWELL'S LETTERS AND SPEECHES, with Elucidations, &c. 3 vols., 18s.

LIVES OF SCHILLER AND JOHN STERLING. 1 vol., 6s.

CRITICAL AND MISCELLANEOUS ESSAYS. 4 vols., £1 4s.

SARTOR RESARTUS AND LECTURES ON HEROES. 1 vol., 6s.

LATTER-DAY PAMPHLETS. 1 vol., 6s.

CHARTISM AND PAST AND PRESENT. 1 vol., 6s.

TRANSLATIONS FROM THE GERMAN OF MUSÆUS, TIECK, AND RICHTER. 1 vol., 6s.

WILHELM MEISTER, by Göethe. A Translation. 2 vols., 12s.

HISTORY OF FRIEDRICH THE SECOND, called Frederick the Great. 7 vols., £2 9s.

LIBRARY EDITION COMPLETE.

Handsomely printed in 34 vols., demy 8vo, cloth, £15 3s.

SARTOR RESARTUS. With a Portrait, 7s. 6d.

THE FRENCH REVOLUTION. A History. 3 vols., each 9s.

LIFE OF FREDERICK SCHILLER AND EXAMINATION OF HIS WORKS. With Supplement of 1872. Portrait and Plates, 9s.

CRITICAL AND MISCELLANEOUS ESSAYS. With Portrait. 6 vols., each 9s.

ON HEROES, HERO WORSHIP, AND THE HEROIC IN HISTORY. 7s. 6d.

PAST AND PRESENT. 9s.

CARLYLE'S (THOMAS) WORKS.—LIBRARY EDITION—*Continued.*

OLIVER CROMWELL'S LETTERS AND SPEECHES. With
Portraits. 5 vols., each 9s.

LATTER-DAY PAMPHLETS. 9s.

LIFE OF JOHN STERLING. With Portrait, 9s.

HISTORY OF FREDERICK THE SECOND. 10 vols.,
each 9s.

TRANSLATIONS FROM THE GERMAN. 3 vols., each 9s.

EARLY KINGS OF NORWAY; ESSAY ON THE POR-
TRAITS OF JOHN KNOX; AND GENERAL INDEX. With Portrait
Illustrations. 8vo, cloth, 9s.

PEOPLE'S EDITION.

37 vols., small 8vo, 2s. each vol.; or in sets, 37 vols. in 19, cloth gilt, £3 14s.

SARTOR RESARTUS.	LATTER-DAY PAMPHLETS.
FRENCH REVOLUTION. 3 vols.	LIFE OF SCHILLER.
LIFE OF JOHN STERLING.	FREDERICK THE GREAT. 10 vols.
OLIVER CROMWELL'S LETTERS AND SPEECHES. 5 vols.	WILHELM MEISTER. 3 vols.
ON HEROES AND HERO WORSHIP.	TRANSLATIONS FROM MUSÆUS, TIECK, AND RICHTER. 2 vols.
PAST AND PRESENT.	THE EARLY KINGS OF NORWAY; Essay on the Portraits of Knox; and General Index.
CRITICAL AND MISCELLANEOUS ESSAYS. 7 vols.	

SARTOR RESARTUS. Cheap Edition, crown 8vo, sewed, 1s.

SIXPENNY EDITION.
4to, sewed.

SARTOR RESARTUS. Eightieth Thousand.
HEROES AND HERO WORSHIP.
ESSAYS: BURNS, JOHNSON, SCOTT, THE DIAMOND NECKLACE.
The above in 1 vol., cloth, 2s. 6d.

DICKENS'S (CHARLES) WORKS.
ORIGINAL EDITIONS.
In demy 8vo.

THE MYSTERY OF EDWIN DROOD. With Illustrations by S. L. Fildes, and a Portrait engraved by Baker. Cloth, 7s. 6d.

OUR MUTUAL FRIEND. With Forty Illustrations by Marcus Stone. Cloth, £1 1s.

THE PICKWICK PAPERS. With Forty-three Illustrations by Seymour and Phiz. Cloth, £1 1s.

NICHOLAS NICKLEBY. With Forty Illustrations by Phiz. Cloth, £1 1s.

SKETCHES BY "BOZ." With Forty Illustrations by George Cruikshank. Cloth, £1 1s.

MARTIN CHUZZLEWIT. With Forty Illustrations by Phiz. Cloth, £1 1s.

DOMBEY AND SON. With Forty Illustrations by Phiz. Cloth, £1 1s.

DAVID COPPERFIELD. With Forty Illustrations by Phiz. Cloth, £1 1s.

BLEAK HOUSE. With Forty Illustrations by Phiz. Cloth, £1 1s.

LITTLE DORRIT. With Forty Illustrations by Phiz. Cloth, £1 1s.

THE OLD CURIOSITY SHOP. With Seventy-five Illustrations by George Cattermole and H. K. Browne. A New Edition. Uniform with the other volumes, £1 1s.

BARNABY RUDGE: a Tale of the Riots of 'Eighty. With Seventy-eight Illustrations by George Cattermole and H. K. Browne. Uniform with the other volumes, £1 1s.

CHRISTMAS BOOKS: Containing—The Christmas Carol; The Cricket on the Hearth; The Chimes; The Battle of Life; The Haunted House. With all the original Illustrations. Cloth, 12s.

OLIVER TWIST and TALE OF TWO CITIES. In one volume. Cloth, £1 1s.

OLIVER TWIST. Separately. With Twenty-four Illustrations by George Cruikshank. Cloth, 11s.

A TALE OF TWO CITIES. Separately. With Sixteen Illustrations by Phiz. Cloth, 9s.

*** *The remainder of Dickens's Works were not originally printed in demy 8vo.*

DICKENS'S (CHARLES) WORKS.

LIBRARY EDITION.

In post 8vo. With the Original Illustrations, 30 vols., cloth, £12.

			s	d.
PICKWICK PAPERS ... ... 43 Illustrns.,	2 vols.	16	0
NICHOLAS NICKLEBY ... ... 39 ,,	2 vols.	16	0
MARTIN CHUZZLEWIT ... ... 40 ,,	2 vols.	16	0
OLD CURIOSITY SHOP & REPRINTED PIECES 36 ,,	2 vols.	16	0
BARNABY RUDGE and HARD TIMES ... ... 36 ,,	2 vols.	16	0
BLEAK HOUSE... ... ... 40 ,,	2 vols.	16	0
LITTLE DORRIT ... ... 40 ,,	2 vols.	16	0
DOMBEY AND SON ... ... 38 ,,	2 vols.	16	0
DAVID COPPERFIELD ... ... 38 ,,	2 vols.	16	0
OUR MUTUAL FRIEND ... ... 40 ,,	2 vols.	16	0
SKETCHES BY "BOZ" ... ... 39 ,,	1 vol.	8	0
OLIVER TWIST ... ... 24 ,,	1 vol.	8	0
CHRISTMAS BOOKS ... ... 17 ,,	1 vol.	8	0
A TALE OF TWO CITIES ... ... 16 ,,	1 vol.	8	0
GREAT EXPECTATIONS ... ... 8 ,,	1 vol.	8	0
PICTURES FROM ITALY & AMERICAN NOTES 8 ,,	1 vol.	8	0
UNCOMMERCIAL TRAVELLER ... . 8 ,,	1 vol.	8	0
CHILD'S HISTORY OF ENGLAND ... ... 8 ,,	1 vol.	8	0
EDWIN DROOD and MISCELLANIES ... ... 12 ,,	1 vol.	8	0
CHRISTMAS STORIES from "Household Words," &c. 14 ,,	1 vol.	8	0

THE LIFE OF CHARLES DICKENS. By JOHN FORSTER. With Illustrations. Uniform with this Edition. 10s. 6d.

A NEW EDITION OF ABOVE, WITH THE ORIGINAL ILLUSTRATIONS, IN CROWN 8vo, 30 VOLS. IN SETS ONLY.

DICKENS'S (CHARLES) WORKS.

THE "CHARLES DICKENS" EDITION.

In Crown 8vo. In 21 vols., cloth, with Illustrations, £3 16s.

		s.	d.
PICKWICK PAPERS	8 Illustrations	4	0
MARTIN CHUZZLEWIT	8 ,,	4	0
DOMBEY AND SON	8 ,,	4	0
NICHOLAS NICKLEBY	8 ,,	4	0
DAVID COPPERFIELD	8 ,,	4	0
BLEAK HOUSE	8 ,,	4	0
LITTLE DORRIT	8 ,,	4	0
OUR MUTUAL FRIEND	8 ,,	4	0
BARNABY RUDGE	8 ,,	3	6
OLD CURIOSITY SHOP	8 ,,	3	6
A CHILD'S HISTORY OF ENGLAND	4 ,,	3	6
EDWIN DROOD and OTHER STORIES	8 ,,	3	6
CHRISTMAS STORIES, from "Household Words"	8 ,,	3	6
SKETCHES BY "BOZ"	8 ,,	3	6
AMERICAN NOTES and REPRINTED PIECES	8 ,,	3	6
CHRISTMAS BOOKS	8 ,,	3	6
OLIVER TWIST	8 ,,	3	6
GREAT EXPECTATIONS	8 ,,	3	6
TALE OF TWO CITIES	8 ,,	3	0
HARD TIMES and PICTURES FROM ITALY	8 ,,	3	0
UNCOMMERCIAL TRAVELLER	4 ,,	3	0
THE LIFE OF CHARLES DICKENS. Numerous Illustrations.	2 vols.	7	0
THE LETTERS OF CHARLES DICKENS	2 vols.	8	0

DICKENS'S (CHARLES) WORKS.

THE ILLUSTRATED LIBRARY EDITION.

Complete in 30 Volumes. Demy 8vo, 10s. each; or set, £15.

This Edition is printed on a finer paper and in a larger type than has been employed in any previous edition. The type has been cast especially for it, and the page is of a size to admit of the introduction of all the original illustrations.

No such attractive issue has been made of the writings of Mr. Dickens, which, various as have been the forms of publication adapted to the demands of an ever widely-increasing popularity, have never yet been worthily presented in a really handsome library form.

The collection comprises all the minor writings it was Mr. Dickens's wish to preserve.

SKETCHES BY "BOZ." With 40 Illustrations by George Cruikshank.
PICKWICK PAPERS. 2 vols. With 42 Illustrations by Phiz.
OLIVER TWIST. With 24 Illustrations by Cruikshank.
NICHOLAS NICKLEBY. 2 vols. With 40 Illustrations by Phiz.
OLD CURIOSITY SHOP and REPRINTED PIECES. 2 vols. With Illustrations by Cattermole, &c.
BARNABY RUDGE and HARD TIMES. 2 vols. With Illustrations by Cattermole, &c.
MARTIN CHUZZLEWIT. 2 vols. With 40 Illustrations by Phiz.
AMERICAN NOTES and PICTURES FROM ITALY. 1 vol. With 8 Illustrations.
DOMBEY AND SON. 2 vols. With 40 Illustrations by Phiz.
DAVID COPPERFIELD. 2 vols. With 40 Illustrations by Phiz.
BLEAK HOUSE. 2 vols. With 40 Illustrations by Phiz.
LITTLE DORRIT. 2 vols. With 40 Illustrations by Phiz.
A TALE OF TWO CITIES. With 16 Illustrations by Phiz.
THE UNCOMMERCIAL TRAVELLER. With 8 Illustrations by Marcus Stone.
GREAT EXPECTATIONS. With 8 Illustrations by Marcus Stone.
OUR MUTUAL FRIEND. 2 vols. With 40 Illustrations by Marcus Stone.
CHRISTMAS BOOKS. With 17 Illustrations by Sir Edwin Landseer, R.A., Maclise, R.A., &c. &c.
HISTORY OF ENGLAND. With 8 Illustrations by Marcus Stone.
CHRISTMAS STORIES. (From "Household Words" and "All the Year Round.") With 14 Illustrations.
EDWIN DROOD AND OTHER STORIES. With 12 Illustrations by S. I. Fildes.

BOOKS PUBLISHED BY

DICKENS'S (CHARLES) WORKS.

THE POPULAR LIBRARY EDITION
OF THE WORKS OF
CHARLES DICKENS,

In 30 Vols., large crown 8vo, price £6; separate Vols. 4s. each.

An Edition printed on good paper, each volume containing 16 full-page Illustrations, selected from the Household Edition, on Plate Paper.

SKETCHES BY "BOZ."
PICKWICK. 2 vols.
OLIVER TWIST.
NICHOLAS NICKLEBY. 2 vols.
MARTIN CHUZZLEWIT. 2 vols.
DOMBEY AND SON. 2 vols.
DAVID COPPERFIELD. 2 vols.
CHRISTMAS BOOKS.
OUR MUTUAL FRIEND. 2 vols.
CHRISTMAS STORIES.
BLEAK HOUSE. 2 vols.
LITTLE DORRIT. 2 vols.
OLD CURIOSITY SHOP AND REPRINTED PIECES. 2 vols.
BARNABY RUDGE. 2 vols.
UNCOMMERCIAL TRAVELLER.
GREAT EXPECTATIONS.
TALE OF TWO CITIES.
CHILD'S HISTORY OF ENGLAND.
EDWIN DROOD AND MISCELLANIES.
PICTURES FROM ITALY AND AMERICAN NOTES.

DICKENS'S (CHARLES) WORKS.

HOUSEHOLD EDITION.

In 22 Volumes. Crown 4to, cloth, £4 8s. 6d.

MARTIN CHUZZLEWIT, with 59 Illustrations, cloth, 5s.
DAVID COPPERFIELD, with 60 Illustrations and a Portrait, cloth, 5s.
BLEAK HOUSE, with 61 Illustrations, cloth, 5s.
LITTLE DORRIT, with 58 Illustrations, cloth, 5s.
PICKWICK PAPERS, with 56 Illustrations, cloth, 5s.
OUR MUTUAL FRIEND, with 58 Illustrations, cloth, 5s.
NICHOLAS NICKLEBY, with 59 Illustrations, cloth, 5s.
DOMBEY AND SON, with 61 Illustrations, cloth, 5s.
EDWIN DROOD; REPRINTED PIECES; and other Stories, with 30 Illustrations, cloth, 5s.
THE LIFE OF DICKENS. By JOHN FORSTER. With 40 Illustrations. Cloth, 5s.
BARNABY RUDGE, with 46 Illustrations, cloth, 4s.
OLD CURIOSITY SHOP, with 32 Illustrations, cloth, 4s.
CHRISTMAS STORIES, with 23 Illustrations, cloth, 4s.
OLIVER TWIST, with 28 Illustrations, cloth, 3s.
GREAT EXPECTATIONS, with 26 Illustrations, cloth, 3s.
SKETCHES BY "BOZ," with 36 Illustrations, cloth, 3s.
UNCOMMERCIAL TRAVELLER, with 26 Illustrations, cloth, 3s.
CHRISTMAS BOOKS, with 28 Illustrations, cloth, 3s.
THE HISTORY OF ENGLAND, with 15 Illustrations, cloth, 3s.
AMERICAN NOTES and PICTURES FROM ITALY, with 18 Illustrations, cloth, 3s.
A TALE OF TWO CITIES, with 25 Illustrations, cloth, 3s.
HARD TIMES, with 20 Illustrations, cloth, 2s. 6d.

A New Edition of
CHARLES DICKENS'S WORKS.

Messrs. CHAPMAN & HALL beg to announce an Edition of CHARLES DICKENS'S WORKS, entitled:—

THE CABINET EDITION.

To be completed in 30 vols. small fcap. 8vo, Marble Paper Sides, Cloth Backs, with uncut edges, price Eighteenpence each.

A Complete Work will be Published every Month and each Volume will contain Eight Illustrations reproduced from the Originals.

CHRISTMAS BOOKS, One Vol.,
MARTIN CHUZZLEWIT, Two Vols.,
DAVID COPPERFIELD, Two Vols.,
Are now Ready.

DICKENS'S (CHARLES) WORKS.
MR. DICKENS'S READINGS.
Fcap. 8vo, sewed.

CHRISTMAS CAROL IN PROSE. 1s.	STORY OF LITTLE DOMBEY. 1s.
CRICKET ON THE HEARTH. 1s.	POOR TRAVELLER, BOOTS AT THE HOLLY-TREE INN, and
CHIMES: A GOBLIN STORY. 1s.	MRS. GAMP. 1s.

A CHRISTMAS CAROL, with the Original Coloured Plates, being a reprint of the Original Edition. Small 8vo, red cloth, gilt edges, 5s.

ONE SHILLING EACH. Reprinted from the Original Plates.
A CHRISTMAS CAROL. Fcap. cloth, 1s.
THE CHIMES: A Goblin Story. Fcap. cloth, 1s.

The Cheapest and Handiest Edition of
THE WORKS OF CHARLES DICKENS.
The Pocket-Volume Edition of Charles Dickens's Works.
In 30 Vols. small fcap. 8vo, £2 5s.

New and Cheap Issue of
THE WORKS OF CHARLES DICKENS.
In pocket volumes.

PICKWICK PAPERS, with 8 Illustrations, cloth, 2s.
NICHOLAS NICKLEBY, with 8 Illustrations, cloth, 2s.
OLIVER TWIST, with 8 Illustrations, cloth, 1s.
SKETCHES BY "BOZ," with 8 Illustrations, cloth, 1s.
OLD CURIOSITY SHOP, with 8 Illustrations, cloth, 2s.
BARNABY RUDGE, with 16 Illustrations, cloth, 2s.
AMERICAN NOTES AND PICTURES FROM ITALY, with 8 Illustrations, cloth, 1s. 6d.
CHRISTMAS BOOKS, with 8 Illustrations, cloth, 1s. 6d.
MARTIN CHUZZLEWIT, with 8 Illustrations, cloth, 2s.

List of Books, Drawing Examples, Diagrams, Models, Instruments, etc.,

INCLUDING

THOSE ISSUED UNDER THE AUTHORITY OF THE SCIENCE AND ART DEPARTMENT, SOUTH KENSINGTON, FOR THE USE OF SCHOOLS AND ART AND SCIENCE CLASSES.

CATALOGUE OF MODERN WORKS ON SCIENCE AND TECHNOLOGY. 8vo, sewed, 1s.

BENSON (W.)—

PRINCIPLES OF THE SCIENCE OF COLOUR. Small 4to, 15s.

MANUAL OF THE SCIENCE OF COLOUR. Coloured Frontispiece and Illustrations. 12mo, 2s. 6d.

BRADLEY (THOMAS), of the Royal Military Academy, Woolwich—

ELEMENTS OF GEOMETRICAL DRAWING. In Two Parts, with 60 Plates. Oblong folio, half-bound, each part 16s.
Selections (from the above) of 20 Plates, for the use of the Royal Military Academy, Woolwich. Oblong folio, half-bound, 16s.

BURCHETT—

LINEAR PERSPECTIVE. With Illustrations. Post 8vo, 7s.

PRACTICAL GEOMETRY. Post 8vo, 5s.

DEFINITIONS OF GEOMETRY. Third Edition. 24mo, sewed, 5d.

CARROLL (JOHN)—

FREEHAND DRAWING LESSONS FOR THE BLACK BOARD. 6s.

CUBLEY (W. H.)—
A SYSTEM OF ELEMENTARY DRAWING. With
Illustrations and Examples. Imperial 4to, sewed, 3s. 6d.

DAVISON (ELLIS A.)—
DRAWING FOR ELEMENTARY SCHOOLS. Post
8vo, 3s.
MODEL DRAWING. 12mo, 3s.

DELAMOTTE (P. H.)—
PROGRESSIVE DRAWING-BOOK FOR BEGINNERS.
12mo, 3s. 6d.

DYCE—
DRAWING-BOOK OF THE GOVERNMENT SCHOOL
OF DESIGN: ELEMENTARY OUTLINES OF ORNAMENT. 50 Plates. Small folio, sewed, 5s.; mounted, 18s.
INTRODUCTION TO DITTO. Fcap. 8vo, 6d.

FOSTER (VERE)—
DRAWING-BOOKS:
Forty-six Numbers, at 2d. each.
DRAWING-CARDS:
Freehand Drawing: First Grade, Sets I., II., III., 1s. each.
Second Grade, Set I., 2s.

HENSLOW (PROFESSOR)—
ILLUSTRATIONS TO BE EMPLOYED IN THE
PRACTICAL LESSONS ON BOTANY. Post 8vo, sewed, 6d.

JACOBSTHAL (E.)—
GRAMMATIK DER ORNAMENTE, in 7 Parts of 20
Plates each. Unmounted, £3 13s. 6d.; mounted on cardboard, £11 4s. Th Parts can be had separately.

JEWITT—

HANDBOOK OF PRACTICAL PERSPECTIVE. 18mo, 1s. 6d.

LINDLEY (JOHN)—

SYMMETRY OF VEGETATION: Principles to be Observed in the Delineation of Plants. 12mo, sewed, 1s.

MARSHALL—

HUMAN BODY. Text and Plates reduced from the large Diagrams. 2 vols., £1 1s.

NEWTON (E. TULLEY), F.G.S.—

THE TYPICAL PARTS IN THE SKELETONS OF A CAT, DUCK, AND CODFISH, being a Catalogue with Comparative Descriptions arranged in a Tabular Form. Demy 8vo, 3s.

OLIVER (PROFESSOR)—

ILLUSTRATIONS OF THE VEGETABLE KINGDOM. 109 Plates. Oblong 8vo. Plain, 16s.; coloured, £1 6s.

POYNTER (E. J.), R.A., issued under the superintendence of—

THE SOUTH KENSINGTON DRAWING SERIES.

FREEHAND—ELEMENTARY ORNAMENT: books 6d., cards, 9d. each.

FREEHAND—FIRST GRADE: books 6d., cards 1s. each.

FREEHAND—SECOND GRADE: books 1s., cards 1s. 6d. each.

FREEHAND—PLANTS FROM NATURE: books 6d., cards, 1s. each.

FREEHAND—HUMAN FIGURE, ELEMENTARY: books 6d.

FREEHAND—HUMAN FIGURE, ADVANCED: books 2s. each.

FREEHAND—FIGURES FROM THE CARTOONS OF RAPHAEL: four books, 2s. each.

FREEHAND—ELEMENTARY PERSPECTIVE DRAWING. By S. J. CARTLIDGE, F.R.Hist.S. Books 1s. each; or one volume, cloth, 5s.

REDGRAVE—

MANUAL AND CATECHISM ON COLOUR. Fifth Edition. 24mo, sewed, 9d.

ROBSON (GEORGE)—

ELEMENTARY BUILDING CONSTRUCTION. Oblong folio, sewed, 8s.

WALLIS (GEORGE)—

DRAWING-BOOK. Oblong, sewed, 3s. 6d.; mounted, 8s.

WORNUM (R. N.)—

THE CHARACTERISTICS OF STYLES: An Introduction to the Study of the History of Ornamental Art. Royal 8vo, 8s.

ELEMENTARY DRAWING COPY-BOOKS, for the Use of Children from four years old and upwards, in Schools and Families. Compiled by a Student certificated by the Science and Art Department as an Art Teacher. Seven Books in 4to, sewed:

Book I. Letters, 8d.
 ,, II. Ditto, 8d.
 ,, III. Geometrical and Ornamental Forms, 8d.

Book IV. Objects, 8d.
 ,, V. Leaves, 8d.
 ,, VI. Birds, Animals, &c., 8d.
 ,, VII. Leaves, Flowers, and Sprays, 8d.

⁎⁎ Or in Sets of Seven Books, 4s. 6d.

PRINCIPLES OF DECORATIVE ART. Folio, sewed, 1s.

DIAGRAM OF THE COLOURS OF THE SPECTRUM, with Explanatory Letterpress, on roller, 5s.

COPIES FOR OUTLINE DRAWING:

LARGE FREEHAND EXAMPLES FOR CLASS TEACHING. Specially prepared under the authority of the Science and Art Department. Six Sheets. Size 60 by 40. 9s.

DYCE'S ELEMENTARY OUTLINES OF ORNAMENT, 50 Selected Plates, mounted back and front, 18s.; unmounted, sewed, 5s.

WEITBRICHT'S OUTLINES OF ORNAMENT, reproduced by Herman, 12 Plates, mounted back and front, 8s. 6d.; unmounted, 2s.

MORGHEN'S OUTLINES OF THE HUMAN FIGURE, reproduced by Herman, 20 Plates, mounted back and front, 15s.; unmounted, 3s. 4d.

TARSIA, from Gruner, Four Plates, mounted, 3s. 6d., unmounted, 7d.

ALBERTOLLI'S FOLIAGE, Four Plates, mounted, 3s. 6d.; unmounted, 5d.

OUTLINE OF TRAJAN FRIEZE, mounted, 1s.

WALLIS'S DRAWING-BOOK, mounted, 8s., unmounted, 3s. 6d.

OUTLINE DRAWINGS OF FLOWERS. Eight Plates, mounted, 3s. 6d.; unmounted, 8d.

COPIES FOR SHADED DRAWING:

COURSE OF DESIGN. By Ch. Bargue (French), 20 Sheets, £2 9s.
ARCHITECTURAL STUDIES. By J. B. Tripon. 10 Plates, £1.
MECHANICAL STUDIES. By J. B. Tripon. 15s. per dozen.
FOLIATED SCROLL FROM THE VATICAN, unmounted, 5d.; mounted, 1s. 3d.
TWELVE HEADS after Holbein, selected from his Drawings in Her Majesty's Collection at Windsor. Reproduced in Autotype. Half imperial, £1 16s.

COLOURED EXAMPLES:

A SMALL DIAGRAM OF COLOUR, mounted, 1s. 6d.; unmounted, 9d.
COTMAN'S PENCIL LANDSCAPES (set of 9), mounted, 15s.
„ SEPIA DRAWINGS (set of 5), mounted, £1.
ALLONGE'S LANDSCAPES IN CHARCOAL (Six), at 4s. each, or the set £1 4s.
RADDE COLOUR SCALE, in case, £1.

SOLID MODELS, &c.:

*Box of Models, £1 4s.

A Stand with a universal joint, to show the solid models, &c., £1 18s.

*One Wire Quadrangle, with a circle and cross within it, and one straight wire. One solid cube. One Skeleton Wire Cube. One Sphere. One Cone. One Cylinder. One Hexagonal Prism. £2 2s.

Skeleton Cube in wood, 3s. 6d.

18-inch Skeleton Cube in wood, 12s.

*Three objects of *form* in Pottery:

 Indian Jar,
 Celadon Jar, } 18s. 6d.
 Bottle,

*Five selected Vases in Majolica Ware, £2 11s.

*Three selected Vases in Earthenware, 18s.

Imperial Deal Frames, glazed, without sunk rings, 10s. each.

*Davidson's Smaller Solid Models, in Box, £2, containing—

2 Square Slabs.	Octagon Prism.	Triangular Prism.
Oblong Blocks (steps).	Cylinder.	Pyramid, Equilateral.
Cubes.	Cone.	Pyramid, Isosceles.
Square Blocks.	Jointed Cross.	Square Block.

SOLID MODELS, &c.—*Continued.*

*Davidson's Advanced Drawing Models, £9.—The following is a brief description of the Models:—An Obelisk—composed of 2 Octagonal Slabs, 26 and 20 inches across, and each 3 inches high; 1 Cube, 12 inches edge; 1 Monolith (forming the body of the obelisk) 3 feet high; 1 Pyramid, 6 inches base; the complete object is thus nearly 5 feet high. A Market Cross—composed of 3 Slabs, 24, 18, and 12 inches across, and each 3 inches high; 1 Upright, 3 feet high; 2 Cross Arms, united by mortise and tenon joints; complete height, 3 feet 9 inches. A Step-Ladder, 23 inches high. A Kitchen Table, 14½ inches high. A Chair to correspond. A Four-legged Stool, with projecting top and cross rails, height 14 inches. A Tub, with handles and projecting hoops, and the divisions between the staves plainly marked. A strong Trestle, 18 inches high. A Hollow Cylinder, 9 inches in diameter, and 12 inches long, divided lengthwise. A Hollow Sphere, 12 inches in diameter, divided into semi-spheres, one of which is again divided into quarters; the semi-sphere, when placed on the cylinder, gives the form and principles of shading a dome, whilst one of the quarters placed on half the cylinder forms a niche.

*Davidson's Apparatus for Teaching Practical Geometry (22 models), £5.

*Binn's Models for Illustrating the Elementary Principles of Orthographic Projection as applied to Mechanical Drawing, in box, £1 10s.

Miller's Class Drawing Models.—These Models are particularly adapted for teaching large classes; the stand is very strong, and the universal joint will hold the Models in any position. *Wood Models*: Square Prism, 12 inches side, 18 inches high; Hexagonal Prism, 14 inches side, 18 inches high; Cube, 14 inches side; Cylinder, 13 inches diameter, 16 inches high; Hexagon Pyramid, 14 inches diameter, 22½ inches side; Square Pyramid, 14 inches side, 22½ inches side; Cone, 13 inches diameter, 22½ inches side; Skeleton Cube, 19 inches solid wood 1¾ inch square; Intersecting Circles, 19 inches solid wood 2¼ by 1½ inches. *Wire Models*: Triangular Prism, 17 inches side, 22 inches high; Square Prism, 14 inches side, 20 inches high; Hexagonal Prism, 16 inches diameter, 21 inches high; Cylinder, 14 inches diameter, 21 inches high; Hexagon Pyramid, 18 inches diameter, 24 inches high; Square Pyramid, 17 inches side, 24 inches high; Cone, 17 inches side, 24 inches high; Skeleton Cube, 19 inches side; Intersecting Circles, 19 inches side; Plain Circle, 19 inches side; Plain Square, 19 inches side. Table, 27 inches by 21½ inches. Stand. The set complete, £14 13s.

Large Compasses, with chalk-holder, 5s.

*Slip, two set squares and T square, 5s.

*Parkes's Case of Instruments, containing 6-inch compasses with pen and pencil leg, 5s.

*Prize Instrument Case, with 6-inch compasses pen and pencil leg, 2 small compasses, pen and scale, 18s.

6-inch Compasses, with shifting pen and point, 4s. 6d.

* Models, &c., entered as sets, can only be supplied in sets.

LARGE DIAGRAMS.

ASTRONOMICAL:

TWELVE SHEETS. By JOHN DREW, Ph. Dr., F.R.S.A. Sheets, £2 8s.; on rollers and varnished, £4 4s.

BOTANICAL:

NINE SHEETS. Illustrating a Practical Method of Teaching Botany. By Professor HENSLOW, F.L.S. £2; on rollers and varnished, £3 3s.

CLASS.	DIVISION.	SECTION.	DIAGRAM.
Dicotyledon ..	.. Angiospermous ..	Thalamifloral ..	.. 1
		Calycifloral ..	.. 2 & 3
		Corollifloral ..	.. 4
		Incomplete ..	.. 5
	Gymnospermous ..	.. ..	.. 6
Monocotyledons	.. Petaloid ..	.. Superior ..	.. 7
		Inferior ..	.. 8
	Glumaceous ..	.. ..	.. 9

* Models, &c., entered as sets, can only be supplied in sets.

BUILDING CONSTRUCTION:

TEN SHEETS. By WILLIAM J. GLENNY. £1 1s.

LAXTON'S EXAMPLES OF BUILDING CONSTRUCTION, containing 32 Imperial Plates, £1.

BUSBRIDGE'S DRAWING OF BUILDING CONSTRUCTION. 36 Sheets, 9s. Mounted on cardboard, 18s.

GEOLOGICAL:

DIAGRAM OF BRITISH STRATA. By H. W. BRISTOW, F.R.S., F.G.S. A Sheet, 4s.; on roller and varnished, 7s. 6d.

MECHANICAL:

DIAGRAMS OF THE MECHANICAL POWERS, AND THEIR APPLICATIONS IN MACHINERY AND THE ARTS GENERALLY. By Dr. JOHN ANDERSON. 8 Diagrams, highly coloured, on stout paper, 3 feet 6 inches by 2 feet 6 inches. Sheets £1; mounted on rollers, £2.

DIAGRAMS OF THE STEAM-ENGINE. By Prof. GOODEVE and Prof. SHELLEY. Stout paper, 40 inches by 27 inches, highly coloured. 41 Diagrams (52½ Sheets), £6 6s.; varnished and mounted on rollers, £11 11s.

MACHINE DETAILS. By Prof. UNWIN. 16 Coloured Diagrams. Sheets, £2 2s.; mounted on rollers and varnished, £3 14s.

SELECTED EXAMPLES OF MACHINES, OF IRON AND WOOD (French). By STANISLAS PETTIT. 60 Sheets, £3 5s.; 13s. per dozen.

BUSBRIDGE'S DRAWINGS OF MACHINE CONSTRUCTION. 50 Sheets, 12s. 6d. Mounted £1 5s.

PHYSIOLOGICAL:

ELEVEN SHEETS. Illustrating Human Physiology, Life Size and Coloured from Nature. Prepared under the direction of JOHN MARSHALL, F.R.S., F.R.C.S., &c. Each Sheet, 12s. 6d. On canvas and rollers, varnished, £1 1s.

1. THE SKELETON AND LIGAMENTS.
2. THE MUSCLES, JOINTS, AND ANIMAL MECHANICS.
3. THE VISCERA IN POSITION.—THE STRUCTURE OF THE LUNGS.
4. THE ORGANS OF CIRCULATION.
5. THE LYMPHATICS OR ABSORBENTS.
6. THE ORGANS OF DIGESTION.
7. THE BRAIN AND NERVES.—THE ORGANS OF THE VOICE.
8 & 9. THE ORGANS OF THE SENSES.
10 & 11. THE MICROSCOPIC STRUCTURE OF THE TEXTURES AND ORGANS.

HUMAN BODY, LIFE SIZE. By JOHN MARSHALL, F.R.S., F.R.C.S. Each Sheet, 12s. 6d.; on canvas and rollers, varnished, £1 1s. Explanatory Key, 1s.

1, 2, 3. THE SKELETON, Front, Back, and Side View.
5, 6, 7. THE MUSCLES, Front, Back, and Side View.

ZOOLOGICAL:

TEN SHEETS. Illustrating the Classification of Animals. By ROBERT PATTERSON. £2; on canvas and rollers, varnished, £3 10s.

PHYSIOLOGY AND ANATOMY OF THE HONEY BEE.
Two Diagrams. 7s. 6d.

NEW NOVELS.
(To be had at all Libraries.)

BY THE HON. MRS. HENRY CHETWYND.

MRS. DORRIMAN. By the HON. MRS. HENRY CHETWYND.
3 vols.

BY GEORGE GISSING.

ISABEL CLARENDON. By GEORGE GISSING. 2 vols.
[*In April.*

BY MRS. BERENS.

A WOMAN WITH A PAST. By MRS. BERENS. 3 vols.
[*In April.*

BY S. LAING.

A SPORTING QUIXOTE; or, The Life and Adventures of the Hon. Augustus Fitzmuddle, afterwards Earl of Muddleton. By S. LAING. 2 vols.

BY ARTHUR GRIFFITHS.

THE THIN RED LINE. By ARTHUR GRIFFITHS. 2 vols.
[*In April.*

BY COLONEL FIFE-COOKSON.

BAYLERBAY; OR, STRANGERS IN TURKEY. By COLONEL FIFE-COOKSON. 2 vols.
[*In April.*

BY MRS. EDWARD KENNARD.

KILLED IN THE OPEN. By MRS. EDWARD KENNARD, Author of "The Right Sort," "Straight as a Die," etc., etc. 3 vols.

THE FORTNIGHTLY REVIEW.
Edited by T. H. S. ESCOTT.

THE FORTNIGHTLY REVIEW is published on the 1st of every month, and a Volume is completed every Six Months.

The following are among the Contributors:—

SIR RUTHERFORD ALCOCK.
MATHEW ARNOLD.
PROFESSOR BAIN.
SIR SAMUEL BAKER.
PROFESSOR BEESLY.
PAUL BERT.
BARON GEORGETON BUNSEN.
DR. BRIDGES.
HON. GEORGE C. BRODRICK.
JAMES BRYCE, M.P.
THOMAS BURT, M.P.
SIR GEORGE CAMPBELL, M.P.
THE EARL OF CARNARVON.
EMILIO CASTELAR.
RT. HON. J. CHAMBERLAIN, M.P.
PROFESSOR SIDNEY COLVIN.
MONTAGUE COOKSON, Q.C.
L. H. COURTNEY, M.P.
G. H. DARWIN.
SIR GEORGE W. DASENT.
PROFESSOR A. V. DICEY.
RIGHT HON. H. FAWCETT, M.P.
EDWARD A. FREEMAN.
SIR BARTLE FRERE, Bart.
J. A. FROUDE.
MRS. GARRET-ANDERSON.
J. W. L. GLAISHER, F.R.S.
M. E. GRANT DUFF, M.P.
THOMAS HARE.
F. HARRISON.
LORD HOUGHTON.
PROFESSOR HUXLEY.
PROFESSOR R. C. JEBB.
PROFESSOR JEVONS.
ANDREW LANG.
EMILE DE LAVELEYE.

T. E. CLIFFE LESLIE.
SIR JOHN LUBBOCK, M.P.
THE EARL LYTTON.
SIR H. S. MAINE.
DR. MAUDSLEY.
PROFESSOR MAX MÜLLER.
G. OSBORNE MORGAN, Q.C., M.P.
PROFESSOR HENRY MORLEY.
WILLIAM MORRIS.
PROFESSOR H. N. MOSELEY.
F. W. H. MYERS.
F. W. NEWMAN.
PROFESSOR JOHN NICHOL.
W. G. PALGRAVE.
WALTER H. PATER.
RT. HON. LYON PLAYFAIR, M.P.
DANTE GABRIEL ROSSETTI.
LORD SHERBROOKE.
HERBERT SPENCER.
HON. E. L. STANLEY.
SIR J. FITZJAMES STEPHEN, Q.C.
LESLIE STEPHEN.
J. HUTCHISON STIRLING.
A. C. SWINBURNE.
DR. VON SYBEL.
J. A. SYMONDS.
THE REV. EDWARD F. TALBOT
(Warden of Keble College).
SIR RICHARD TEMPLE, Bart.
W. T. THORNTON
HON. LIONEL A. TOLLEMACHE
H. D. TRAILL.
ANTHONY TROLLOPE.
PROFESSOR TYNDALL.
A. J. WILSON.
THE EDITOR.

&c. &c. &c.

THE FORTNIGHTLY REVIEW *is published at* 2s. 6d.

CHAPMAN & HALL, LIMITED, 11, HENRIETTA STREET, COVENT GARDEN, W.C.

CHARLES DICKENS AND EVANS [CRYSTAL PALACE PRESS.

www.ingramcontent.com/pod-product-compliance
Lightning Source LLC
Chambersburg PA
CBHW030741230426
43667CB00007B/803